CW00923384

MILITARY ORIENTALISM

CRITICAL WAR STUDIES SERIES

Series Editors

Tarak Barkawi (Centre of International Studies, Cambridge University) and Shane Brighton (Birkbeck College, University of London)

War transforms the social and political orders in which we live, just as it obliterates our precious certainties. Nowhere is this more obvious than in the fate of truths offered about war itself. War regularly undermines expectations, strategies and theories, and along with them the credibility of those in public life and the academy presumed to speak with authority about it. A fundamental reason for this is the frequently narrow and impoverished intellectual resources that dominate the study of war.

Critical War Studies begins with the recognition that the unsettling character of war is a profound opportunity for scholarship. Accordingly, the series welcomes submissions from across the academy as well as from refl ective practitioners. It provides an open forum for critical scholarship concerned with war and armed forces and seeks to foster and develop the nascent encounter between war and contemporary approaches to society, history, politics and philosophy. It is a vehicle to reconceive the fi eld of war studies, expand the sites where war is studied, and open the field to new voices

DAVID KILCULLEN

The Accidental Guerrilla—Losing Small Wars in the Midst of a Big One

PATRICK PORTER

Military Orientalism—Eastern War Through Western Eyes

PATRICK PORTER

Military Orientalism

Eastern War Through Western Eyes

HURST & COMPANY, LONDON

First published in the United Kingdom in 2009 by
C. Hurst & Co. (Publishers) Ltd.,
41 Great Russell Street, London, WC1B 3PL
© Patrick Porter, 2009
All rights reserved.
Printed in India

The right of Patrick Porter to be identified as the author of this publication is asserted by him in accordance with the Copyright, Designs and Patents Act, 1988.

A Cataloguing-in-Publication data record for this book is available from the British Library.

ISBNs
978–1–85065–960–0 *casebound*
978–1–85065–959–4 *paperback*

www.hurstpub.co.uk

'We are facing an army of barbarians in Korea, but they are barbarians as trained, as relentless, as reckless of life, and as skilled...as the hordes of Genghis Khan.'

(Hanson Baldwin, *New York Times*, July 1950)

'The Oriental tradition, however, had not been eliminated...On September 11, 2001 it returned in an absolutely traditional form. Arabs, appearing suddenly out of empty space like their desert raider ancestors, assaulted the heartlands of Western power, in a terrifying surprise raid.'

(John Keegan, October 2001)

'American ground troops are going to have to learn to be more like Apaches.'

(Robert Kaplan, 2004)

'What do they know, this bunch of flip-flop, dress-wearing bastards... Fuck, they actually know what they are doing.'

(Corporal Quentin Poll, Afghanistan, 2006)

As America and its allies fear military failure abroad, culture is being touted as the key to strategy and even the essence of warfare. The War on Terror has revived interest in the foreign and the bizarre. But what is the relationship between war and culture? And what drives our fascination in the first place? Our fixation with the exotic nature of our enemies is powerful but often misleading. Powerful, because we articulate anxieties about the West through visions of the enemy, as irrational fanatic, noble savage, mystical genius, or timeless primitive. Misleading, because 'Eastern' warriors are mostly not static cultural captive. They are dynamic strategic actors. From Imperial Japan to the Taliban, from warlords to suicide bombers, we find people breaking traditions and remaking cultures in pursuit of victory. Culture is better approached not as a clear script for action, but as an ambiguous repertoire of ideas through which people make strategy. It is this lack of cultural determinacy that helps explain why war is so full of surprises.

CONTENTS

ACKNOWLEDGEMENTS

A thousand thanks to Michael Dwyer at Hurst for making the whole project possible and steering it through, and to Columbia University Press for agreeing to co-publish. Thanks also to the editors, Tarak Barkawi and Shane Brighton, for the honour of including this in their 'Critical War Studies' series.

Others also contributed in many ways. For their advice, criticism and support, I am indebted to Dan Neep, Theo Farrell, Jeannie Johnson, Alex Marshall, Mark Adams, Rob Dover, Huw Bennett, Paul Domjan, Chris Tripodi, Huw Davies, Niall Barr, Vanda Wilcox, David Betz, Katherine Brown, Derek Gregory, Tim Bird, Pauline Kusiak, Jeni Mitchell, Stephen Biddle and Robert Saunders.

I am also grateful to participants in forums at the Institute for National Strategic Studies in Washington, on 'Governance and Intelligence' at Loughborough University, at the International Studies Association Conference, New York, and at the Defence Studies Department at Staff College for their helpful comments on earlier versions of the argument.

This book would not have been possible without the help of the staffs of various archives, including the National Army Museum, the National Archives, the Liddell Hart Archive, the National Security Archive and the Hoover Institution.

Three chapters draw on articles in *War and Society, Parameters* and *Orbis*; thanks to the editors and publishers for their permission to re-publish them in a much expanded form in this book.

I am also grateful to the officers at Staff College for their curiosity, intelligence and humour. Without their influence, this could not have been written.

To Ronald Ridley, Nick Stargardt, Adrian Gregory, John Moses and Hew Strachan, great mentors and teachers, go my lifelong thanks.

They and two great Colleges, Ormond and Magdalen, set me on the path of cultural and strategic history.

For their love and solidarity, thanks to my parents Brian and Muriel, and my sister Emily. For easing all burdens, this book is dedicated to my wife Andrea.

INTRODUCTION

Pepsi Cola versus Death

War is a political act. In the tradition of the Prussian soldier Carl von Clausewitz, it is an outgrowth of power struggle, where people clash in a vortex of passion, calculation and chance. But down the ages, and in Clausewitz's lifetime, war also appeared as a cultural act. Armed conflict is an expression of identity as well as a means to an end. When Spain's *Conquistadores* arrived in Meso-America in 1519, invaders and locals eyed each other with bewilderment. The Aztecs were dismayed by the men who ambushed the unarmed, killed from a distance with canon and crossbows, wearing armour over torsos that should be bare and painted. The Spanish saw the hosts as primitives who fought to capture and cannibalise their victims.[1] Combat, whether for Christian imperialism or a hungry Sun-God, was a ritual where societies' traits were violently affirmed. How people fight reflects who they are.

Today, the gap between enemies again seems vast. The foe's strangeness, accentuated by war, grabs the headlines. As one young Afghan fighter bragged, 'The Americans love Pepsi Cola, but we love death.'[2] Western soldiers emerge from bases containing fast food and cinemas to battle fighters dreaming of an Islamic Caliphate. The stealth bomber is countered by the suicide bomber. According to one American general, today's wars are 'culture wars' at the 'edge of the empire.'[3] The US Marine Corps names its terrorist enemy as a 'primordial form of warfare.'[4] When militaries and states speak of culture, they often mean difference and separation, rather than resemblance and linkage. The shock of the September 11 attacks was widely seen as alien fanaticism. It was a strike by premodern zealots, or 'Islamist descendants from the ancient Arab heartland', on icons of modernity.[5] This invasion from the unknown inspired Steven Spielberg's remake of *War of the Worlds*.[6] Some argue that Bin Laden's mass-casualty terrorism was senseless, inspired by religious fury without rational, political purpose.[7] To them, the atrocity was the work of a death cult, staging a theatre of horror for its own sake. Confronted by televised beheadings, *jihad* seems to emanate from pathologies we can hardly understand, and a will we cannot match.[8] Some maintain that Oriental enemies, from Islamist terrorists to tribal warriors, wage war not as a rational instrument but for religio-cultural self-expression.[9]

The primeval fanatic is as crude a caricature as the cowardly Westerner. Al Qaeda may seem like a medieval throwback from another world. But it is highly modern, spawned out of globalisation and its circulation of ideas and methods. No matter how strange, no war culture is an island. And its murderous methods do not just enact its identity, but have a dark strategic logic.[10] This book examines Western visions of others' warfare, and how visions of themselves often stare back. It explains—and questions—our obsession with the exotic and the bizarre. It is about two related themes. Firstly, it asks what draws Western observers to 'Eastern' war. Secondly, it challenges some approaches to culture which persist in militaries, the academy, and public life.

This is an old story. But it finds few overarching studies.[11] A rich body of scholarship has already grown around 'Orientalism', the ways Westerners define themselves in relation to an 'Other.' In this agenda for research, war is mostly in the background. Yet war is a potent site of Orientalism. In and through war, people formulate what it means to be Western or non-Western. This is a time of furious debate over barbaric terrors and our response to them. Events have shaken the naïve utopianisms of the 1990s, whether the dream of the peaceful global village, post-national cosmopolitanism, or the 'end of history.' Serious minds return to the forces of faith, blood and soil, and how these manifest themselves in conflict. To give perspective, it might help to ask how Westerners have gazed on Eastern war, from morale to morality, tactics to strategy, casualty tolerance to authority, from ancient Persia to the Taliban.

Since recorded history began, the clash of the West and the Rest seized the popular imagination. War between Achaeans and Trojans raged in Homer's *Iliad*, the epic poem. Though Homer cast them as similar, later Greeks (and Turks) treated that war as the struggle of Europe and Asia. The Greco-Persian wars of the fifth century BC hardened this division in Western consciousness. This conflict was the original question for Herodotus, who wrote to understand why Greek and barbarian 'fought against one another.' For him, culture had great explanatory power, 'custom is king.' Persia's armies reflected their civilisation: fierce, opulent and servile.[12] The collision of Persian 'hordes' and Greek hoplites came to symbolise the clash of freedom and autocracy. War was of, by and for civilisation.

Conflicts with strange enemies, endlessly recalled and mythologised in art, literature and film, help define the West's cosmology. Sioux warriors encircling Custer's men to push back the frontier; Zulus charging into the rifle volleys of South Wales Borderers; unseen Afghans, 'like hungry wolves', hunting the few survivors of a British invasion;[13]Aztec priests tearing out their captives' hearts; Japanese *kamikaze* pilots writing poems before shedding flesh 'like a cherry blossom from the bough.'[14] Easterners provoke mixed reactions. They can inspire fear and envy, as predators or exemplars, zealots or noble savages. At times, they become ideal-types, symbols of valour through which the West can regenerate itself. Before crossing the Iraq border in 2003, tank crews of the Sixty-Fourth Armour Regiment re-enacted this past, saying prayers before performing a Seminole Indian war dance.[15]

It would be saying too much to claim that the West defines itself purely through the non-Western 'Other.' The West grew also through its own internal conflicts, such as the Renaissance, the Reformation, industrial and political revolutions, and the Enlightenment.[16] But the 'Wild East' has played its part in generating the West's sense of self. The nature of others' warfare remains a highly charged political question.[17] As well as a means of survival, war is a medium through which we judge the calibre of our own and other civilisations. The Declaration of Independence, America's foundational statement of self-definition, brands natives as barbarians whose 'known rule of warfare is an undistinguished destruction of all ages, sexes and conditions.'[18] Such judgements can have a concrete impact on policy. Images of the military East have shocked policymakers, such as the US administration official after China's attack in Korea in 1950. 'I was brought up to think the Chinese couldn't handle a machine...suddenly, the Chinese are flying jets!' At other times, it has underpinned alliance choices. American diplomats in the 1950's reasoned that they should opt for Pakistan over India because Hinduism was effeminate and passive, whilst Islam was masculine and robust.[19]

The very idea of the 'West' continually replenishes itself through war. In 1917, the US government asked colleges to give courses on Western Civilisation to returning servicemen, teaching them what they had fought for.[20] The concept of the West was institutionalised in NATO, the alliance founded in 1949. Energised by the Korean and Vietnam wars, the Soviet threat from the East was then linked with the 'yellow' peril of Oriental despotism.[21] In our own time, the Oriental enemy has been reconfigured, from the godless communism of the Cold War to the warlordism and zealous Islamism of the twenty-first century. While these do not draw the same kinds of counter-mobilisation as fascism or Soviet communism, the 'War on Terror' helps reformulate the West.

Popular and elite culture is still drawn to the relationship between Western identity and conflict. Hollywood draws huge profits from films about wars and alien cultures, such as *300, The Last Samurai, Black Hawk Down, Rambo II* and *III*, and *Dances with Wolves*. The book market, as recent titles about the battles of Lepanto, Thermopylae or Constantinople suggest, has an appetite for the idea of the Occident embattled by the Orient, while sales have risen of T.E. Lawrence's account of the Arab Revolt.[22] Novels about Spartan heroism against Eastern hordes are favourites in the US military.[23] For thousands of Australian backpackers, Gallipoli memorial services are sacred rites. The martial roots of Western identity are still an obsession. This book is a symptom of that obsession.

This is despite, or because, the notion of the West is a changing concept with arbitrary borders.[24] The West exists as a loose imagined community. But it has been the 'Old West', the synthesis of classical, Christian and Germanic cultures, or the 'New West' with its triad of reason, liberty and progress. It has been defined around blood, soil, language, religion, political institutions, or social organisation. Its membership has altered, as have its frontiers, which have been drawn in Cyprus, Ethiopia, the Volga or the Dardanelles.[25] Yet its self-identity thrives on existential crisis. Self-styled Westerners summon historic struggles in defining moments. The Alamo, the 1836 siege between Mexico and Texan rebels, was dubbed America's Thermopylae.[26]

We live in belligerent times but also culturally complex times. The 'identity craze' reflects the uncertainties and insecurities of a world where people and ideas constantly cross boundaries. When identity seems a powerful force but is hard to demarcate neatly, mythologised war offers clear battle lines. This longing for clarity helps explain the popularity of Samuel Huntington's *Clash of Civilisations* thesis, where cultural affinity is the prime source of conflict.[27] It explains the underlying violence of Andrew Roberts' *History of the English Speaking Peoples*, where the Anglosphere is a cultural unity remobilising in every generation against new outside forces of unreason.[28] Civilizations define themselves most sharply through their clashes.

War's power to express and reproduce cultural identity is also evident in the enduring appeal of 'decisive battle.' This idea bemuses sceptical scholars. But it lives on in outlets such as commercial television. It gives battle a world-historical significance, where great issues were decided not by vast impersonal forces, but by armies or navies amassed as envoys of their civilisations, fighting while history 'hung trembling in the balance.'[29] In real history, battles are often indecisive, civilizations overlap, and political opportunism may trump cultural fidelities. Often, states and powers do not behave as culturally bounded actors, hence convenient alliances between Ottomans and Venetians, Crusaders and Fatimid Sultans, or modern Shi'ite Iran's security co-operation with Christian Armenia.[30] Yet the mythic memory of battle, with its dichotomous, crystallising nature, lends order to history's messiness.[31] It sustains the fiction of enclosed civilizations, 'watertight under an eternal sky.'[32]

In our fascination with decisive battle and the making of the West, we are heirs to a genre of nineteenth-century literature, epitomised in Edward Creasy's 1851 classic, *The Fifteen Decisive Battles from Marathon to Waterloo*.[33] Six of these featured clashes between the bearers of Western civilisations against Orientals, summoned under Hannibal, Attila, or the Umayyadd Caliphate. A Victorian triumphalist, Creasy wrote to trace the rise of Anglo-Saxon power.[34] Non-Western peoples turned up chiefly to be defeated. Creasy retold battle stories to stiffen British resolve and promote a sense of imperial mission.

One hundred and fifty years later, American historian Victor Davis Hanson added *Carnage and Culture* to this genre.[35] He argued that Western civilization, birthed by the competitive citizen-soldiers of classical Greece, created a distinctive, deadly 'Western way of war.' Hanson credited the West's military dominance to its strengths of political freedom, consensual government, capitalism, self-criticism, scientific inquiry, and civic militarism. But Hanson wrote to warn the West as well as praise it. After a century of catastrophic wars between Westerners, and now with nuclear weapons, the greatest danger was the West turning its lethality on itself. Hanson treated battles more as 'landmark' reflectors of cultural traits rather than 'decisive' agents. But armed clashes were still the spine of history. This powerfully stated argument clearly touched a nerve, becoming a national best-seller and translated into a dozen languages.

Today, a swathe of opinion, from theorists to practitioners, argues that we should turn back to culture as a code stone for understanding warfare, particularly the profound 'otherness' of foreigners.

The Cultural Turn

Culture is again on the lips of scholars, soldiers and statesmen. For many reasons, there has been a 'cultural turn' towards an anthropological approach to war. 'Culture matters', we are frequently told, while philosopher Sun Tzu's advice to 'Know your enemy and know yourself,' is a standard cliché in works on insurgency and terrorism.[36] According to the Chinese sage, mastering war demands self-knowledge and an accurate reading of the enemy, a dialectical exercise that will reward the strategist with victory upon victory.

But why culture, and why now? Historically and today, the rediscovery of culture is a response to imperial crisis. The latest culturalism of the US military has been touted as 'revolutionary.'[37] But this is only the latest rebranding of the idea. In 1940, after wars with 'strange people' from Nicaragua to China, the American Marine Corps produced its *Small Wars Manual*, urging the study of natives' 'racial characteristics.'[38] This was a response to fears of revolution and Axis subversion in Latin America, and to allegations of brutality in the Caribbean that had led to congressional inquest and public outcries.[39] Before that, the Indian Mutiny of 1857 prompted British officers to 'know the natives' better, generating handbooks categorising India's social groups and loyalties. Lord Roberts, the celebrated Field Marshal 'of Kabul and Kandahar', later warned Lord Kitchener that the officer corps must grasp the 'ideosyncrasies of the Natives.'[40] Well into the twentieth century, guidebooks were published with taxonomies of local tribes.[41] Colonel Charles Callwell, British authority on 'small wars', believed that calamitous defeat by Zulus at Isandlwhana in 1879 showed the need to know their 'habits, the customs, and the mode of action on the battlefield.'[42] To learn culture was to keep power and forestall catastrophe. The embrace of culture grew out of a colonial legacy whose influence continues, but its new incarnations replace the language of 'race' with 'culture.'[43]

The Cold War, and the fear of nuclear apocalypse, gave new momentum to the study of strategic culture and America's investment in 'area studies.' Given the extreme danger of misreading enemies, nuclear strategist Bernard Brodie claimed '...good strategy presumes good anthropology and sociology.'[44] In this spirit, Jack Snyder and others found in the Soviet elite a unique outlook towards nuclear doctrine, a predisposition to preemptive and offensive use of force formed by centuries of insecurity and authoritarianism.[45] Anthropological-strategic knowledge, applied to 'small wars', could also be about interacting with a dangerous superpower.

Today, crisis again motivates the embrace of culture. America's strategic failure, so the argument goes, springs from cognitive failure to understand foreign societies in Asia and the Middle East. Though its conventional military strength outguns its opponents, the US struggles to translate tactical battlefield supremacy into lasting political triumph. American leaders fear that it is losing the propaganda war to a weaker and backward enemy. As Defence Secretary Robert Gates asked in embarrassment, 'How has one man in a cave managed to outcommunicate the world's greatest communication society?'[46] General David Petraeus, the former commander of Multi-National Force Iraq, leads soldier-intellectuals in a reform movement to improve the military's skill at lesser wars, especially counterinsurgency (COIN). The new *Counterinsurgency Field Manual (FM 3–24)*, operational from 15 December 2006, mentions 'culture' 88 times and 'cultural' 90 times in 282 pages, calling for 'agile, well-informed, culturally astute leaders.'[47] *The Manual* marks a significant departure from the technical-organisational thrust of previous American doctrine. It is a response to the near-implosion of Iraq, where an insurgency mutated into horrific communal violence, while NATO tries to navigate the tribal world of Afghanistan and a resurgent Taliban. It reflects the realisation that satellites can yield information but people must interpret its meaning. And in the future, culture might be vital in increasingly complex battlespaces, such as the convulsive megacities of the Third World.[48] Moreover, cultural literacy appeals as a theoretical underpinning for high statecraft, as the US seeks to contain the nuclear ambitions of North Korea and Iran. All this has opened the way for a teaching moment, where theorists of culture can get a hearing.[49]

But the focal point of the cultural turn is the 'War on Terror.' Six years after the invasion of Iraq, and eight years after the 9/11 attacks, critics argue that the war has proven strategically illiterate.[50] To be sure, there have been successes. The US-led coalition has struck body-blows against Al Qaeda as a network, an ideology and a movement. It has toppled a patron in Afghanistan while offering a democratic alternative. It has killed and captured talented agents, constraining its ability to operate in the First World, while Al Qaeda's overreaching brutality now alienates Iraqi and Muslim opinion. Yet the costs of this war are high. It has killed and tortured too many people, drained too much money and political capital, and inflamed global tensions. These failures flow partly from conceptual confusion. It is a war formulated on supersized, global principles at the expense of local knowledge. It is a war declared on a tactical method rather than an identifiable group, for utopian rather than achievable goals, with little grasp of ends, ways and means. Political leaders have reformulated the 'War on Terror' to the 'Long War' to the 'Global counterinsurgency' to define its complexity. But in schizoid fashion, the same leaders periodically declare victory, turning-points and missions accomplished. Cultural literacy might be an answer to this disarray.

The cultural turn is also a reaction against the illusions of the pre-9/11 era. American military strategy of the 1990s was marked by the technology-driven quest for a 'Revolution in Military Affairs' (RMA), where the American colossus would prevail against armies in the field by exploiting its material and systemic strengths. Knowledge of the battlespace, precision munitions, rapid mobility and decision-making would paralyse the enemy and lift the fog of war.[51] But neither the doctrine, training and tools designed to counter the Soviet threat, nor the RMA revolution seems capable of dealing with current wars. American advantages have been offset by the indirect methods its enemies employ, by the gangland of urban warfare, in which industrial might or superior firepower do not guarantee success, and by their enemies' amorphous shape. Prepared for conventional battles against a clear adversary, surgical invasion and swift, overwhelming strikes, America's military was unprepared for post-invasion disorder in Iraq, and for prolonged contact with complex foreign societies. The revolution in military technology is answered by a cultural counter-revolution.

Soldiers distressed by failures in Iraq and Afghanistan are drawn to culture as the missing answer. In testifying before Congress, Major

General Robert H. Scales called for 'culture-centric warfare', arguing that the Iraq crisis requires 'an exceptional ability to understand people, their culture, and their motivation.'[52] Returning from Afghanistan, British soldier Leo Docherty claimed that conventional forces should be replaced by clusters of 'Afghan experts', immersed in the country with a 'profound knowledge of local culture, language and politics.'[53] Major General Peter Chiarelli described an 'Arab and Iraqi culture' grounded in 'inherent corruption (by Western standards)'and extreme concepts of 'honour above all', so much so that "lying" to defend one's honour is a cultural norm—something that we, with our Western value set, cannot comprehend.'[54] Pentagon studies blame 'cultural insensitivity' for fuelling insurgencies in Iraq and Afghanistan, while the US Army War College now studies 'failed states in Africa, the Middle East, and Central Asia that may become breeding grounds for terrorists.'[55]

Strategy is a practical affair, about the optimal way of configuring a nation's resources towards its goals. Washington is willing to pay for cultural expertise if it will provide effective solutions. US Defence Secretary Robert Gates has already authorised $40 million to expand the Human Terrain System of anthropologists working with the military, increasing teams from six to twenty-eight.[56] The 2006 *Quadrennial Defence Review* judged cultural intelligence about the Middle East and Asia as 'critical to prevail in the long war and to meet 21st century challenges', while Donald Rumsfeld noted the military's need for 'foreign language skill and regional and cultural expertise.'[57] The US State Department's new Chief Strategist for counter-terrorism, David Kilcullen, has a doctorate in political anthropology.[58] Within military discourse, culture is approached as a dimension of warfare that can be operationalised, by integrating anthropological training into education and campaign planning.[59] Private military companies such as BAE Systems, Hicks & Associates, and Mitre Corporation advertise for cultural experts and linguists. Culture serves two, overlapping purposes, as a way of explaining the enemy's thought and behaviour, and as a basis for interacting with foreign societies. By knowing the turf, the intricacies of tribes, religion, customs, and collective memory, it is hoped America and its allies need no longer be ignorant armies that clash by night.

To some, culture is the essence of strategy, even the key to strategic salvation, because it can bridge military power and ultimate victory.[60] Tony Corn lays the errors of the Iraq war at the door of American

Clausewitz-worship, arguing that we should replace classical strategy with anthropology. This 'will shed light on the grammar and logic of tribal warfare', creating the 'conceptual weapons necessary to return fire.'[61] Campaigning for President, Senator John McCain said that understanding foreign cultures is 'a strategic necessity,' vowing to create an 'Office of Strategic Services' with a programme of language and anthropological study.[62]

This 'culturalism' is a moving target, defined in different ways and articulated at different levels of magnitude and sophistication. It varies from attempts to isolate cultural traits and their impact on strategy, to wider conceptualisations where culture is almost omnipresent.[63] In the US and UK, notions of culture-centric war are taking hold beyond military circles.[64] Before the military re-discovered anthropology, political scientists had already been drawn to the concept of strategic culture.[65] Works by Elizabeth Kier on interwar French and British doctrine, Isabell Hull on the rapacious routines of the Imperial German Army, or Waheguru Sihdu on the ancient roots of Indian strategy argued that national or organisational strategies are culturally determined, generated by long-term political evolution, experience or geography.[66] Before them, historians such as Basil Liddell Hart and Russell Weigley identified British and American 'ways of war.'[67] Strategic culture theory traces continuities back to core texts, from Sun Tzu's *Art of War* in China's warring states period, to Kautilya in ancient India, to Thucydides' commentary on the Peloponnesian war and Clausewitz' *On War* in the Napoleonic era.[68]

There is now a rich literature on strategic culture. Studies by Theo Farrell on the Irish military, Peter Katzenstein on Japan, Jack Snyder on Soviet nuclear strategy, Ken Booth on the role of ethnocentrism in strategy, are indispensable. These works share a conviction that culture is critical to the central questions of strategy, such as how resources are translated into military power,[69] how decision-makers think, how nations prepare for war and how material things and ideas affect one another. The spirit of all these works is to correct the delusional idea of an acultural, universal 'strategic man.'[70] While they stress the role of ideas and identity, they do not fall prey to determinism or dogmatism, are aware of the changeability of culture, and the different levels at which culture can operate, at the global, national, organisational or normative levels, the gaps between declaratory symbolic culture (what people say about themselves) and actual behaviour, and the methodological difficulties of proving the role of culture as an independent causal agent.[71] They ask who are the keepers of strategic culture, and by what mechanisms it is passed on. Though they recognise the role of human agency in breaking free of cultural constraints, they are more impressed by the power of those constraints. In this view, because cultures are a semi-permanent force of beliefs and norms rooted in the past, they usually change only slowly or at critical junctures, and lag behind changes in surrounding conditions.[72] Culture in this view strongly mediates the effects of the wider security environment on state policy. Culture means that strategic behaviour is not fully responsive to externalities. As yet, there is no firm consensus on how malleable cultures are, a question that this book revisits.[73]

Cultural approaches also come in more ambitious, 'metacultural' forms, where culture is almost destiny. Fresh military histories and studies of counter-insurgency pitch culture not only at the level of nation-states, but across trans-national civilisations. They identify sets of concepts and behaviour that separate East from West, sketching the East as an unbroken strategic tradition that unites dispersed societies from Sun Tzu's China, medieval Arabia, modern Turkey, to the Arab and Islamic insurgencies of today. Along these lines, the *Cambridge History of Warfare* has a successful Western way of war as its organising principle.[74] John Keegan argued that war is culture by other means, that Oriental warfare is 'different and apart from European warfare', relying on 'evasion, delay and indirectness.'[75] Christopher Coker argues that Westerners historically preferred direct battle fought without guile to smash the enemy, whereas the 'Islamic' way of war chose standoff weapons, deceit and attacking enemy cohesion.[76] Paul Bracken claims Eastern war was 'embodied by the stealthy archer', unlike the archetypal Western swordsman 'charging forward, seeking a decisive showdown, eager to administer the blow that will obliterate the enemy.'[77] The plot of these sweeping narratives is about Western dominance, as titles such as *The Triumph of the West* suggest.[78]

But because of recent difficulties faced by the American model of war-making, the notion of a Western way of war has become less triumphalist. Orientals appear not so much as inferior, but as sophisticates ready to confound the West and its witless impatience. Against a West infatuated with the sword, Muslims have fashioned a new 'Islamic way of war', exploiting Western weaknesses, with techniques from terror to propaganda, economic warfare to subversion.[79] Others see an older Eastern tradition. John Poole uses the idea of an 'Eastern thought process' didactically to criticise Western war, arguing that Orientals generate effective light infantry, and fight indirectly with encirclements, dispersal, and trickery.[80] This has been endorsed by William Lind, another theorist:

> The Oriental way of war is far more sophisticated. It plays across the full spectrum of conflict—the moral and mental levels as well as the physical. Even at the physical level, it relies on the indirect approach, on stratagem and deception, far more than on simple bombardment. Seldom do Asians fall into mindless *Materialschlacht* or 'body counts'; and while Oriental armies often can (and have) taken many casualties, their tactics at the small-unit infantry level are often cleverly designed to spare their own men's lives in the face of massive Western firepower.[81]

Robert Cassidy sees an 'Eastern way of war' rooted in the philosophies of Sun Tzu and Mao Tse-Tung, marked by 'reliance on indirectness, perfidy, attrition and protraction', and is 'inherently more irregular, unorthodox, and asymmetric than our traditional conception of war.'[82] 'Inherently' is a very strong word, implying an almost hereditary tradition. (As we will see, this overlooks the long history of Western commanders using deception and indirect methods, from Themistocles to Schwarzkopf). Implicitly or explicitly, much of this popular culturalism takes a 'primordialist' view of culture. That is, it sees culture as an immobile, unified set of ideas and instincts, a natural 'given' force created by traditions and collective experiences, where identity is more or less fixed by inherited, socially transmitted factors.

Though culturalist approaches vary wildly, all versions agree on some fundamentals: that culture at some level profoundly shapes choices, that people think and act as they do largely because of who they are. In the language of security studies, cultural theories claim that 'ideational' factors (i.e. ideas and norms) explain things better than 'realism', the approach that stresses objective interests and material balances of power. Like-minded historians look primarily to inherited and habitual preferences, derived from the past, to explain behaviour, and see this as the stream in which other variables swim, such as the personalities, contingencies and quirks of a situation.

This cultural turn is also part of wider debates about the nature of war and international politics. Is it an ethnocentric error to speak of universal principles of strategy? The poles of this debate are usefully marked by Michael Handel, for whom strategy has a global, objective logic, and Ken Booth, who argues that strategy is heavily dependent on cultural context.[83] The belief in cultural specificity takes more popular form in Robert Kaplan, who argues that Herodotus with his eye for ethnographic detail speaks more to the present than Thucydides' generalisations about war and human nature.[84] The return to cultural specifics is also driven by a backlash against the Bush administration. Bush's vision of a world remade in America's image, some argue, has caused all the trouble. All this restages the argument between the universalism of Enlightenment thought and Romanticism, with its stress on the original 'genius' of each people.

The debate about war and culture also goes to the heart of Anglo-American relations. Both the US and UK are doing the heavy lifting in current operations, and are strongly invested in the issue. Given America's overwhelming military strength, Anglophiles claim that cultural skill is what Britain, as junior but more seasoned partner, can bring to the table. This ticklish subject touches deeper questions about the eclipse of British power. What is Britain's strategic role, with its empire gone and its armed forces shrunk? Etched into much Atlantic discourse is the notion that Britain as enlightened Greece can refine the military might of America's uncouth and untutored Rome, the old hegemon educating the new about handling the natives. Ironically, American soldier-scholars such as Lt Col John Nagl helped create this image of British superiority. Despite their reluctance to acknowledge empire and the differences in the time-scale and context of their imperial role, American proconsuls and strategists consciously reach back to British experience. This Anglophile critique of American performance was repeated back by a British audience, such as Brigadier Nigel Aylwin-Foster.[85] This reworks an older dialogue between Britain's colonial past and America's imperial present. It surfaced before the Gulf War of 1991,[86] and was recently revived by Prince Andrew, who complained that the counsel of British colonial wisdom could have prevented failure in Iraq.[87] Despite the unhappy legacies of British partition, America's own long experience with 'small wars', despite the arbitrariness of contrasting American failure in Vietnam with British success in Malaya, this transatlantic dialogue persists. It is another way that the argument about culture is also an argument about the West.

Definitions: Orientalism and Culture

Before outlining my argument, some concepts need to be clarified. 'Orientalism' refers to the history of how Westerners have historically defined, represented and schematised the 'Orient' or 'East', and defined themselves around it, whether as a geographic entity, a particular culture, or as a distinctive value system. It is about the dialogic relationship between 'Self' and 'Other', and how perceptions of the East are bound up with Western debates about the West. In this sense, I mean Orientalism as the dynamics of cultural perception within a complex set of relationships, as opposed to a coherent, single ideology, or as opposed to the approach of Edward Said, who defined it as a continuous 'system of ideas' and 'imaginative geography.'[88] Orientalism in this study is not a monolith, but is a plural and shifting set of epistemological ideas, attitudes and practices. It contains themes that are time-bound and distinctive to their historical context and themes that are recast and reintroduced over space and time. It is also inflected in many different forms and is often marked by ambiguities and contradictions. It is reflected in abstract thought as well as policy, from intelligence analysis to the hiring of indigenous forces, from proposals for Western military reform to coercive diplomacy.

What is culture? This is a concept that should be handled with care. Anthropologists, especially those outside the military, are increasingly uncomfortable with the term.[89] There are many models on offer, ranging from the laconic notion that culture is 'the way we do things around here', to Clifford Geertz's evocative claim that 'man is an animal suspended in webs of significance he himself has spun.'[90] Sociologist Max Weber's work was seminal. With the metaphor of train tracks, Weber argued that ideas work like 'switchmen,' defining the ideal and material interests that drive action.[91] Ethnographers coming after Weber, such as Claude Levi-Strauss and Geertz, saw culture as a value orientation, an abstract system of meanings and oppositions. For Geertz and others, culture is a system of symbols, social structures, institutions, norms, values and codes, that people use to order their world, which are learned, socially transmitted or inherited rather than genetic.[92] Crucially for the study of strategy, this 'classic' view sees culture as a given social fact, or in Durkheim's terms, received from the past and passed on to the future.

Since then, the academic understanding of culture has evolved. Later theory approaches culture as a more dynamic and unstable interplay between structure and practice, ideas and behaviour. To understand the role of culture, we can build on a sophisticated body of revisionist anthropological and historical work that emerged in the 1980's and

1990s. This scholarship challenged the view of culture as a world of meaning that is old, bounded and unified, shaped primarily by internal logic, discretely packaged within a certain ethnic, territorial or even civilisational space, reigning over its people. In its place, it conceives culture not just as a system of meanings, but as a dialectical relationship between system and practice. This 'performative' approach recognises that culture is not so much 'logical, coherent, shared, uniform, and static' but is 'a sphere of practical activity shot through by wilful action, power relations, struggle, contradiction, and change.'[93] Modern anthropological work has shown that even societies deemed 'simple' and tribal are highly mutable, full of internal ruptures and power struggles, and made by borrowings from outside as well as internal drives.[94]

What does culture mean when it is related to strategy? 'Culture' in the strategic context has been defined as 'a distinct and lasting set of beliefs [and] values' and preferences regarding the use of force, its role and effectiveness in political affairs.[95] This includes an array of factors, such as prevailing attitudes, habits and values of the military and its parent society, geopolitical position, historical experience, political development, and received wisdom. Strategic culture theory typically assigns several characteristics to culture. These include *continuity* over time, an enduring set of *values and behaviour*, rooted in memories, ideas, particular conditions, and by features *distinctive* or *peculiar* to specific societies.[96] But as will be argued here, cultures at war contain rival and clashing narratives, taboos that can be enforced or ignored, and porous borders across which new ideas and practices are smuggled. Therefore I define culture as *an ambiguous repertoire of competing ideas that can be selected, instrumentalised, and manipulated, instead of a clear script for action*. Within this process strategy is made.

The Argument

This book tackles cultural approaches to war for several audiences: specialist academic literature, militaries and the wider public domain.

For the specialist literature on strategic culture, this book offers three fresh approaches. Firstly, in asking again how culture 'works' in wartime, it turns attention back to culture 'in motion', exploring how cultures change within the mutual hostility of wartime. Strategic culture should be appreciated as the dynamic product of reciprocal interactions as well as a set of internal ideas and influences. People bring their cultures with them to the battlefield, but they and their enemies also remake each other. Scholars who work on strategic culture would acknowledge this, but place greater emphasis on the internal drives and inner anatomy of a society at war, with the occasional disruptive impact of strategic 'shocks' such as Pearl Harbor or 9/11. By contrast, I place greater weight on the impact of external stimuli and the dynamic action/reaction reciprocity of war. Culture, as many sociologists and anthropologists conceive it, is a constitutive phenomenon, created by the relation between different animate bodies, rather than a bounded tradition. In this respect, scholarship on strategic culture has some catching up to do, and military debate to a greater extent, with the social sciences.[97] As well as rethinking flawed versions of culture, one purpose of this book is to 'marry' better models of culture, with the world of military policy and analysis that is rediscovering the concept.

Secondly, where strategic culture literature places greater weight on the logical consistency, unity and coherence of culture and its influence on actors,[98] I emphasise the contradictions within culture, the multiplicity of strategic cultures in one country or society, and the way it is politically usable. In arguing for a more fluid and contested version of culture, my argument stands on the shoulders of social scientist Alastair Johnston, who argues that culture can contain conflicting codes of statecraft that elites selectively apply, and historian Brian McAllister Linn, who portrays the organisational culture of the US Army as a mixed bag of competing martial traditions.[99] When conflicts arise between culture and calculations about the utility of action, culture can be remade to serve utility. This is a question of emphasis rather than absolute difference between the existing literature and my own argument.

Thirdly, I analyse the observer as well as the observed. A major obstacle to accurate cross-cultural perception is the problem of analytical objectivity. As Ken Booth warned decades ago, sound insight into other cultures requires a degree of self-distanciation.[100] That is, the observer must become more aware of their own cultural perspective and quirks, and achieve distance from them, in order to appraise others more successfully. The study of military Orientalism can help this difficult task. I try to turn attention to what drives our interest in non-Western warfare in the first place, to understand the eye of the beholder. By unpacking the range of assumptions and myths through which Westerners gaze on the military East, and engage in a critical dialogue with our own preconceptions, this can heighten the observers' consciousness of their own mental baggage and further enrich their analysis.

While the academy has already generated strong challenges to a historical and flawed versions of culture, these have not conquered the field. There is still a serious strain of academic opinion that approaches culture in problematic ways. It is produced by mainstream figures from prestigious institutions who publish in respected outlets. These works are not homogenous, but all accept primordialist, meta-cultural versions of culture, or see culture as the soul of modern war. Their ideas also have a notable influence and impact beyond, from public debate to military policy and at senior levels of government. Because this body of opinion continues to attract prominent scholars and because it enjoys a strong public reception, it deserves to be answered.

A brief sample of this might include: Thomas Johnson and Chris Mason, whose work on the 'mystical' Taliban appears in *Orbis*; Christopher Coker, of the London School of Economics, who identifies 'Islamic' vs. 'Western' ways of war; the latest *Cambridge History of Warfare*, edited by Geoffrey Parker, which is organised around the concepts of the Western way of war and its continuity as a strategic tradition; work on tribal warfare by Andrea Dew and Richard Schultz Jr. the Director of the international security studies program at Tufts University's Fletcher School, which has been endorsed by terrorism and intelligence experts Bruce Hoffman and Sir Richard Dearlove; Tony Corn, a teacher in the European Studies at the US Foreign Service Institute, who argues that the study of Clausewitz and classic strategy should yield to the study of anthropology; while two grand narratives about culture and war, Robert Kaplan's *Balkan Ghosts* and Victor Hanson's *Carnage and Culture* both influenced American Presidents. Kaplan's fatalist work on the inevitable ethnic blood feuds of the Balkans intellectually reinforced President Clinton's initial decision not to intervene in Bosnia.[101] Hanson's work on the democratic West's military advantages intellectually reinforced the Bush Administration's confidence of success in the Iraq war.[102]

Such ideas also cut across scholarly, professional military and political audiences. The civilian academy plays a part in shaping how the American military conceptualises culture. *Field Manual 3–24*, for example, was written with the assistance of academics. It was published by a prestigious university press at Chicago and became an Amazon bestseller, marking the intersection of three audiences—public, academic and state-military—all invested in a debate about wars against shadowy adversaries in faraway places. One participant was Montgomery McFate, who straddles the academic and military worlds as a cultural anthropologist, a professorial instructor at Johns Hopkins School of Advanced International Studies, and co-founder of the US military's 'Human Terrain Team' system, and who describes Al Qaeda as a primordial force. In both the academy and the public sphere, the culture debate is not over. If anything, despite decades of revisionist scholarship, sweeping ideas about culture are thriving. It is not too late to show that culture in its relationship to war turns out to be contested, ambiguous and politicised.

To summarise:

- Westerners have debated about themselves, their own societies and policies, through visions of the Orient. The history of 'military Orientalism', the fascination for Eastern ways of war, is also a history of Western anxieties, ranging from fear to envy to self-criticism;
- Culture is an ambiguous repertoire of competing ideas that can be selected, instrumentalised, and manipulated, instead of a clear script for action. At war, even actors regarded as conservatives may use their culture strategically, remaking their worlds to fit their needs. Warfare has a discipline of its own that often forces its participants to remake their culture. Those with the will and capacity can make choices, compromise or violate taboos or values for reasons of utility, acting despite tradition not because of it. Cultural realism, which sees culture as fluid and malleable, does a better job of explaining this relationship than 'primordialist' versions, where culture is a clear, semi-permanent tradition that acts on its subjects;
- Theories of strategic culture have much to offer. Culture is an influential variable that can shape war aims, define victory and conflict termination, rank preferences and geostrategic priorities, and constrain choices. But an unbalanced preoccupation with difference and separation, or with the exotic nature of non-western war, can be a poor basis for understanding how people behave. By depicting culture as a unitary force that drives behaviour, we may oversimplify the relationship between culture and action, and damage our ability to watch people acting strategically;

- Warfare has a reciprocal dynamic. Rather than being the by-product of separate and discrete autonomous cultures, it is shaped also by the reactive processes of competition, imitation and globalisation. Culture is shaped by externalities, such as the interpenetration of ideas and influences across boundaries. While the rhetoric of war may be one of hostility and mutual abhorrence, the practice of war is often convergence;
- The typology of 'cultural realism' can help us avoid two extremes. The first is neo-realism, with its concept of global 'strategic man', where culture hardly matters. The second is cultural determinism, where people are almost prisoners of culture, and where strategy and war are bound only by culturally specific norms. With a cultural realist approach, culture can still be powerful. How else could we explain why actors so often appeal to it? But it is also malleable, giving actors greater choice. We can observe the continual interactions and trade-offs between power and identity, tradition and calculation, by seeing culture as something forever remade.[103] In turn, the ability of actors to make effective strategy through culture depends on a range of variables. These include: *time* that is necessary for warring peoples to change; *motive*, where war applies enough interaction and critical pressure to encourage change; the *capacity* to make change, which may be limited by circumstances and resources; and *skilful leadership* that recognises how to use culture.

Some Caveats

This is not an attempt at exhaustive history, which I happily leave to others. Thanks to the author's linguistic limitations, its main focus is on examples from the Anglosphere. That is where the military debate is most intense. But hopefully this imbalance will be corrected by future works on French, Spanish or other Western military Orientalisms. Also, unlike some attempts to interpret Orientalism, it does not deny the possibility of knowledge. Although I argue that perceptions of the Other are often partly a projection of one's own fears and dreams, I do not conclude that nothing is knowable and that inquiry is hopeless. We do not have to abandon the pursuit of historical knowledge to recognise that there often was (and is) a self-reflexivity to written observations of foreign military cultures. Neither is the book an in-depth policy proposal, although some policy implications are suggested at the end. Despite its critical approach, this is not an Olympian work that talks down to others as though the author is infallible. Such is the power of Orientalism, that this book is probably tinged by the very images and myths that it seeks to challenge. Exotic images of the enemy are hard for anyone to block out. This is precisely why it is important to argue against ahistorical myths rather than deny them.

This is a historians' study of the relationship between culture, strategy and war, that draws on past and present cases. As well as an overview chapter, I make some incisions as case studies in greater depth. These include Western perceptions of a Far Eastern ally (Japan from 1904–1910), an historic example for imitation from the Mongolian steppes (Chinggis Khan's army as Westerners saw it in the interwar period), a Central Asian enemy far away (the Taliban through American eyes from 2001), and an Arab adversary nearby (Hizballa through Israeli eyes in 2006). These cases show different impulses that have driven Western fascination, tracing their influence on observers from the military to academe, explaining how and why it has gripped the imagination, and the misconceptions it can breed.

This book is offered in the spirit of friendly criticism. There is *prima facie* evidence that the 'cultural turn' has paid real dividends, as militaries teach themselves to think harder about the human environment in which they operate. In Iraq, it has made American operations in places like Mosul more humane and discriminate, enabled overstretched forces to depress the level of violence, while skilful interaction has helped create a realignment of Sunni tribes against Al Qaeda in Iraq.[104] These gains may be fragile and temporary, but we can applaud the efforts of the US military to reform itself. Hopefully, the argument here can assist this movement, by showing how a 'cultural realist' approach can help, refining our understanding of culture with sober political awareness and a little creative skepticism. It is not a question of whether culture matters, but *how* it matters, and how to conceptualise it.

Mass producing individuals who are schooled in languages, equipped with local knowledge and anthropologically literate is an expensive task. It demands investment of time, money, energy and resources, diverted from other activities, not least keeping the fighting edge. It is vital, therefore, that this education does not create a misleading conception of culture. We can approach culture as a discrete resource that can be pressed into military service, as a matter of the military learning the social ecology of where they operate. Or we can understand wartime culture as a set of moving relationships that the military helps to constitute. As this study shows, the relationship is volatile. Awareness of the dynamics of that relationship, as well as knowledge of local customs, must be part of an effective pedagogy of the subject.

This is important because the cause of culturally-informed war will suffer if it is oversold, as strategic air power and information technology once were. Implicit in some military/strategic analysis is the notion that single moments of cultural illiteracy determine whole wars.[105] This view implies an optimism, that wars can be won if only we learn to push the right semiotic buttons. It is worth remembering the example of Prime Minister Anthony Eden, whose occupation of Suez in 1956 inflamed Arab nationalism, created an international crisis, drained British influence in the region, and highlighted the decline of British power. The same man was also a gifted Orientalist, fluent in Farsi and Arabic, with an Oxford First in Oriental studies. If technology cannot replace strategic judgement, neither can cultural knowledge.

Chapter Outline

In Chapter 1, I provide an overview of military Orientalism, surveying the different contexts in which Westerners have observed the 'Wild East.' While the rhetoric of imperialist hegemony is part of this tradition, it does not account for the richness or the complexity of this history, which lacks a single ideological drive. I argue that Westerners have voiced their fears about themselves, their survival, identity and values, through different visions of non-western warfare.

Chapter 2 shows the strengths and weaknesses of prevailing versions of the new culturalism. By losing sight of the dynamic and unstable nature of this relationship, culturalism risks being politically naïve, overlooking the many moments where strategic cultures do not control actors, but where actors remake their cultures. Culture emerges as a powerful weapon of war that can be instrumentalised.

Chapter 3 examines the opinions of British military observers of Japan, during and after the Russo-Japanese war (1904–5). These observers appraised Japan's military performance through a social investigation. They linked Japan's fighting ability to its demographic base, its political value system, and its concepts of citizenship. Instead of seeing Japan's way of war as intrinsically different and culturally specific, they claimed that it could be imitated. They stressed the role of Japanese institutions in shaping its military excellence, such as its education system, its war memorial culture, and its cult of the emperor. Above all, domestic political issues shaped British perceptions. The image of Japan became a rhetorical standard by which to criticise perceived defects in British culture. They feared that the British Empire was threatened by urbanisation, industrialisation and liberalism, and believed Japan showed how to combine warrior values with modernity.

Chapter 4 examines Western images of the Mongols, remembered as nomadic predators who threatened civilisation. Paradoxically, their way of fighting also inspired Western visionaries, who believed that the Mongols showed how to reunite the two forces, firepower and movement, that had been tragically divorced on the western front in the Great War. Interwar armour theorists, such as Basil Liddell Hart, linked the mobile warfare of the Asia steppes with the potential of modern mechanised forces. The Mongols at his hands became an ideal-type of warrior that reflected his ambitions for tanks and aircraft: self-sufficient, indirect and boundlessly mobile. This said as much about Western fears as it did about Mongol warfare.

Chapter 5 argues that the Taliban, often depicted as exotic enemies wedded to traditionalism, are in fact cultural realists. Throughout the US-led war in Afghanistan, some specialists and pundits emphasised their cultural peculiarities. They depicted the Taliban as tribalists or Islamic mystics, incomprehensible in 'Western' terms. But the Taliban's shifting attitudes in three areas—education, propaganda and suicide bombing—shows that even cultural conservatives trade tradition for victory.

Chapter 6 is about the July 2007 War between Israel, the Middle East's premier military power, and Hizballa, Lebanon's Islamist para-military political movement. In two ways, Israel failed to know the enemy. The main body of the IDF, whose optic was the experience of fighting Palestinian irregulars, under estimated Hizballa. Supposedly primitive theocrats, they fought as hybrids with an advanced structure, operational methods and technological expertise. An underlying notion of an undifferentiated 'Arab' strategic culture proved false. This was also a war of perception, and the battlespace spanned visual images played for a global audience. Although Israeli military minds believed they could smash and discredit Hizballa, Hizballa proved to be a dynamic strategic actor rather than a passive enemy, and seized control of the war's narrative.

Before examining these moments in modern military history, the next chapter introduces the history of the 'Wild East.'

1

THE EMBATTLED WEST

By 1945, the image of Japanese soldiers had transformed. As a British training pamphlet described, the ape became superman:

> The Japanese soldier is, after all, a human being...Before the war started he was classified as a rather fine type of almost human ape, imitative, brave, but without originality, capable only of fighting according to the set exercises of the book and easily beaten by the superior resources and initiative of the white races.
>
> After the considerable battering the white races represented in the Far East received in the four months following Pearl Harbour, opinion...swung the other way. The Jap became a superman, a master of jungle warfare, capable of living for months on a handful of rice, brilliant, resourceful and entirely without fear.[1]

As this suggests, Orientalism can be highly fluid. This chapter explores some of the myriad ways Westerners have gazed on the military 'East'. Representations of the Orient at war, from the texts of strategic thinkers, military observers or anthropologists, to the fiction of popular culture, show us how perceptions have been made, ruptured and redrawn. Orientalism is neither uniform nor necessarily consistent, but draws strength from its ambivalence, its ability to sustain contradictory ideas and images. At times, Westerners have made accurate insights into others' warfare, and they have also made distorted judgments about enemies, judgments which reflect the Western self-image refracted through Orientalism. Throughout, they have debated about themselves—their own warfare and society—through visions of the Orient.

This chapter has four parts. First, it tracks the concept of 'Orientalism' and shows that the East figured in the strategic imagination since antiquity, but not always in straightforwardly supremacist or imperialist ways. Second, it shows how the dynamic interaction of conflict creates a hybridity of war cultures. Third, it examines one of the most important contexts, the period of European and American colonialism, when Western powers became dominant over much of the 'East.' Finally, it looks at two seminal moments of the twentieth century, when Western interest in exotic warfare intensified: the Pacific war with Imperial Japan and the Balkan wars of the 1990s.

Western Confidence, Western Crisis

Power relations between Western and non-Western states have changed continually. In the era of European expansionism and colonial conquest, Westerners glimpsed the East from a position of strength. But for long periods before, they were underdogs. Parthians, Arabs, Mongols, Mamelukes, Magyars, Seljuk Turks, Safavids or Ottomans eclipsed their power. From the Western Roman Empire's collapse until the European conquests of the sixteenth century, non-Westerners dominated land warfare for the most part, though Europeans were more competitive at sea.[2] In response, Western perceptions of the East took many forms. Confidence, fear, empathy, horror, the worldly and apocalyptic can all be found. The focus has moved between the material, (weapons systems, logistics and technology), to the intangible (fighting morale, social cohesion, or attitudes to authority and self-sacrifice). Westerners watched Oriental warfare from different vantage points, as observers up close, or from a distance, through literature, iconography and film. Orientalism is a filter through which a variety of claims can be made. It has alternately worked to warn, to celebrate, to educate or mobilize its audience. What unifies these claims is that the image of the enemy is created through a dialogue of the 'other' and the self.

The word 'Orientalism' has meant many things. It originally referred to experts on Eastern languages, art and literature, from Turkey to Arabia to the whole of Asia. It also came to indicate a way of dealing with the Orient, particularly attached to the East India Company. It now refers to the politics of how and why outsiders, especially Westerners, have represented near- and far-Eastern societies. During decolonization after World War Two and the challenges to European hegemony in India, Algeria or Egypt, it took on new meanings. In the work of Edward Said, A.L. Tibawi, Abdel-Malek and Raymond Williams, 'Orientalism' denoted the distinction between East and West as an epistemological concept. These scholars were variously formed by Gramscian ideas of cultural hegemony, Derridan textual deconstruction, or Foucault's view of the inextricable link between power and knowledge. But in common, they argued that 'knowing' the East is a delusional and suspect activity. They argued that it operates on several fronts, as a value system of ideas and assumptions about the 'East', a style of thought, a 'saturating hegemonic system', and a tool of imperialism.[3]

The doyen of this movement was Edward Said. In his study of French and British representations of the Middle East in the nineteenth and twentieth centuries, and subsequent writing on Israel and American foreign relations, he charged that Western portrayals of the Oriental 'Other' were essentially imperialistic, casting Easterners as inferiors: emotive, tribal, irrational, and sensuous, inclined to extremism and violence.[4] They were fallen civilizations ripe for rule. Despite its claim to disinterested inquiry, scholarship rhetorically normalized and legitimized a set of binary constructions, contrasting European (and then American) rationality, capitalism and maturity with non-European primitivism and immaturity. This exploitative form of knowledge, Said argued, revived ancient prejudices. It was peddled by European colonialists, scholars and others in the late eighteenth and nineteenth centuries, an age of European expansionism, before it was taken up by the United States. Archeologists and novelists assisted the agenda of proconsuls, viceroys and mercantile overlords, because they approached the East from a position of power. Orientalism supported 'Occidental self-affirmation, domination and ascendancy.'[5] One of the few scholars to study Orientalism in a martial context, Tarak Barkawi, argues that the West needs and defines itself against the imagined Orient, so that the West is 'always in a superior position.'[6]

Said's original hypothesis, that Orientalist scholarship was the handmaiden of empire, is strongly challenged.[7] As historians such as John MacKenzie argue, relationships within imperial culture were historically unstable and took many forms. And the Orient was not always central to European consciousness. For Britain over a considerable period, the 'Other' to mobilize against was not primarily the Orient, but France, whether Roman Catholic or revolutionary, as well as internal ethnic and class 'Others.'[8] Neither was the nexus between scholars and imperialism always as simple. The founding fathers of modern anthropology were hardly the 'Colonel Creighton' colonialists targeted by Said.[9] Scholars in the area, like Edward Granville Brown, Lewis Henry Morgan or Bronislaw Malinowski were anti-imperialist in their opinions. Said himself later modified his position, moving from 'Orientalism' to the concepts of 'hybridity' and 'colonial discourse', showing how Western identities were built through borrowings from the Orient, albeit in a framework of inequality.[10]

To be sure, there has long been an intimate association between some scholarship and military conquest. European colonial administrators employed anthropology to classify and dominate their subjects, even if the relationship was looser than Said allowed.[11] Well before anthropology became a self-conscious discipline, Orientalism intellectually spearheaded empire. An ensemble of scholars accompanied Alexander of Macedon's invasion of the Persian Empire (334–323BC). On the heels of his murderous campaign into the heart of Asia, there were architects, botanists, geographers, astronomers, zoologists, and mathematicians. Historians, poets and rhetoricians acted as well-paid propagandists.[12] Napoleon Bonaparte, an imitator of Alexander, invaded Egypt in 1798 with the scientific *Institut d'Égypte* and an entourage of ethnographers, artists and antiquarians. Scholars oversaw the looting of ancient objects and broadcast Napoleon's civilizing and modernizing mission.[13]

Linkages between power and cultural knowledge entered English vocabulary. The term 'Middle East' is an ethnocentric label which places the West at the centre of the world. Often used as though it were an objective fact, it was created to define the geography of power from a Western vantage point. American geostrategist Admiral Alfred Thayer Mahan first coined the phrase in 1902. Mahan wanted to improve on 'Orient', distinguishing the Arabian peninsula from the 'Near East' of Bulgaria and the Balkans and the 'Far East' of China and Japan. The Middle East was the vital chokepoint that joined Africa with Asia. It contained the arteries and supply routes between East and West, with the coaling stations and coastlines needed for maritime reach. To 'know' the East was to know the gateway to power.[14]

Today, critics still implicate scholarship with imperialism. Anthropologists accuse colleagues working with the US military of weaponising their profession into a tool of spying and torture, servicing a 'kill chain' rather than enlightening the waging of war. This repeats the accusation that power and scholarship are dangerously yoked.[15] Yet even as Westerners have at times acted as the enablers and court historians of imperialism, they have been inspired by other impulses. Orientalism is not necessarily aggrandizing or triumphalist. This is shown by the text where Said began, *The Persians*, a play by an Athenian war veteran about an Asian enemy.

The literary heritage of Western Orientalism begins with the Greco-Persian wars. In 472BC, Aeschylus' *The Persians* was first staged in Athens. It was eight years after the battles of Salamis, Plataea and Mycale thwarted the Persian emperor Xerxes' attempt to conquer Greece. For the Athenians and other allied city-states, victory seemed a miraculous deliverance. Greek resistance on land and sea, galvanized by the Spartan-led holding action at Thermopylae, would be celebrated as a struggle for liberty against barbarian interlopers. It became central to Athenian and later Western self-definition, 'the supremely Greek achievement.'[16] Aeschylus portrayed the war from the view of the Persian court. News of defeat arrives and lamentation follows. The Chorus summons the spirit of Darius, Xerxes' majestic father, who scolds his son's arrogance. The Persian king is ruined. For Said, *The Persians* launched Western self-exaltation, dumping onto Asia 'the feelings of emptiness, loss, and disaster.'[17]

To an extent, this is a play of self-celebration. Aeschylus contrasts Greek virtues with Persian vices. He anticipates Orientalist tropes by distinguishing Persians and Greeks with sharply drawn lines.[18] The Persians are 'dangerous men, too many to number', who have vowed to 'throw slavery's yoke firm on the Greeks.' The East, under an enslaving tyrant, is bathed in luxury. Xerxes' Persians are a natural land power, but their despot violates the natural order, bridging the Hellespont to govern the sea. At war, naturally free peoples combat natural slaves. The battle narrative contrasts Greek hoplites with Persian bowmen, citizen-soldiers with heavy shield and spear juxtaposed against Eastern archers.[19] Possibly in order not to spoil the picture of a culture clash, Aeschylus plays down the 'Asiatic' Greeks, the Ionians, whom Xerxes employed in his invasion force. Greek ships appear with the spreading dawn, associated with light and the Persians with darkness. Athens' navy rows into battle singing an anthem to political freedom, liberating their fatherland, people and sacred sites. Defeat checks Persia's power, and robs Asia of its splendour.

It is understandable that Aeschylus celebrated this victory as a vital day's work. After all, Aeschylus himself had fought at both Salamis and Marathon, *The Persians* was written by a survivor of Marathon, a real historical battle ten years earlier in which Aeschylus' own brother was killed. No-one needed to construct the fact that the largest empire known in its time had attacked the small city-states of Greece and that the consequences of defeat would have been mightily unpleasant. The Greek alliance contained slave-owning oligarchies such as Sparta, and victory opened the way for Athens' brutal imperialism, but Athenians believed Greek autonomy, constitutional government and survival were at stake, and that defeat would have made them satrapies of an authoritarian world-state.

But Aeschylus does more than affirm patriotism. He fits Persia's defeat into a pattern of moral order in Greek cosmology, where the gods punish overreaching ambition. Aeschylus does not credit the victory at Salamis primarily to the Athenian navy. While Persian names are recited in lists, no individual Greek is named. Persian defeat is willed by heaven. 'It was some Power, something not human' and 'Gods' who 'keep Athens safe for her goddess.'[20] Xerxes in his 'reckless pride' crosses the fatal boundary between Asia and Europe. He is presented as an aberration rather than a typical Persian, with Darius a contrasting voice of prudent restraint. It is unclear whether Xerxes' plight is supposed to evoke our sympathy in an Aristotelian sense. Nevertheless, Aeschylus' Darius reminds his son not of Athenian greatness but of hubris, defining this as a global law.[21] After Salamis, Darius predicts that 'blood poured out on Plataia's battleground by Dorian spears, so great the pile of bones' shall be 'speechless warnings that those who must die not overreach themselves.'[22] Alongside parochial celebration, we are left with a message of universality. Xerxes may be exotic, but he is a type Greeks would recognize in their own drama, the ruinously arrogant autocrat.[23]

Aeschylus both asserts and challenges the polar differentiation of Greek versus Persian. That Persia could be portrayed in this ambiguous way makes sense in a broader context. The Hellenic and Persian worlds were antagonistic but also interlocked, through mutual political interference, military recruitment, exiles and defections, and Persian rule over Greek cities. The context for Athens was euphoria about its new prospects as a rising power. Before the first performance of the *Persians*, the Delian League was formed, for mutual protection and an offensive against backpedalling Persia, whose power in the region was being eclipsed.[24] Through Xerxes' downfall, Aeschylus invites the audience at Athens to reckon with the dangers of imperial ambition.

Since the Classical empires, Orientalism served to question Western supremacy as well as affirm it. The Orient can appear yielding and weak, or as the place where empires go to die. Unease and the fear of decline have bothered modern imperial visionaries. Compare Rudyard Kipling, the celebrated poet of empire, with Ralph Peters, retired officer and advocate of America's global power. Kipling as a Victorian and Edwardian believer in the 'White Man's Burden' feared that power inevitably receded, that Britain would be punished for 'frantic boast and foolish word,' and that its costly, overstretched forces would be picked off by 'home-bred hordes.' Similarly, Peters warns that America, with its naive technologism and its elite's loss of vigour, is menaced by fanatics with superior will, driven by an 'angry god', and armed with the suicide attack, the wonder weapon of the age.[25] If Orientalism is a language about power, it is a site of anxiety over the vulnerability of that power as well as its effective projection.

Because Orientalism is a mixed bag of self-glorification and self-doubt, it can underpin different policies. Consider the contrasts in America's debates over war against Iraq in 1991 and 2003. During the war in Iraq from March 2003, supporters of the invasion claimed it would be a 'cakewalk', President Bush declared the end of major combat operations under the banner 'Mission Accomplished', later taunting Iraqi insurgents to 'Bring it On.'[26] War in Afghanistan in October-November 2001 had scattered the Taliban with few American casualties. This created a climate of intoxication, emboldening Bush about invading Iraq.[27] In Bush's triumphal vision, ultimate victory was assured because America was on the right side of God and history.

By contrast, public debate before the 1991 Gulf War was filled with defeatism rather than triumphalism. As America prepared for its first duel against Iraqi ruler Saddam Hussein, retired military generals, professional analysts and former diplomats issued dire forecasts. The US, they feared, was headed for a quagmire in the Gulf. The military would be 'bled dry' with losses of up to 45,000 casualties. Saddam with his petro-dollars commanded a million troops, the fourth largest army in the world, armed with chemical weapons. As the crisis escalated, the US would resort to tactical nuclear weapons. The conflict would waste the post-Cold War 'peace dividend.' It would polarize and bankrupt American society at home and humiliate and isolate it abroad.[28]

Misleading images of the Orient played a role in these predictions. Experts on the Middle East warned that America would meet disaster because it misunderstood the 'Arab mind.' James Atkins, former ambassador to Saudi Arabia, claimed America's inability to fathom 'inscrutable' Arabs would bring disaster. George Ball, former ambassador to UN, used the stereotype of Arab duplicity, claiming Saddam was a cunning haggler 'conditioned by the psychology of the Middle Eastern bazaar.' Saddam would fragment America's alliances. Remembering crusades and colonialism, or Mongol Hulagu Khan who sacked Baghdad in 1258, Arabs would desert America. Pan-Arab identity would dictate policy.

But events unfolded differently. The US won the support of many Gulf States as it assembled an international coalition. It expelled Saddam's invading forces from Kuwait after only four days of land war and with minimal losses. Few commentators judged accurately that American forces would gain air supremacy, and prove to be better equipped, better trained and more adept at mobile armoured battles.[29] For their part, Arab states, among them Egypt, Saudi Arabia and Syria, looked past the history of Western invasion and colonialism, identifying their interests with the US, seeing fellow Arab Saddam as a threat to the regional balance of power. Saddam presented himself as the defender of Arab-Islamic civilisation. But for Arab rulers, their security as power-seeking states trumped considerations of cultural ties to Iraq, and they surmounted their history to block his ambitions.[30] Arab politics, like any politics, turned out to be a complex process of negotiated interests. Ironically, it was the American ex-Ambassadors, with their claim to cultural expertise, who succumbed to misleading stereotypes of the Arab 'mind', seeing Saddam not as miscalculating despot but as inscrutable genius, and Arab governments not as flexible strategic actors but as captives of ancient history. This was not the first time, or the last, that those claiming intimate knowledge of 'Oriental psychology' would be wrong.[31]

Ideas of exotic war shift partly because they reflect how Westerners see themselves and their own way of warfare. Over centuries, there have been competing ideas of 'primitive' war. As Europe increasingly made contact with the non-European world, observers often believed they had glimpsed 'early man.' They speculated over what newly discovered cultures revealed about human nature. Natives from pre-Columbian America to Papua New Guinea became subjects for this argument, that gathered pace in the sixteenth century, as the likes of More, Montaigne and Machiavelli, later followed by Rousseau and

Montesquieu, were drawn to warfare beyond Europe. Visions of 'primitive' man informed philosophical speculation. The Hobbesian tradition saw these societies as primordially violent, because war was rooted in pre-civilised 'Nature' and was made possible by a lack of sovereign order. Others believed that early human society lived in social harmony; this suited their view that war is a violation of original innocence.

In more utopian visions, primitive man either rarely waged war, or circumscribed war within strict parameters. Writing in the 1570s, Montaigne praised the warfare of the Brazilian Atlantic Coast as 'both simple and pure', waged not for material gain but for the display of valour. Thomas More's Utopians waged war through intelligence and wit, rather than bloodshed.[32] For Rousseau, philosopher of the French Enlightenment, humans were naturally peaceable. Materialist corruption, wealth and territorial lust turned them to conflict. The West became the womb of violence. This 'noble savage' myth grew as an idea with which to condemn predatory materialism. The archeological record has not been kind to this myth. Fatality rates in the Amazon or Papua New Guinea were four to six times higher than those experienced by modern nations, and prehistoric villages in North America and Europe had fortifications and their inhabitants' skeletal remains bore the blows of weapons.[33] The notion that primitive man lived in tranquility was fantasy, but it powerfully informed Western self-criticism.

As an alternative to the 'noble savage' tradition, there is the view of Western exceptionalism, where non-Western cultures are naturally, irrationally violent. Commentators have claimed that Iraqis, Afghans, Yugoslavs, Amerindians, Somalis, Turks, or Japanese are particularly predisposed to war.[34] While wars have raged through these histories, most striking is the view that this makes them different from the West. This is based narrowly on the recent peace of Europe and North America. For centuries, Europe was a centre of internal violence, ethnic cleansing, pogroms, feuds and vendettas, and then imperial expansion, mechanized slaughter and chemical warfare, and the birthplace of fascism and industrial-scale genocide. Even when it achieved internal peace in the Cold War, this was thanks largely to exhaustion from two world wars, the transfer of power to America and the Soviet Union, and the nuclear deterrent. For its part, the United States was founded by a revolutionary war, preserved by a civil war, expanded by frontier wars and defended in a 'Total War.' What society does *not* have a bloody past?

If organised violence is the common experience of humanity, rather than the result of Oriental character or Western misdevelopment, then a narrow focus on cultural peculiarities has a limited value in explaining it. For one thing, this approach wrongly treats cultures as autonomous and separate. At its crudest, Orientalism petrifies history into antique and static traditions, hardly changed by a changing environment. By reducing the history of warfare to separate worlds, it ignores the interconnections that constitute warfare. Therefore, we should consider how warring cultures reshape one another.

The Hybridity of War

Strategy is about the struggle for survival as well as identity. It is a competitive, imitative exchange. Fear of losing out in an arms race or in military modernization or conflict itself makes adaptation, and re-education, vital. States and polities study, spy and copy from one another, adapt desirable features of others' militaries, seek advisors to help import weapons systems, doctrines or military style. Military organisations derive from the culture of their parent societies, but they are also part of a worldwide profession of state-based militaries that borrow from each other.[35] In the nineteenth century, the successful British Navy and the Prussian-German Armies became compelling models. Mao in his theory of liberation strategy and 'people's war' was inspired by reading Clausewitz. Ottomans hired European military advisors, while their Janissary corps inspired European powers to develop military music and marching in step. Vietnam's anti-colonial reform movement forged its vision of revolutionary struggle partly from the exploits of George Washington and Abraham Lincoln, and mediated ideas of Social Darwinism and Marxist-Leninism with Confucian idealism and Maoist guerrilla warfare.[36]

As the American frontier experience suggests, contact with new terrain and societies remakes cultures and creates new ones. In the Seven Years' War (1756–63), American Indians fought alongside and against European regulars, and their methods mingled. French and British militaries learnt that European methods had to be adapted to forests and vast distances, and a different indigenous host. Regulars would have to travel faster and lighter, exploiting cover and concealment.

New formations of light infantry exchanged their red coats for green or brown clothes, shaving their heads and sometimes painting their skins like the Indians, while Indians trained regulars and traders.[37] Indian warfare also adapted to the newcomers. In 1763, Pontiac's attack on Fort Detroit incorporated European battlefield and siegecraft techniques.[38]

The practice of scalping demonstrates how societies integrate foreign practices, even ones they deem barbaric. Although the removal of body parts has a long history in European warfare, during the French and Indian War (1754–1760) European fighters assumed that scalping originated with the natives, 'this horrible custom was practiced by these savages alone, and sprang from their own barbarism.'[39] But Europeans then took up the method. They paid native allies or mercenaries to scalp as a way of encouraging aggression and counting bodies, while frontiersmen and Christian ministers also scalped. The economic system of bounties expanded the practice, so that tribes for whom scalping was unfamiliar or a rarity now increasingly practised it. What had been a more ritualized, elaborate ceremonial practice among native Americans now evolved into a systematic market of mutilation.[40] Conflict among the pre-Columbian native peoples of Amazonia, which long predated Western conquest, was intensified and reworked by European intrusion. The introduction of firearms, Western manufactures (such as steel cutting tools) and the pursuit of unlimited profit had a dramatic impact. Head-hunting amongst the Jivaro, formerly a limited and ritualized activity, became rampant because the European demand for shrunken heads and a 'Western demand for exotica' was 'capitalizing the killers.'[41] Paradoxically, war can drive cultures closer together.

In the wars of the eighteenth century, professional armies were organized and clothed in similar ways, and had more in common with their adversary counterparts than the civilian world. Hungry and frustrated European armies, without adequate supply lines, besieged, starved and slaughtered non-combatants.[42] The greatest hostility flowed more often along military vs. civilian lines than national culture.[43] Today, for reasons of practical utility or symbolic nationhood, nations of the poorer 'Global South' frequently pursue capital-intensive militarization, creating professional forces, over 'labour-intensive' militarization, which creates lightly armed militias.[44] Worldwide markets, the flow of knowledge and technology, and education enable the spread of weapons systems and at least an outward 'sameness.' Today, Western forces and their adversaries may not share a professional culture. Yet as the next chapter shows, enemies as bitter as the US and militant Islam reshape one another, even while they call each other names.

Because competition can have homogenizing effects, war can prompt recognition as well as 'Othering.' 'War...is not simply a clash of Others, made possible by an ignorant horror of difference. The warrior looks out at the enemy and sees men who are, in crucial respects, recognizably like himself.'[45] Even though he wrote that 'East is East', Rudyard Kipling saw that the East/West divide dissolved on the battlefield, in the affinities between professional soldiers and tribesmen on the North-West Frontier: 'But there is neither East nor West, Border, nor Breed, nor Birth/When two strong men stand face to face, tho' they come from the ends of the earth.'

As this hints, social class as well as trans-cultural difference create points of similarity and recognition. There can be a horizontal cultural divide between societies at war, but there can also be a vertical class divide between commanders and those who fill the ranks. Europe's medieval warrior aristocracy in wars against Muslim forces might find more to recognize in the elites that commanded the enemy than in their own social inferiors. Hence they distinguished between the Muslim masses, who were treacherous heretics, and some individuals who were chivalric heroes. The *Chanson de Roland*, an eleventh-century epic about a Saracen ambush of the Christian Roland and his army at Roncevaux in 778, treats the Saracens as criminals, but describes the Emir of Babylon as nearly the mirror-image of the Frankish knight: '...for his courage he's famous far and near/Were he but Christian, right knightly he'd appear.'[46] After 1187, when Saladin defeated a Crusading Army at Hattin, recaptured Jerusalem and gave safe conduct to the surrendering Christians, *Chansons de geste* and chronicles claimed that Saladin had ideal Frankish qualities. Some went further, branding him an honorary Christian who had secretly been dubbed a knight.[47] With these gestures, the enemy could be assimilated and its success more easily explained.

In a conscious dialogue, Westerners have looked to the enemy's strengths in order to criticize themselves. The success of non-Western powers such as the Ottoman empire from the fifteenth to the seventeenth centuries also prompted study as educational examples. This state had well-organised and well-disciplined armies, and excelled at siegecraft and fortifications. Echoing Machiavelli, military observers of early modern Europe were dissatisfied with their own undisciplined and volatile mercenary armies, and looked with envy at Turkey's alternative system.[48] They contrasted their unruly mercenaries with the good order, courage and self-control of Ottoman forces.[49] There were also religious explanations for Ottoman success, appearing in the work of Martin Luther and lasting into the seventeenth century. The might of the Turkish enemy could be seen as a symptom of Western corruption.[50]

Declinists who worry about the fall or decay of the West have been drawn to the figure of the Oriental or native warrior. In the face of distressing change, such as the Industrial Revolution and the coming of the modern world, the Eastern hero came to symbolise the West's lost virtues. Consider Hollywood treatments of cross-cultural encounters, *Dances with Wolves* and *The Last Samurai*. In both, a white American soldier, a forlorn cavalry officer or jaundiced mercenary, drifts from a corrupt and insane white world. He encounters a formidable martial people, whether Japanese or Native American. Their antique code of honour is contrasted with the cold-blooded brutality of those that seek their destruction. Nathan Algren, played by Cruise, is disturbed by American frontier massacres and drawn to the exotic mystique of the samurai, just as Kevin Costner's John Dunbar admires the purity of the Sioux. The nomadic white hero rediscovers his soul in the precapitalist, pristine barbarian.[51] He enters their society, assimilates to their culture, and joins their twilight struggle to resist capitalist modernity, in the Satsuma rebellion against the Meiji regime in 1877, or against the Federal Army's expansionism. The final scenes of the *Last Samurai*, where uniformed soldiers slaughter charging Samurai with machine guns, unmistakably anticipate the Western Front of World War One, and the theme of a nobler chivalric world annihilated by mechanized butchery.

Older versions of the 'going native' genre were more predatory tales where joining the 'savages' enabled the hero to battle against them. Ron Howard's *The Missing* is one of the more recent of this version, about a white man who becomes an Apache before hunting down a diabolical redskin slaver. By contrast, *The Last Samurai* recalls the atrocities of white society and is a more liberal and guilt-stricken update to the tradition. But it is in essence a 'Western', true to the classic motif of 'going native.' Ed Zwick, director of *Last Samurai*, was inspired by Kurosawa Samurai films, which were in turn inspired by American Westerns. The historical detail of the samurai or native Americans matters far less than their usefulness as symbols for the Western experience. In *The Last Samurai*, Cruise's character likens the Samurai both to the Spartans at Thermopylae and the Sioux he battled under Custer. Classical Greek, native American and Japanese icons are fused into a generic heroic type. To Zwick, *The Last Samurai* is about America's 'collapsing societal values. There does seem to be a certain rot that I can't help but be aware of.'[52] Ancient and anti-rational, the noble savage becomes a figure of reactionary nostalgia.[53] By valorizing the Oriental, the filmic frontier-crossing story expresses unease with the modern West.

The image of the eternal warrior standing outside time proved popular. Myths of ancient continuity were long attached to Japan's *Samurai*, who have also been portrayed—and portrayed themselves—in folkloric terms, as a sword-wielding and honour-bound aristocracy, valuing reputation above material interest and pursuing social stature through war. In America, cheap novels and Wild West shows, and works of anthropology and history, portrayed natives of the North American Plains as nomadic warriors who cared more about personal honour than about material interests, the 'mythic counterparts of Anglo cowboys.' Their warfare, supposedly, was a functionalist game, expressive rather than instrumental, waged out of individualized militarism and a predisposition to violence. They were the famed buffalo hunters, a great horse culture, who rode like their ancestors for raids, revenge, and glory.[54]

But these ideas were ahistorical. Samurai in the thirteenth and fourteenth century may have thirsted for social esteem and ceremonial display. But they were willing to withdraw from battle or change sides, cared strongly about payment and reward, and committed suicide less often than is thought. They were at least as likely to act as calculating soldiers of fortune as men who followed the way of death. It was the Samurai of the seventeenth century who romanticized their forbears in order to justify their privileges in peacetime.[55] Plains Indians waged war for collective material interest, such as economic markets in New Mexico, as well as personal glory. They maintained honour codes and protocols of etiquette, but within a material framework for wars, and fought for hunting rights, access and tribute. Moreover, their horse culture was not ancient or an incremental evolution from primordial times, but a relatively late innovation that arrived via Spanish contact from the South and West, and the firearm from French, British and American contact in the North and East. Though they were confused for timeless hunters, the tactics they employed against white settlers in the nineteenth century were the result of the dislocating impact of new technology, the transition from agriculture to nomadism, and increasing competition for land.[56] By the time Custer's Seventh Cavalry rode out to attack the Greasy Grass encampment in 1876, war had altered the worlds of whites and natives.

Because these ideas of the eternal warrior hold such power as ways of criticizing the West, scholarship can challenge but not fully exorcise them. The relatively recent experience of European and American empire, and the enduring reality of frontier battles, leaves us with images and ideas that still resonate.

Savage Wars of Peace: the Colonial Context

As Europeans conquered the earth, military Orientalism entered a new era. The gunpowder revolution and industrialization empowered conquerors, and long-range naval power gave them a global reach. Conquest of the Americas was followed by races to dominate India, Africa, China and the Asia-Pacific. In the United States, the end of the Civil War was followed by penetration of the country's interior, while victory over Spain created opportunities for expansion in Latin America, the Philippines and Hawaii. The frontier became a place of exotic terrors in the minds of imperial powers.

'Small wars' against indigenous peoples rarely posed an existential threat to Western powers. But they proved dangerous in other ways. Defeat or failure at the hands of a supposed inferior provoked self-examination, even disturbing the concept of Western identity. One rhetorical way of handling defeat was to adopt enemies as a recognizable hero, or present them as kindred Westerners. In 1896 at Adowa, Ethiopians surrounded and killed 262 Italian officers and 4,000 men, bringing down the Crispi government. It was the greatest disaster in European colonial history. So Europeans transformed Ethiopians into a fellow Christian and European power surrounded by Islamic hordes, portraying them as racially Caucasian, darkened by the equatorial sun.[57]

Defeats, disasters and atrocities abroad could bring down governments. They strained social cohesion, and drew debate over the costs and morality of empire. The climax of imperialism, dated roughly between 1885 (the Berlin Congress) and 1914 (the First World War), was also an anxious time of rivalry and tension among European powers. Competing priorities of home defence and state spending, and doubts over the benefit of fighting wars on the periphery, meant popular opinion could only be mobilized for short, decisive wars. Wars could jeopardise the physical and mental capacity of the population to defend and police the empire. Empire created its own antibodies. Dissidents, journalists and politicians criticised colonial warfare, such as the indictment of British methods by the liberal MP J.A. Hobson.[58] Paradoxically, expansionism was powered by the very anxieties over decay and decline that it created.[59]

As examples, Germany's campaigns against the Herero and Maji-Maji rebellions in 1904–6 outraged the Reichstag which refused to pass the budget. A campaign in Algeria waged to save the Bourbon Restoration instead unleashed protests in France and political collapse in 1830. Napoleon III was weakened by expensive adventures in Mexico, while the Third Republic's attempt to seize Tunisia resulted in the fall of Prime Minister Jules Ferry. Benjamin Disraeli's government was mortally wounded by William Gladstone's 'Midlothian' campaign against the Zulu War of 1879–80 and the Afghan War of 1878–80.[60] The United States would taste this during the Vietnam War. A nation with an identity of anti-imperialism was polarised in a war denounced as an imperialist venture that poisoned the republic's soul. Wars on the periphery, which governments rarely wanted to support with more than a small fraction of national resources, impacted on the capital cities and core of empires, also known as the 'metropole,' upsetting confidence in the nation's civilizing mission and its doctrines of imperial destiny, whether *Pax Romana, Pax Britannica* or 'Manifest Destiny.'[61]

In hindsight it may appear that European and American conquest was inexorable. A common preconception of colonial wars is that Western military advantage was overwhelming. In *Blackadder*, Captain Edmund recalls the battle of Mboto Gorge, where his regiment fought '10,000 Watusi warriors armed to the teeth with Kiwi fruit and guava halves.' But this reflects a period when the technological gap between European and native defender was widening. It was not ever thus. For long, instead of fighting in radically foreign ways, natives could compete on familiar terms. In the pre-industrial age, expeditionary forces were resisted by enemies such as the native Americans with flintlock muskets, and more lethally by Indians, who were able to generate their own powder, bullets, muskets and sometimes artillery. This parity applied particularly before the introduction of breech-loading rifles in the 1860's. It was often difficult for Europeans to close down technology transfer, or to seize a monopoly on their weaponry and skills. Indigenous forces hired European advisors, traded their coveted goods for weapons, or were armed by rival powers or colonists who lacked manpower. And the defender's climate, remote location and terrain could logistically impede invaders, as Europeans often remained sea-bound and struggled to move heavy artillery inland.

Symmetry and 'sameness' might feature in these campaigns alongside asymmetry. So in the 2nd Maratha War (1803–5), British commanders Lake and Wellsley expected to fight against irregulars with mounted warriors and guerrilla methods. But the Marathas employed modern weapons systems to wage devastating conventional war. At the battle of Assaye on 23 September 1803, Wellesley's army suffered casualties of more than 30%. In his later incarnation as the Duke of Wellington, he judged it to be his hardest battle.[62] In New Zealand, the Maori exploited Britons' assumptions that they would fight as traditionalists. Instead of staying in their traditional wooden palisades (their *pa*) to provide easy targets for British artillery, they turned the *pa* into decoys and improvised a subterranean system of trench defence and tunnels that anticipated the Western front of World War One.[63] Adaptive enemies refused to behave according to cultural preconceptions.

The experience of empire helped a particular idea to coagulate, the distinction between soldiers and warriors. Soldiers were disciplined, organized and directed for instrumental purposes and expediency. Warriors, by contrast, were peoples for whom conflict had a meaning of its own. Warfare was a calling, affirming a way of life and expressing existential values.[64] The warrior was a primitive but embodied qualities that were endangered in the West. After the battle of Omdurman in 1898, where British firepower slaughtered Sudanese Dervishes, the triumph 'of the arms of science over barbarians' also called forth primal courage. The savages were mad yet 'gallant', charging and 'yelling like fiends.'[65]

A classic text of military Orientalism, from the 'high renaissance' of the colonial era, was Colonel C.E. Callwell's *Small Wars*, comparable with French Lt. Colonel Alfred Ditte's *Observations sur les Guerres dans les Colonies*.[66] Callwell distinguished between savage and civilised modes of warfare. Savage wars were waged by alien cultures operating by different rules, while savages were easily impressed by 'a bold and resolute procedure.'[67] Because Asiatics were unable to fight in more limited conventional ways, and were readily coerced by shows of vigour, it was necessary to abandon norms of restraint to subdue them. 'Uncivilised races' mistook 'leniency' for 'timidity,' so that 'fanatics and savages must be thoroughly brought to book and cowed or they will rise again.'[68] With this argument, Callwell echoed and reinforced an attitude endemic in European imperialism, the linkage between a society's mode of war and its degree of civilization, and correspondingly, the kind and intensity of violence that was justified in meeting it. Once a philosophical argument about the nature of humanity, the notion of primitive warfare was transmuted into a system of military thought.[69] Callwell's *Small Wars* supplied a permissive ideology which enabled imperial armies to justify the level of force based on the enemy's perceived barbarity.

The idea that the enemy is singularly obsessed with strength and weakness, impressed only by dash and brutal treatment, has been applied to many disparate foreign cultures. Like Russian General M.D. Skobolev, who believed that hitting Asians hard kept them quiet, American General Douglas MacArthur claimed special insight into 'Oriental psychology' and its tendency to admire 'aggressive, resolute and dynamic leadership.'[70] Of the Arabs, a senior US officer with the 4th Infantry Division claimed that 'The only thing these sand niggers understand is force and I'm about to introduce them to it.'[71] Culture becomes the excuse to reach for the revolver.

But this rhetoric is more than an excuse, licensing aggression that might otherwise seem reprehensible, such as indiscriminate violence or breaching non-combatant immunity. It is attractive also because it enables people to think of themselves as civilized while practising brutality. This logic can be seen in the title of a document from Britain's Air Ministry in January 1922, that speculated that the best forms of 'frightfulness' to be applied in 'savage warfare' to make rootless nomads 'behave themselves' would be psychological terror: 'Suggested Systems of Attack against Uncivilized Tribes.'[72] In this world view, where the violence of savages is primal and unsophisticated, the West is guided by strategic rationality.

Apart from 'savage' and 'civilized', there were peoples in between. Imperialist commentators often taxonomized subject peoples as 'martial races.' Indian Sepoys, Punjabi Sikhs or Nepalese Gurkhas were enlisted as defenders of empire. Contemporaries saw in them the valour that made them 'noble exemplars of the True Military Tradition.'[73] A nineteenth-century form of martial race theory spread through a growing market of opinion of journals, popular fiction and handbooks about heroic peoples. Major-General C.J. Mellis, writing of his expedition in East Africa in 1896, weighed the abilities of different races—Arabs who 'won't stand and fight but bolt when you are in their neighbourhood', then distinguished between Punjabis and Pathans, the former 'good chaps' of pluck and spirit, the latter loathsome 'hulking undisciplined brutes.'[74] Whole peoples were assigned modal personalities.

These ideas helped shape recruitment patterns. Especially between 1880 and 1914, populations thought to be culturally or biologically predisposed to war increasingly made up the native infantry, so that by 1893, 44% of the Native Indian Army was recruited from perceived 'martial races', while by 1914 it rose to three-quarters.[75] Army officers believed that racial qualities existed, yet also believed that other processes improved their quality, such as conversion from Hindu to Sikh, combining essentialist rhetoric about intrinsic traits and the constructionist view that racial traits were malleable. Martial race theory also provided images of foreign warriordom through which observers could seek the regeneration of their own society. As in a mirror, political officers projected onto the Pashtun tribal mind their own code of Victorian public-school values, where frontier fighters were animated by 'honor', 'courage' and 'word.'[76]

The Indian Mutiny of 1857 was a critical moment in defining these hierarchies. High-caste sepoys of the Bengal Army who had rebelled were recast as disloyal cowards and were excluded from later recruitment, while the Sikhs and Gurkhas who helped to crush the uprising were idealized. The Eden Commission Report of 1879 described the Punjab as the 'home of the most martial races of India' and 'the nursery of our best soldiers.' British officer G.F. MacMunn's description of the Punjabi shows how observers saw exotic warriors through the prism of ideas about British class and manhood:

> The Punjabi generally, but especially the Sikh, has become a world wide adventurer...tall, well-knit men, with their long hair pulled up under the headdress, their beard and whiskers neatly curled up close to the face, and their

military bearing all stamp the man...As a fighting man, his slow wit and dogged courage gave him many of the qualities of the British soldier at his best.[77]

This romantic view of frontier society transcended foreigners, and likened sub-continental warriors to Highland soldiers. Sikhs, Afghans or Pathans were both superior and inferior. Superior, because the British believed them to be untamed primitives who had not been polluted by commerce, and that their savagery endowed them with honour and simplicity. Inferior, as colonial rhetoric infantilized them, seeing their stupidity as they key to their obedience. Because the natives lacked civil society, it was held that they needed British officers to orchestrate them into a coherent force. Authorities such as Lord Roberts feared education and urbanization as centres of nationalist subversion, so the Indian Army rarely recruited from towns or cities. The British chose to recruit from remote regions, where most recruits were illiterate, reinforcing stereotypes about their stupidity.[78] Recruiting as a practice created a self-fulfilling theory.

If war is both an expression of identity and a practical a tool for success, the two phenomena can clash. Westerners, thinking of themselves fighting fairly, found themselves fighting cultures that refuse to observe their protocols. When primitive methods seemed effective, they could be adopted. Thus when fighting the naturally 'treacherous' Afghans, one report from 1925 advised, 'nothing is more effective' than the 'adoption by our troops of some of their own "slim" methods' including ambushes and feints, so that 'do unto Afghans as they do unto you' would get results.[79] Reports about the Japanese army in Malaya in World War Two portray an enemy 'full of low cunning' who carried out 'ruses', but this duplicity could be copied to counter them. British forces must 'play him at his own game.'[80] Callwell defined fanatics as undisciplined and disorganized but brave, such as Afghan Ghazis or Algerians. This enemy might have to be impersonated in order to be defeated. 'The hostile tactics are essentially aggressive, and inasmuch as they involve substitution of shock action for fire action, the regular forces are compelled, whether they like it or not, to conform to the savage method of battle.'[81] Thus a tension developed between the desire to distinguish imperial power from the fanaticism that subverted it, and the recognition that 'fanatics' could force others to fight on their terms. To a degree, it was necessary to become the enemy to defeat it.

Britain's operations in Somalia illustrate some of the contradictions that accompanied the Orientalism of frontier wars. Rebels and opponents were frequently described as insane or 'fanatics.' The word 'fanatic' was not only applied to intense ideological belief systems, but also to almost any act of rebellion.[82] Col J.E. Gough feared that a British withdrawal to the coast would enable the Mullah to become 'a formidable fanatical Mahomedan power.'[83] 'Notes for Guidance for the Camel Corps' of 1930 still warned of the 'fanatical uprising of all the Somali tribes.'[84] Not all observers agreed. One officer cautioned that 'the Mullah's conduct throughout was the perfectly rational conduct of an extremely ambitious and extremely capable man.'[85] The question of whether the enemy was rationally directed or a chaotic horde was never finally resolved. [86] But it was in moments of battle that the issue came into sharp focus.

In the iconography of cross-cultural wars, the focal point is frequently the fighting. Famous battles between East and West remain legendary. These clashes include Thermopylae (480BC), Roncevaux Pass (778), Constantinople (1452), Tenochtitlan (1519), Lepanto (1571), The Alamo (1836), Little Big Horn (1876), Rorke's Drift (1879), and Gallipoli (1915) all of which were immortalized in literature and film. These battles became the stuff of adventure stories and public titillation. These battles enjoyed a lucrative market, whether in oral tradition or in mass entertainment, and were also bestowed with a deeper significance.

In these episodes, we can see a loose but strong archetypal narrative. Trapped and outnumbered Western combatants must fight an enemy horde against the odds. With the exception of Thermopylae, which happened on the edge of Hellenic soil, these battles usually occur in distant or frontier territory. The heroes must defend outposts or isolated positions as a result of a botched excursion or intelligence failure. Their heroism or martyrdom occurs in outer darkness. Given the odds against them, the expedition can be seen as an essentially defensive struggle. Against Mohammed Ahmed, the Mahdi ('the Guide'), who in Islamic eschatology signalled the return of the Messiah and waged *jihad* against British forces, the *Pall Mall Gazette* depicted General Charles Gordon in the Sudan standing 'Alone, in a black continent, dauntless and unfaltering...holding the capital of the Sudan against beleaguering hordes.'[87] The isolated heroes affirm the best of civilisation precisely in the place where civilisation is subverted by alien practices such as human sacrifice, slavery, child soldiers, scalping, cannibalism or suicide attack. Because the foe is momentarily stronger, the overdog becomes the underdog for the day. The Western audience is brought to imagine its own vulnerability.

The battle might result in victory or defeat. Regardless, the virtuous few fighting the massed enemy embody the self-sacrifice necessary to sustain civilisation. In the United States, battles against native forces were invested with an existential importance. The defeat and death of Custer and his Seventh Cavalry at the battle of Little Big Horn, a militarily minor event, became a touchstone of American identity. Of battles on American soil, only Gettysburg received as much writing. At the Centennial of America's foundation, a time of internal class strife and economic distress, war between redskin and pale-face became central to divining the meaning of history. Custer's fall shocked some as a blow to the struggle against the savagery of the plains; others saw the defeat as an exemplary sacrifice that should unify a fractured society. Little Big Horn nourished a longer-term 'frontier ideology', an idea of righteous struggle against barbarism through which Americans judged subsequent conflicts at home and overseas, whether against striking workers or Vietnamese Communists. The landscape of battle became a meaningful space through which America's fate could be articulated.[88] The battle, indeed, had something for everyone. For American Indians, their victory stood for brave anticolonial resistance.[89] For white society, Custer's tragic heroism, and an adversary who put up a fight, ennobled the war to tame the landscape and create a bicoastal nation. Conquest could be won by virtue as well as firepower and coercion.

The residue of frontier struggles supplies a language through which to interpret American wars abroad. American soldiers might take the frontier with them. The metaphorical language of 'Indian Country' was and is pervasive in US military discourse. It jumbles meanings, suggesting chaotic and dangerous territories that must be pacified, war against non-white peoples, guerrilla and terrorist forms of combat, and ultimate victory.[90] It has resurfaced in successive expeditionary wars, including wars against Japan, North Vietnam and Iraq. In 1942, a military observer in Malaya described Japan's onslaught of movement, surprise and encirclement: 'It is like Indians fighting with Tommy guns.'[91] Today's 'Indian Country' and the 'red Indian' metaphor are transported to the Middle East. Ambushed in Nasirlyali, Iraq, in

March 2003, Sergeant James Riley instinctively used similar terms, 'We were like Custer. We were surrounded.'[92]

The writer and adventurer Robert Kaplan uses the Indian wars to define today's world as a global extension of the American frontier. US forces take up their missionary burden, bringing order into 'zones of sheer chaos.'[93] And as in 1876, Kaplan uses the frontier as an idea with which to educate American society at home. This is also about the dialogue between civil society and its military defenders. Kaplan insists that, just like the nineteenth-century wars, noisy liberal critics need to acknowledge the dangerous nature of the frontier. Kaplan also is attracted to Indian resistance methods. He uses the metaphor of light-armed, mobile Indians as an ideal-type to criticise the structure of the American military. American forces, he suggests, should be more like Apaches. By developing small units of dexterous soldiers, they can reform their military from a 'dinosaurian, Industrial Age beast to a light and lethal instrument skilled in guerrilla warfare.' The barbarian is both the enemy and the model for military transformation.

Because the West in these battles faces daunting odds, the heroic formula becomes about numbers as well as rhetoric. Obviously, being outnumbered in the event of victory amplifies the glory of the victors, while in defeat it highlights their valour. Ever since antiquity, commanders and their admirers have stressed the enemy's size as a measure of their achievement, at times claiming suspicious ratios. Herodotus estimated that Xerxes in his invasion had mobilized 2,641,610 fighting men. Yet Hans Delbrück, with the benefit of comparative orders of march showed that if Herodotus were right, the Persian marching column would have to have been 420 miles long. As the first troops were arriving at Thermopylae, the last would have just marched out of Susa.[94] Hagiographies of Hernan Cortes, such as William Prescott's bestselling *History of the Conquest of Mexico*, claimed that the calibre of Spanish-Christian civilization was demonstrated in the ability of the Conquistadores to conquer the masses of Mexico with only a tiny expeditionary force.[95]

These claims are historically misleading and serve to obscure other contributing factors for military success. Western skill and discipline were clearly an important ingredient in battlefield supremacy. Yet other circumstances beyond the battlefield were destructive of native anticolonial resistance. One reason battle narratives could focus on a small number of Westerners was precisely that colonial militaries recruited indigenes as fighters or spies. Despite modern talk of the 'clash of cultures', some Indians chose to cross cultural boundaries and assist Custer's multinational frontier army.[96] Conquest was also helped by the devastation of disease and the exploitation of local divisions. Success owed much to the unspectacular, such as the creation of small expeditionary parties with tinned food, potable water, and way stations. Systemic problems played a part, such as the difficulty natives had in permanently mobilizing and feeding an army, or in the American Indians' case, the cumulative demographic impact of white settlement and the railroad. Yet in the focus given to landmark battles, these things were marginalized, unwittingly or deliberately, in order to make Western militaries the main actor in the drama, and a moment of combat as the pivotal event.

Many mythologised battles were indecisive, and were assigned meaning beyond their military significance. Gallipoli was a failed Entente campaign to storm the Dardanelles, seize Istanbul and break Ottoman Turkey's control of the sea route to Russia. Yet it became the core of a creation myth in Australia and New Zealand. In Australia's case it was cast as the baptism of former penal colonies into nationhood through the sacrifice of a volunteer army. A successful minor episode, Rorke's Drift, entered British hagiography as an heroic effort. The outnumbered defenders showed nerve and discipline to hold out for twelve hours. But they had advantages, devising a strong defensive position with vast stores of ammunition. In the ordinary course of events, it would only have received limited attention in regimental history. Here their efforts were lionised because the battle served a political purpose. The government celebrated it to distract attention from another recent disaster, Isandhlwana, where Zulus with the two 'horns' of double encirclement annihilated a British battalion. That defeat by naked savages shocked the British public. To assuage national distress, more medals were awarded at Rorke's drift than any battle in history.[97] Heroism is not only a physical or moral act, it is a process of 'social creation' that relies on recognition by a wider audience.[98]

While we should be cautious of exact parallels, some meanings invested in these historic battles rhyme with more recent cases. Consider the battle of Mogadishu (1993), the aborted American-led operation in Somalia dramatized in *Black Hawk Down* (2001). The film presents the American soldiers as heroes on the edge of darkness. Thrust into a post-apocalyptic cityscape, they are frustrated by the ruthless warlords and the enemies' freedom to operate, set against their own restrictive rules of engagement. While this story was stylistically and contextually different from nineteenth-century 'frontier fight' tales, it shares at least one important feature: it is directed at the home front, through the figure of the alienated soldier. Even the most restrained versions of this genre depict the soldiers sympathetically as representatives of civic duty, Christian valour or raw courage for the education of citizens at home. The story is as much a commentary on domestic society as well as the nature of the far-off enemy.

Public appetite for this kind of heroism is reflected in the growing legend of 'Operation Red Wing', a battle between four US Navy SEALs against 150 Taliban fighters in the Afghan mountains in 2005. It has already produced a bestselling eyewitness account (*Lone Survivor*), while Universal Pictures has purchased the film rights.[99] This text captures the ambivalences of Western perceptions of culturally alien war. Deployed to Afghanistan, Marcus Luttrell's SEAL team endures extraordinary hardships. Releasing three Afghans they come across, Luttrell is convinced the same three inform the Taliban, who hunt his team and kill his comrades. Americans are endangered because they show mercy and play by '*our* rules, the rules of the Western countries, the civilized side of the world.'[100] Luttrell sees his men as victims of a tripolar conflict between the barbaric Taliban, the weak American homefront and his beleaguered men caught in the middle. A combination of irresponsible media, paralyzing liberalism and ignorant citizenry at home will leave America's military helpless to combat merciless fanatics. The frontier battle is fought to defend the West's moral standards, but the same standards make America vulnerable:

> In the global war on terror, we have rules, and our opponents use them against us. We try to be reasonable; they will stop at nothing. They will stoop to any form of base warfare: torture, beheading, mutilation. Attacks on innocent civilians, women and children, car bombs, suicide bombers, anything the hell they can think of. They're right up there with the monsters of history.
>
> And I ask myself, Who's prepared to go furthest to win this war? Answer: they are. They'll willingly die to get their enemy. They will take it to the limit, any time, any place, whatever it takes. And they don't have rules of engagement.[101]

As well as horror, there is a whiff of envy here. Such is the enemy's barbarity that the civilized must abandon their restraints to combat it. So he justifies torture on these grounds, and later when wounded and sheltered in a village, even contemplates a suicide bomb attack on some Afghan villagers should the Taliban arrive to execute him. At the heart of this is a scathing attack on liberal opinion in America. Luttrell deploys the image of the monstrous Taliban as a foil to attack part of the American 'self', in this case the naïve humanists at home.

Not all frontier heroism tales are so explicitly ideological. Compared to some heroic tales, the films *Zulu* (1964) and *Black Hawk Down* (2001) are more muted in justifying war.[102] Dennis Showalter notes that 'In both, a small self referencing body of professional soldiers stands off an overwhelming enemy in an alien land for reasons never given. 'Why us? Asks a young and bewildered Tommy. 'Because we're here, lad' replies the grizzled colour-sergeant. 'No one else. Just us.'[103] The soldiers do little preaching but, like Leonidas and the three hundred Spartans, are exemplars, obedient to their countries' laws. *Black Hawk Down*, whose tag line is 'Leave no Man Behind', investigates the same bond of soldiers stranded in a surreal foreign city. Bound by their comradeship, dislocated combatants convey unease with the society that sent them. Eric Bana's character makes a low-key speech about the physical and moral distance of American Rangers from their compatriots at home. Frontier tales are retold to educate a wayward society.

Thus far, we have seen how Orientalism operated in the context of colonialism and empire, and some of the ideas that evolved out of those legacies. But in the twentieth century, Orientalism had to adjust to a new challenger who abruptly shattered the white man's domination of Asia.

The Twentieth Century: 'Yellow Peril' and 'Ancient Hatreds'

The rise and fall of Imperial Japan is a major episode in the history of military Orientalism. It is widely seen as a moment of cultural error, one of the gravest intelligence failures and underestimations of non-Western military power in history. The resulting war in the Pacific between the United States, the British Empire and Japan became defined as a brutal race conflict in which Japan seemed the strangest of enemies, one that militarised the taboo of suicide. This same conflict is also closely tied to the discipline of anthropology. In America, war with Japan stimulated the boom of 'whole culture' studies, where social scientists tried to identify the national character of societies. Cultural-anthropological studies of warring nations were sponsored by the US government through bodies such as the Committee for National Morale, which sought to leverage the insights of anthropology to help wartime mobilisation, and propelled a generation of American Japanologists to academic and bureaucratic positions.[104]

We now know much about how foreigners analysed Japanese military power.[105] In the interwar years, it was once said, Western estimates of Japanese military power were perverted by racism. Outsiders fell into the trap of under-estimating Japan, and its will and ability to challenge Anglo-American power.[106] This folly was punished by the shock of Pearl Harbor in December 1941. Japan pounded the forces of complacent Great Britain, the United States and the Netherlands, overwhelmed limited garrisons at Malaya and Singapore, and seized an empire from the Philippines to the Dutch East Indies. Written off as an uncreative and inferior people, Japan innovated in naval aviation, night combat and amphibious warfare.

Yet as new research shows, the record of pre-war Western perception is more subtle.[107] The history of Anglo-American perception of Japan was an ambivalent combination of accuracy and error. Opinion in the Military Intelligence Directorate of Britain's War Office, for example, was far more balanced. In the interwar period, vulgar stereotypes existed among more junior officers about the Japanese' poor eyesight and balance, and their non-adaptive 'national character.' This was only one of several strains of opinion, however. Japanophiles stressed their capacity to learn and innovate and to make quick decisions, their powers of endurance, their *espirit de corps*, their capacity for night attacks, and their greater studiousness than British counterparts.[108] Some reports recognised the dangers inherent in deteriorating relations with Japan and the need for the ability to project power in the region.[109] The problem was that these professional insights were not generally appreciated among British officers.

Where experts inaccurately perceived Japan, this was often for reasons other than bigotry. It was due also to Japanese secrecy and security restrictions, to linguistic barriers, and in Britain to the bias of colonial interpretation of intelligence towards internal policing. A degree of racial complacency may be inferred from the general assumption that Japan would not take the gamble of challenging Anglo-American power in the region. But rather than uniform racism, ethnocentrism and mirror-imaging were the main intellectual failings. On the grand strategic level, some neglected the fact that Japan should not be judged against the standard of Western Europe, with its limited force-to-space ratio and its stress on heavy firepower, but in terms of the vast and undeveloped areas of Asia, where Japan's ethos of manoeuvre, morale and speed made more sense.[110] Another distorting factor was the different way Japan approached field exercises and manoeuvres. The IJA used these activities as tests of efficient staff work, scripting and rehearsing them, rather than as tests of initiative. Similarly, amphibious landings were practised as assaults on undefended rather than fortified positions, a difference that misled observers preoccupied with the Gallipoli precedent.[111]

The Pacific War has been characterised as a process of barbarization, where both sides saw the enemy as a radical 'other.'[112] Its unanticipated aggression led to a brutal war in the Pacific (1941–45) where both sides mobilised their citizens around dehumanising propaganda. Japan's hyper-nationalist, suicidal army was regarded as an expression of its national psychology from time immemorial. Scientific racism and essentialist views of national character bred mutual incomprehension and helped to create a war without mercy. This Japan reinforced, by emphasizing its own uniqueness, its preordained right to rule inferior races, and its radical 'otherness.' With slave labour camps, firebombing and nuclear obliteration, the war accentuated the sense of cultural antagonism. It was perceived as a clash of radically different cultures.

Kamikaze suicide attacks (officially known as *tokkotai* or Special Attack Units) were the most potent symbol of Japan's 'otherness.' In reality, there was only a limited supply of willing *kamikaze* pilots. Young pilots praised as willing sacrificial heroes were actually being coerced or forced to volunteer for the *tokkotai* operations rather than volunteering. Some refused but their refusal was ignored. Other pilots on missions tried to return or land on water, while others such as Hayashi Ichizo who obeyed also protested against the official ideology: 'I cannot say that the wish to die for the emperor is genuine, coming from my heart. However, it is decided for me...' In a psychological questionnaire two months after Okinawa started, one third of the members of one *tokkotai* unit remained undecided and felt conflicted.[113] Yet outwardly, those on the receiving end could not know about these ambivalent feelings and internal reluctance, and the tactic looked alien and fanatical. Recalling Japan's desperate attempts to coerce the

Allies, and the ambivalent impression it left, US Vice Admiral Charles R. Brown described 'a hypnotic fascination to a sight so alien to our western philosophy. We watched each plunging *kamikaze* with the detached horror of one witnessing a terrible spectacle...And dominating it all was a strange admixture of respect and pity.'[114]

But in wartime, images of Japan spanned the extremes. They ranged from the fear created by Japan's early successes, to the belittling hostility of Allied propaganda, to increasingly accurate intelligence assessments and psychological appraisals.[115] In the Pacific War, just as Allied nations painted the enemy as inhuman savages, their intelligence and psyop staff worked to diagnose and rehumanise the 'Jap.' It was a world of polarities and conflicting priorities—the Allies deliberately incited hatred in their populations against Japan, yet also needed accurate ideas of the enemy. Recent scholarship suggests that British, American and Australian intelligence capabilities improved dramatically relative to Japan's over the course of the Pacific War. Why? Partly, Japan had the 'victory disease.' It was a victim of its own previous successes against China and Russia, and the rapid conquests in Asia. The shock of defeats, by contrast, stimulated the Allies into greater effort. Partly it was the ability to overcome cultural stereotypes. While the Allies improved, the IJA was misinformed about its enemies, largely because it was overrun by an arrogant contempt for its Anglo-American foes, reinforced by Tojo militarists' blinding dogma about Japanese supremacy. Partly it was resources. Britain had been preoccupied with the war against Germany, which meant that its once-deprived intelligence efforts in the Far East were stepped up. And partly, the effectiveness of propaganda and psychological operations was based on battlefield successes, so that the former gained strength from the cumulative impact of the latter.[116]

The complexity of Western perceptions of Japan is illustrated in the work of two influential Japanists, American intelligence officer Bonner Fellers and anthropologist Ruth Benedict. Fellers would become the head of psychological war operations under Douglas MacArthur, and American propaganda efforts would be based on his 1935 study, *The Psychology of the Japanese Soldier*. Fellers' study was at some points a crude caricature but strikingly prescient at others. On one hand, he talked down the poor physical traits of Japanese aviators, and the nation's lack of resourcefulness. On the other, he predicted 'suicidal air assaults' ten years in advance, as well as the strengths and weaknesses of Japan's offensive doctrine. Fellers overplayed Japan's 'single personality' in his 1935 study, but also recognised that Japanese traits were malleable, not permanent and inbred. Fellers recognised the 'mythohistory' of Japanese militarism. Japan's intensifying brand of nationalist militarism was a creation of state indoctrination, promoted by the likes of General Araki Sadao, a nationalist who was war minister, army minister and education minister during the 1930s.

In his later wartime orientation manual, *Answer to Japan*, Fellers placed greater stress on the role of the 'gangster militarists' whom he distinguished from the rest of the Japanese population, as the true aggressors who had duped their Emperor and country into war. Towards the war's end, Fellers argued US policy should separate these men from the Emperor in order to make peace. Fellers also saw that the aversion of Japanese combatants to surrender was due partly not to inbred traits but to the military policy of spreading 'scare stories' of enemy torture. And this severe code was itself a recent, radical reinvention. Early in 1941, General Tojo issued an official military code instructing Japanese soldiers not to stay alive in dishonour, promising that sacrifice would make Japanese warriors divine and perhaps admit their spirits to the 'Patriots' Shrine' in Tokyo. This brutally radicalised the *Bushido* code that had been elaborated in milder form by the liberal internationalist Nitobe Inazo in 1900. Fellers' evolving hypothesis, that Japanese behaviour was primarily to be explained through political and circumstantial context rather than innate peculiarities, has been vindicated.[117] This insight informed his view of American postwar policy towards Japan—if fanaticism could be learnt, it could also be unlearnt.[118]

Ruth Benedict's *Chrysanthemum and The Sword* became a canonical text of 'national character' study. Commissioned by the US government in June 1944, it influenced American post-war policy, particularly its insight that Japan's population could be reconciled to defeat if the Emperor and his divine authority were maintained. It was one of the most eloquent portrayals of a culture, and it noted how the concept of *Bushido* had evolved and been manipulated. It also had its shortcomings. Given wartime circumstances, it was based on scant evidence, as her informants were few and unrepresentative. It overstated the homogeneity of Japan. Benedict's idea of a single Japanese personality reflected the propaganda of Japan's government, that it was 'one hundred million hearts beating as one.'[119] Benedict explained the Pearl

Harbor attack as the symptom of cultural deficiencies, divorced from its immediate diplomatic and political context. So Japan's 'national character' was central to her explanation of the attack. This overshadowed other explanations, such as the nature of Japan's regime that had dismantled the liberalism of the 1920's, or the British, Dutch and American economic embargo, a slow strangulation that gave an aggressive regime the choice of striking America or withdrawing from China and Indo-China.[120] Benedict's study illustrates a central problem encountered by cultural analysts: how to distinguish how a culture portrays itself rhetorically on the surface, and the undercurrents of conflict and contradiction beneath.[121]

After the Cold War, new communal conflicts again fascinated the West. This time, the focus was on mass murder in Africa, in the Caucuses and on Europe's doorstep. Television screens in the 1990s showed graphic images of ethnic cleansing and 'tribal' wars. As the Cold War ended, and with it the constraints of bipolar world order, a range of wars erupted in Africa and the Balkans. Public commentators and state officials 'culturalised' these wars as pure, 'ethnic' struggles, inevitable eruptions of 'ancient hatreds.'[122] The fall of the Soviet Union and Titoist Communism, which had contained these undying conflicts, now enabled their release. Non-Westerners from the former Yugoslavia to Rwanda fought each other not primarily because of immediate security crises, but because their ancestors did. At its most reductionist, they fought because they were 'like that.' Lawrence Eagleburger, a US advisor on Yugoslavia, insisted in September 1992 that the Bosnian war was 'not rational. There is no rationality at all about ethnic conflict. It is gut, it is hatred; its not for any common set of values or purposes.'[123] This fatalism helped prevent international military intervention. General Colin Powell, his influence and prestige heightened by the 1991 Gulf war, staked his opposition to intervention on the idea that war sprang from 'deep ethnic and religious roots that go back a thousand years.'[124] Orientalism served not to spur Western interference, but to block it.

Yet militant ethnicity was not an inherent disease of these cultures. It was a totem and vehicle for violence, but the conflicts had politics at the core, and were generated by cliques rather than whole societies.[125] Those who characterised the wars as Hobbesian conflicts of 'all against all' fail to differentiate between the general population and actual instigators, a triangle of political elites, secret police and underworld opportunists. Violence issued from governments mobilizing often non-ideological paramilitaries and death squads. In the Balkans, this pattern developed because of initial resistance to nationalist incitement. Conventional soldiers mutinied or deserted, and civilians defied conscription. States had to find alternatives, arming minority compatriots in neighbouring states, and recruiting criminals as mercenaries with the promise of unrestricted rapine. While cooperation took place, in the Rwandan genocide over 90% of the population did not participate in the killings. Ethnic identity was coercively imposed on the majority. This explains the surprise and perplexity of minorities in each state, suddenly turned upon by armed militias from once friendly communities. Without guarantees of state protection, the victimized turned to their own paramilitary defenders.

Orientalist images develop most strongly where there is an unwitting collaboration between outsiders and insiders. America's nervous generals and policymakers, reluctant to intervene in 'ethnic' wars, had an interest in portraying these conflicts as inexorable and irrational. Politicians in the same conflicts whipped up the rhetoric of hyper-nationalism, raising the memory of historic wounds and bitter grievances. Op-ed articles and interviews in Washington or New York, and speeches and radio broadcasts in Kigali or Belgrade, both reinforced the same fatalism of inherent violence.

The mythologies of the 'Wild East' are again being reworked in Western visions. In the 'War on Terror', we point to sub-rational Orientals who fight for its own sake, to the time-bound warrior caught in a world of unguided violence, to the inscrutable enemy, and the collision of radically separate cultures. The following chapter explains how these images mislead us.

2

RETHINKING WAR AND CULTURE

To wage war, become an anthropologist. Lose the fetish for Clausewitz, and embrace culture as the way to understand conflict. Or so argue strategists, historians, and officers on both sides of the Atlantic. From the academy to the Pentagon, fresh attention is being focussed on the value of knowing the enemy. To make sense of military-strategic failures in faraway places, they turn back to cultural intelligence, knowledge of the adversary and the host population it fights among. They argue that culture matters and that history shows it. They point to Robert McNamara, who believed that America failed in Vietnam partly because it understood little about that country.[1] We can agree that culture matters. But how does it operate, and how should we conceptualize it?

This chapter examines ahistorical and flawed versions of culture that are asserted by military officers, academics, and even a military anthropologist. It argues that in its more essentialist forms, culturalist approaches paint foreigners as non-dynamic exotic beings fixed in time. In a strategic world of dynamism and hybridity, this will not do. Particularly in relation to the 'war on terror', this flawed approach overstates continuities within cultures in a way that erases lived history. And it misses the interactive and power-political nature of war, which has a culture of its own that can change all parties to a conflict. By drawing sharp lines to separate and distinguish cultures, it overlooks the way ideas travel across boundaries. It misconceives what culture is. And it neglects the ironies of war. Even as they wage holy war, militant *jihadists* draw from a global marketplace of ideas. They borrow from the infidel. Rather than being a continuum with native culture, today's terrorists and insurgents mutate in form, feed off global forces, and flout traditions. But before exploring this, some credit is due to the 'cultural turn.'

Why Culture Matters

In principle, the rediscovery of culture is desirable. It aims to foster awareness among militaries and governments. Cultural agility matters at every level—strategic, operational, and tactical. It matters at a time of occupations of foreign soil, where soldiers are being asked to act as police officers, nation-builders, and peace-brokers. The ability to map out the labyrinth of power structures, networks, and confessional or ethnic perspectives in a foreign society is a vital activity along the spectrum from peacekeeping to counter-insurgency. To an extent, the cultural turn is a needed corrective to technological determinism. And it also promotes the healthy practice of overcoming ethnocentrism to achieve critical distance from oneself, and imagine others' perspectives.

Culture is an influential variable, and culturalism turns attention to the domestic context in which decisions are made, as well as to interstate power relations. Policy is made at home by decision-makers who are formed by particular memories, biases, and values, and is executed by organisations and individuals with their own baggage.[2] Cultural theories remind us that the stakes or 'referent objects' of war, such as 'national interests', war aims or 'victory', are not mere self-evident 'things', but a combination of things and ideas about them.[3] Ideas intervene to define what these mean, and even what the end of a war looks like. Culture may help explain why, for example, Israel with its lack of strategic depth, its small but educated population and its collective memory of security crises, has been drawn to pre-emptive war, offensive operations, high technology and an absolute view of security. Thus a culture has grown around Israel's strategic situation. Israelis inherit a set of assumptions about security and about the use of force, with which to interpret the world.[4] Actors in war are not billiard balls that only operate according to external pressures.

Today's Iraq war demonstrates the strategic costs of misunderstanding the enemy. Both President Bush and Saddam Hussein were victims of their own misperceptions. The Bush administration was misguided by its narrow conception of war and how its invasion would be received in Iraq. It assumed its opponents agreed that the defeat of Iraq's field army would terminate hostilities. It neglected post-invasion strategy as a separate, second-order administrative task. And it refused for too long to admit the existence of an insurgency. For his part, Saddam Hussein was deluded by his own cultural dismissal of America. In his Occidentalist prejudices about the West, he miscalculated that rich America was too casualty averse and timid to risk a full-scale ground invasion of Iraq. He distributed videos of *Black Hawk Down* to his generals.[5] Overthrown, tried and executed, he underestimated American political will, the same error of cultural dismissal that misled ideologues of Nazi Germany and Imperial Japan.[6] Both Bush and Hussein failed, in Clausewitz's words, to grasp 'the kind of war on which they are embarking.'[7]

Just as it turns attention to neglected areas, a stress on culture carries dangers of its own. It can easily be done badly. Ironically, a stress on the peculiarities of others can reinstate stereotypes instead of challenging them. This was seen in the recent Iraq war, where a range of confused opinions about Arabs was on display.

Culture, Colonialism, and Myth

As Iraq was militarily occupied in 2003, a range of cultural explanations emerged for the growing evidence of an insurgency. Some outsiders looked to the natives' national character to explain the conflict. They resisted because, primarily, they were Arabs. To US company commander Todd Brown, the Arab is 'proud' but also a masochist who appreciates being treated violently. 'You have to understand the Arab mind...The only thing they understand is force—force, pride and saving face.'[8] An *Economist* article asserted the view of a timeless Iraqi national character, quoting a retired diplomat to show that after centuries of sectarian strife, Iraqis are bright but disputatious people, only governable by strong men.[9] It was as if Iraqis were distinctive in their internal conflicts or in their resistance to being ruled by others. These statements are less about ethnographic insight and more an assertion of power. You do not have to be Edward Said to see the problem here.

Those who argue most forcefully for the military utility of cultural knowledge can have the most flawed ideas about it. The fine line between cultural intelligence and cultural fiction was shown by American General Anthony Zinni, an enthusiast of culture.[10] Zinni was fixated by the 'proud Arab', hypersensitive to insult. To him, America's 'biggest error' in Iraq was not its ill-conceived occupation which induced anarchy in Iraqi society, but its phrase 'Shock and Awe', an arrogant slogan that inflamed 'Arab pride and Arab manhood.'[11]

This view of pride as a particularly Arab trait is odd, given the historical role of honour and esteem in Western statecraft.[12] The Iranian hostage crisis lingers as a national wound in Washington, for example. And there is little peculiarly cultural about the fact that some Iraqis rebelled. Invasions that breed disorder, with low levels of consent and hostile contiguous territories, have provoked revolt in all sorts of societies. Nationalism as a response to unwelcome foreign occupation is not distinctive to Iraqis or Arabs, but is a largely generic response of modern people, something Spanish Catholics or Indian secularists would recognize. It is misleading to particularize it as an Arab quirk.[13] Zinni, however, portrayed the Iraq insurgency not so much a situational phenomenon, but a backlash of distinctive Arab emotion. Thus his plea for American to 'know the enemy' revived the rhetoric of colonialism in new form, but with a bodyguard of cultural sensitivity.

This is precisely one difficulty with the 'cultural turn' within the military. It can fall prey to ahistorical colonial nostalgia. Havoc in Iraq tempted some analysts to recall a time when Great Powers, particularly Britain, supposedly handled indigenous peoples better. To handle revolt and insurgency, modern soldier-intellectuals looked to a mythologised history of Empire as a guide. American as well as British officers asserted this Anglophilia. In his testimony before Congress in 2004, Major General Robert Scales judged America's current campaigns by the yardstick of the British Empire and its 'small wars.' He urged the US military to follow the footsteps of British soldier-adventurers such as 'China' Gordon and T.E. Lawrence. Britain's success in Basra, he argued, owed much 'to the self-assurance and comfort with foreign culture derived from centuries of practicing the art of soldier diplomacy and liaison.'[14] Scales was playing a similar tune that was sounded when UK forces entered southern Iraq in 2003. The British press and some combatants congratulated themselves for pacifying the region with a lighter footprint, presenting their urban peacekeeping as 'the tactical antithesis to the brutal and aggressive Yanks.'[15] By no means was this view universal. But participants and onlookers—American and British—often spoke of British experience taming American power. Cultural sensitivity, experience and knowledge of the Orient were what the British, as Greece, could teach America, the new Rome.

Because this world view rests on bad history, and an ahistorical view of British colonialism, it is a poor guide to the present. Gordon, Lawrence and Basra are dubious examples of successful cross-cultural statecraft. Gordon was a gifted diplomat and soldier, but was unable to quell a prolonged uprising in the Sudan and allowed himself to be besieged and killed. T.E. Lawrence developed disdain for Arabs, judging them 'a limited, narrow-minded people, whose inert intellect lay fallow in incurious resignation.'[16] If anything, Lawrence's example demonstrates the way cultural immersion can generate contempt. And then there is Basra, which General Scales regards as a model of culturally agile campaigning. What since happened to this city throws doubt on Scales' interpretation. UK forces withdrew to its outskirts in December 2007 almost under siege by mortars and rockets. The new Iraqi police chief reported the legacy he inherits: 'They left me militia, they left me gangsters, and they left me all the troubles in the world.'[17] It took an American-Iraqi military offensive in March 2008, rather than soft urban peacekeeping, to restore order to the city.[18]

A similar myopia is evident in the UK's recent *Joint Doctrine Note 2/07*. The *Note* claims that British 'best practice' counterinsurgency, evolving through Malaya, Kenya, Palestine and Borneo, applied the 'cultural sensitivity' of 'earlier colonial campaigns.'[19] In its desire to enshrine the 'light touch' as a pillar of present COIN practice, the *Note* presents cultural agility as Britain's historical asset, reasoning that because it was important to past success, it is also today. But this is a false history, a repeat of the 'Liberal Lie' that the final campaigns of empire had imbued British COIN doctrine with a 'minimum force' philosophy and unequalled levels of cultural insight.[20] In reality, campaigns like Malaya and Kenya were not culturally sensitive, except in the sense of leveraging local hatreds. Against the Kikuyu ('Mau-Mau') in Kenya, Britain employed interrogation under torture, hangings, indiscriminate bombings of forest, and white settlers or local proxies applied sadistic violence, dismemberment, and killings in custody.[21] In Malaya, there were detentions without trial, executions, jungle bombing campaigns, and forcible resettlement of the population into camps. Divide-and-rule and exemplary punishment marked these campaigns more than 'hearts and minds.'[22] If these campaigns succeeded, it was not because they were discriminate and enlightened.

Restraint and awareness are respectable in themselves. But there is no automatic relationship between cultural sophistication and victory.

'Lesser wars' are about power and survival as well as ideas and identity. History leaves us an uncomfortable insight: that occupations of brutality can succeed. The gentler gamester is not always the soonest winner. America successfully applied terror to crush insurrection in the Philippines (1899–1902), including water boarding and concentration camps, even when the news of atrocities sparked public outrage at home.[23] Conversely, cultural knowledge might not tilt the conflict in one's favour. Against the mutinous American colonies, the British troops spoke the local language, were of the same religion, many were distantly related, and could be tried in a local court for excessive force. But this did not resolve the underlying political conflict. The majority still saw the British as illegitimate occupiers.[24] Anthropology can help deliver success, but it needs a permissive political and strategic context.

War and the Exotic

For a fuller glimpse of problematic approaches to culture, consider the arguments of Montgomery McFate, leading cultural anthropologist with the US military, architect of the Human Terrain System, and avowed critic of ethnocentrism. In calling for cultural awareness, McFate is confident that cultures exist as coherent and separate things. She has defended the US military's use of Raphael Patai's *The Arab Mind* in its teaching curriculum.[25] Patai's study casts Arabs from Algeria to Saudi Arabia as a monolithic people, loveable but infantile, drawn to fantasy and aggression by their language, parenting and music, and acting out a role scripted by their Bedouin origins and climate.[26] It denies diversity or change to the Arab world, and fixes a fictitious 'Arab psyche' as a permanent pathology, isolating Arabs from external influence, modernisation or discontinuity. This view of the gulf between the West and the Rest informs McFate's view of the War on Terror. She claims that America is 'Clausewitizian' in its understanding of war, 'where armed conflict is a rational extension of politics by other means', which is profoundly different to al Qaeda and Iraqi insurgents. These adversaries

> neither think nor act like nation-states. Rather, their form of warfare, organizational structure, and motivations are *determined* by the society and the culture from which they come. Attacks on coalition troops in the Sunni triangle, for example, follow predictable patterns of tribal warfare: avenging the blood of a relative (*al tha'r*); demonstrating manly courage in battle (*al-muruwwah*); and upholding manly honor (*al-sharaf*). Similarly, al Qaeda and its

affiliated groups are replicating the Prophet Mohammed's 7th-century process of political consolidation through jihad, including opportunistic use of territories lacking political rulers as a base, formation of a corps of believers as a precursor to mass recruiting, and an evolution in targeting from specific, local targets (such as pagan caravans) to distant powerful adversaries (for instance, the Byzantine Empire). To confront an enemy so deeply moored in history and theology, the US Armed Forces must adopt an ethnographer's view of the world: it is not nation-states but cultures that provide the underlying structures of political life.[27]

In this determinist view, Mohammed and the Sheiks ride again in the form of Iraqis and Islamists. War is treated as a re-enactment of ancient Oriental impulses. Culture refers to a localised, endogenous process and one's enemies are ultimately predictable. McFate echoes T.E. Lawrence's confidence, that 'knowledge of their prejudices will enable you to foresee their attitude and possible course of action in nearly every case.'[28] And she approaches culture itself as non-dynamic. Despite nodding to 'globalization', McFate's conception of it is limited, as a process of encountering new adversaries, but without cultures changing as a result.[29] The new *American Field Manual on Counter-Insurgency (FM3–24)*, written partly by McFate and influenced by classic ethnography, shares aspects of this view of culture, as logically consistent, bounded, highly integrated, internally coherent, and animated often by a single unifying narrative. In fairness, it acknowledges that culture is learned and therefore changeable.[30] But the balance lies with continuity.

This outlook is flawed in many ways. First, there is the notion that the organisational structure, motivations and methods of America's enemies are determined by their 'society and culture', acting as medieval or tribal throwbacks. For all the exciting cultural inferences McFate draws about intangibles, such as manly honour and blood vengeance, these tribal warriors also pursue material goals. In the Sunni Triangle where McFate sees feuds of pride, kinship, and wounded masculinity, tribes and al Qaeda also fight over the control of revenue, like smuggling and banditry.[31] And identity itself is plural. As one military observer cautions, Iraqi tribalisms must compete with a host of other influences and social forms, including de-tribalised populations and fractures of sect, ethnicity, class and ideology. Tribal influence varies and sheikhs can find their tribes divided.[32] And as demonstrated when RAF spy planes overheard Taliban fighters speaking in West Bromwich and Bradford accents, culture is not easily isolated to the boundaries of local society.[33] Al Qaeda is the product of no single indigenous culture, but is part of an umbrella of linked movements from the Philippines, Indonesia, Morocco and Western Europe. It is formed through global interactions and borrowings, and shapes its warfare through the worldwide circulation of ideas, technology and techniques.

Al Qaeda wages war on America, but it adapts American ideas and draws from non-Muslim strategic thought. Al Qaeda's doctrine of a 'long war', articulated on internet journals and hammered out during struggles from Xinjiang to Eritrea to Bosnia, is inspired partly by Clausewitz and his ideas of the relationship of war and politics, and the 'centre of gravity' that is the enemy' source of strength.[34] During the war in Afghanistan in 2001, a journalist found a copy of Clausewitz's *On War* in an al-Qaeda safe house, with highlighted sections on courage.[35] Its military training camps are full of American books. One of its houses in Afghanistan contained a book *Winds of War*, which collected studies of revolutionary leftist and asymmetric strategic thinking from South America, China and the US, and its theorists are particularly fond of quoting and adapting Mao's 'three stage' concept of guerrilla struggle and the need to mobilise the masses.[36] Black radicals such as Robert F. Williams, a precursor to the Black Panthers, features also in the literature.[37] It prepares its recruits by using the training manuals of American and British Special Forces, doctrinal publications available in open source.[38]

So Al Qaeda's ideas about conflict are not simply determined by indigenous ideas, but are a fusion of religious beliefs with classical, revolutionary and contemporary strategic thought. Sayyid Qutb, an intellectual with a major impact on Salafist jihadist thinking, regarded it as legitimate to learn 'military science' from a non-Muslim.[39] As did the strategist Abu Bakr Naji, who invoked Paul Kennedy's theory of 'imperial overstretch' to explain America's vulnerability. He claimed 'the Sharia permits us to use the plans and military principles of non-Muslims in which there is no sin.'[40] One of Al Qaeda's leading intellectuals and teachers, Abu Mus'ab al-Suri, relied primarily on the Qu'ran and an American book on guerrilla warfare when lecturing at Afghan training camps, adapting leftist guerrilla concepts to his vision of global Islamic jihad.[41] This borrowing can be even more direct. The Abu Sayyaf Group of the Philippines lifted the Brazilian rebel Carlos Marighella's *MiniManual of the Urban Guerrilla*, turning it into the

MiniManual of the Urban Mujahideen by replacing the Marxist words with Islamic words.[42] Abu 'Ubayd al-Qurashi, an aid to Bin Laden who wrote on strategy in the jihadist magazine *Majallat al-Ansar*, drew extensively on Western and non-Islamic sources. As well as Mao and Clausewitz, he used *War of the Flea*, the study of guerrilla warfare by American journalist Robert Taber. He also incorporated the idea of 'fourth generation warfare', a concept created in 1989 in the US Marine Corps *Gazette* to explain the complexity of post-Cold War conflict.[43] Al Qaeda's newsletter announced in 2002 that 'The time has come for the Islamic movements facing a general crusader offensive to internalize the rules of fourth-generation warfare.'[44] Ironically, the idea was created by Bill Lind, an American cultural conservative as well as military mind, and now turns up in al-Qaeda broadcasts.

Al Qaeda's communiqués draw not only on its mythical history, but also from Western critiques of American imperialism, such as Michael Moore and William Blum, and European criticisms of environmental vandalism.[45] In its pursuit of a new world through inspirational violence and its lack of programmatic goals, Al Qaeda owes as much to the revolutionary imagination of nineteenth-century European anarchists as it does to medieval religious wars or ideas of Islamic governance.[46]

Al Qaeda and its affiliates fashion themselves out of the very process of globalization that they claim to dislike. Even this most anti-Western movement is also highly modern. In contrast to Bin Laden's usual image in the US, as a Saudi religious puritan yearning for the seventh century, he is a hybrid that should be familiar to Westerners—part venture capitalist, part creative CEO and part media manipulator. The many groups that make up the conflict in Iraq are differently organised from previous generations. They are as much driven by shared ideology as formal organisation, and with the aid of technology and experience, they have become more horizontal, dispersed and networked in their shape.[47] In this, they adapt prior patterns seen elsewhere. Al Qaeda and its affiliates have more in common with South American narco-terrorist structures, or the model of 'leaderless' small-cell resistance as popularised by antigovernment white supremacists Tom Metzger and Louis Beam (and later taken up by Islamist theoretician Abu Mus'ab Al-Suri), than with the more tightly controlled organisations of the past. Skilled insurgent groups, like neo-Nazis, follow the logic of adaptation and make their movements more complex in order to survive.

One major way that the war of radical Islam goes beyond local traditions is through organised crime, an activity that does not respect borders. From the Moroccan drug traffickers who converted in prison before participating in the Madrid bombings, to the trade in kidnapping and extortion in Iraq, the war is wrapped up with a global black market.[48] And religious ideas can be a cloak for criminal ambitions. The Taliban may claim to embody religious purity but their ranks include opportunist brigands who have grown their beards to fit in.[49] This fusion of criminality and 'culture clash' is one reason not to take the rhetoric of blood and faith at face value. Instead, a more politically aware cultural analysis could reintroduce human agency into the picture, showing how gangsters or crime lords reinvent themselves as jihadists, exploiting and reworking culturally resonant ideas in their pursuit of material power.

In many pragmatic ways, the global market shapes *jihad*. Insurgent groups evolve through a world bazaar of operational knowledge transfer. Groups as disparate as Hizballa, Marxist Columbian rebels and American white supremacists meet in the triborder area of South America to exchange tradecraft.[50] Islamic and non-Islamic groups have used the same designs for car bombs as others from Latin America to the Middle East to Africa.[51] This transfer of technique and skills can be indirect, done through emulation and the accelerating availability of instruction manuals in cyberspace. Or it can be direct collaboration even with former enemies, such as Bin Laden's permission for Muslims to cooperate with Iraq's 'infidel' Saddamists.[52] 'Knowledge traffic' and the marketplace of expertise that schools insurgents in kidnapping or attacks on critical infrastructure, tells us as much about these adaptive movements as does indigenous customs.

It is easy to become exclusively focused on the differences between enemies in the 'war on terror', because they themselves rhetorically assert the profound differences between them. But while they vilify one other, they imitate one another in competition. Both have co-evolved in the realms of strategic ideas, force structure and tactics. In America, Al Qaeda fascinates its opponents as a model of modern propaganda, stimulating new focus on 'information operations.' Former Defence Secretary Donald Rumsfeld argued in early 2006 that America must become more like Al Qaeda by mastering its art of 'strategic communication' (or propaganda), shaping perception and counteracting the enemy's appeal.[53] Al Qaeda's corporate 'franchise' model of organisational resilience and propagandist skill appeals as a model that America can copy.[54] As former presidential advisor and analyst Philip Bobbitt suggests, Al Qaeda 'will employ self-financing operations, rely on coalitions of the willing, and seek preclusive victories. In some ways, they are already showing us how to organize ourselves for victory.'[55] America is also increasingly imitating its enemies' force structure. Especially after the heavy attrition at Tora Bora and Fallujah, insurgents have developed as a mosaic of elusive cells that cannot be smashed with decisive blows. In response, the US invests more in smaller, stealthier groups, just as the French in Algeria reacted to their enemies' decentralisation, because such enemies are difficult to combat with mass.[56] US Special Forces and Army doctrine is trying to narrow the distinction between professional soldiers and warrior cultures, fostering the idea that soldiering is an existential way of life rather than just a utilitarian job.[57] This is not to suggest that the US and its enemies will replicate each other. It suggests that the forces shaping their 'way of war' are exogenous and driven by strategic interaction. As insurgencies respond to conflict, their methods, shape and even purpose mutates. These tendencies are due to many things, but two major forces stand out. There is globalization (or more precisely the latest phase of globalization), which since the advent of mass literacy, the telegraph and the cheap press has been increasing and accelerating the spread of information and ideas, thereby greasing the wheels of mutual influence between enemies. And there is the reciprocal, competitive nature of war itself.

Methods of guerrilla warfare, such as suicide or roadside bombings, are the response to shifting strategic circumstances, rather than the inevitable products of a long-term Arab-Islamic culture. Many Arab states for decades after the Second World War eschewed an indigenous form of asymmetric warfare; instead, from Nasser's pursuit of a Soviet-style military to Saddam's investment in machine-age war, they sought to develop conventional military power. After disappointing results against conventional forces, alternatives such as guerrilla methods proved compelling. If anything, suicide bombing in Arab cultures is a relatively recent innovation. It was historically a taboo and attitudes towards it fluctuate. Majority opinion in many Arab-Islamic countries increasingly disapproves of it, along with Al Qaeda's methods of beheadings and indiscriminate attacks on civilians.[58] Life is made complex for insurgent groups precisely because their techniques do not always line up with their wider constituencies, who do not always endorse their methods.

There is also evidence that insurgents and other stateless actors, rather than being constrained by culture, actually violate norms for practical reasons. For example, Islamist groups, from Hamas to Al Qaeda, have doubly broken with traditional attitudes, to suicide and to female participation, by employing women in increasing numbers as suicide bombers. And this despite religious taboos among male-dominated Islamist movements against employing women in combat. Indicating the trans-national, innovative and highly modern nature of the insurgency, al Qaeda in March 2003 announced a women's suicide division containing Afghans, Arabs and Chechens, coordinated through the internet.[59] Previously, it was primarily nationalist/separatist or leftist movements that featured women as suicide bombers. Religious terrorism was mostly male-dominated. Would-be female combatants like Khawla Bint Al Azoor complained that they were only permitted to give indirect support. She wrote in *Jihad* magazine in 1987 about the struggle with the Soviets that 'I only wish I could give my life and my spirit as a gift to this pure land as a martyr.'[60] But more recently, women such as Chechen 'Black Widows', have entered battle to occupy theatres, bring down civilian airliners, plot the assassination of politicians, and conduct 'martyr operations.' Much media and professional commentary still treats female suicide bombers as an aberration to be explored through their individual profile and motivation.[61] But there is also a practical collective decision made by male-dominated groups to sanction women's participation as the situation changes. Cultural resources can be found to legitimate the participation of women.

Women offer a range of benefits as *jihadists*. Employing them doubles the number of potential recruits; their profile as women defies stereotypes and is below the radar; they are stealthier and harder to detect; they are overlooked by governments and officials thinking in terms of the typical male 'profile' of suicide bomber; they inflict greater psychological impact because of perceptions that they are shocking and atypical; and even shame men into participation.[62] In Iraq, Al Qaeda has increasingly used women as bombers since protective concrete walls and tighter security have made car bombings more difficult.

It is instructive to hear what the sponsors and organisers of female suicide bombing say. Recall the changing attitude of Sheikh Ahmed

Yassin, spiritual leader of Hamas, who initially 'categorically renounced the use of women as suicide bombers' in January 2002. Two years later, after Hamas struck with its first female suicide attack, he justified it on grounds of utility. 'The male fighters face many obstacles, so women can more easily reach the targets...Women are like the reserve army—when there is a necessity, we use them.'[63] Female suicide bombing, once abhorrent, became a compelling method.

To justify these policy changes, those in favour appealed to two cultural resources, the Qur'an and sacred history. If cultures are repertoires with diverse and clashing ideas, what better instance than sacred texts, where conflicting messages, guides to action and symbols can be found to justify almost any act? For the advocate of women's participation in *jihad*, the Qur'an recognizes women's participation, and contains passages about women's equal stats. Within Islamic history, there are precedents of female fighters. The prophet's own wife and granddaughter fought in battles, as did the legendary Nusayba bint K'ab, who fought in the Battle of Uhud in 625, as well as other women who supported jihad through nursing the wounded, donating jewellery, and encouraging their male family members. The heroism of these women became celebrated icons for modern-day imitators.[64] Islamic traditions, like all cultural traditions, can be strategically interpreted. The suicide bomber, stereotyped as a young man in a state of religious exaltation, might be an overlooked woman. Here is a case where assumptions about the culturally static profile of the enemy could prove not only misguided but deadly.

There is an identifiable relationship between doctrinal shifts and strategic developments. Lebanon's Hizballa internally debated suicide bombing after Israel invaded in the summer of 1982 and at first clerics in the movement objected to the new tactic after the first 'martyring' operation. But suicide bombers successfully drove American marines and French paratroopers out of Lebanon and Israel into a narrow zone of southern Lebanon. Such attacks also generated support in competition with Lebanon's rival Shiite Amal movement. This made it an irresistible weapon, which in turn generated fresh theological justifications, and Shiite clerics sanctioned suicide attacks. Then, after Israel withdrew from Lebanon in 1985, the method seemed less compelling and only conventional methods were permitted. As Hizballa's leading cleric announced, self-martyring operations were only permissible if they inflicted enough benefits, 'if they bring about a political or military change in proportion to the passions that incite a person to make of his body an exploding bomb.'[65] The legitimacy of the method rose and fell with the degree of urgency (foreign occupation) and utility (whether the method worked). Culture was remade under pressure.

Tribal War and Primitive Fantasies

Like McFate's interpretation of Al Qaeda and Iraq, mainstream academic studies of tribal war can also misconstrue culture. Scholars Richard Shultz and Andrea Dew, whose work is endorsed by authorities such as Bruce Hoffman, draw on notions of 'primitive warfare' and 'the otherness of others' to argue for an intrinsic difference between Third World warriors and First World soldiers. Schultz and Dew focus on moments of culture clash, such as Mogadishu in 1993, where they show America blundering into Somalia to unleash a tribal vendetta. They argue that America was confused by its Clausewitzian paradigm of war, which fails outside a Western context:

> Traditional warfare...was pervasive and very different from its modern, predominantly Western, counterpart. It did not reflect the Clausewitzian paradigm or Grotian limitations. Tribal and clan chieftains did not employ war as a cold-blooded and calculated policy instrument to achieve state policy objectives. Rather, it was fought for a host of social-psychological purposes and desires, which included conquest, prestige, ego-expansion, honour, glory, revenge, vengeance, and vendetta.[66]

This traditional warfare, they argue, is what tribal societies have returned to in the age of decolonization. 'Otherness' here becomes a euphemism for simplistic stereotypes. Where Western states wage war for policy, stateless Others do so to serve primal psychological longings, such as blood feuds. This revives arguments once in vogue about the 'clash of cultures' between European invaders and Plains Indians, Mexicans or Hawaiians, between natives who were ritual-dominated primitives, immobile or frozen in time, creatures of myth and superstition, and European conquerors who thought and fought strategically.[67]

The problems with such an approach are manifold. First, it is an impoverished idea of Western strategic thought, relying on a shallow misreading of Clausewitz. In distinguishing the West and the Rest, Schultz, Dew and McFate reduce Clausewitz to the concept that war is policy by other means. In a common oversimplification, they relegate Clausewitz to another time of classical inter-state war, where war was the sole business of nation-states and regular armed forces. Given war has fundamentally altered its nature, goes the argument, Clausewitz has little to offer in understanding the complexity of today's *Mad Max* world of low-intensity wars, sub-state actors, and blurred lines.[68] In the post-Clausewitz age, warfare became the expression of fundamental identities and ideologies rather than the 'cost-benefit' pursuit of political interests.[69] Clausewitz belongs to a time of professional soldiers, whereas we need to adjust to a world of warriors.

But Clausewitz did not say that warfare must be a cold-blooded policy instrument of the state. Rather, he insisted that war could not be sanitized in this way: 'it would be an obvious fallacy to imagine war between civilized peoples as resulting merely from a rational act on the part of their governments.'[70] Clausewitz described war not only as a tool of statecraft, but as a form of *Politik*, a word of multiple meaning that encompassed both policy and politics, so that war could be instrumental but also express escalating political struggle over the distribution of power. He viewed war as being shaped by a trinity of reason and instrumentality, passion and hostility, and chance. Revenge or hatred, or national peoples' armies—the revolutionary force of his time—could intensify war, even to the point where costs outstripped gains and where passion submerged reason. He had seen that war and defeat could take on existential meanings of their own. As a Prussian officer, he was also a nationalist radicalised by Napoleon's occupation of his homeland. Recall the burning heat of his 'memorandum of confession' in 1812: 'even the loss of freedom after an honourable and bloody battle secures the rebirth of the people and is the seed of life from which, one day, a new tree will strike firm root...I would be only too happy to find a glorious death in the magnificent fight for the freedom and dignity of the fatherland!'[71] This was the Clausewitz who appealed to later German nationalists, whose twentieth-century wars would be drenched in existential meaning, framing death as sacrifice and the battlefront as the place of moral test and rebirth. Western war culture could be violently expressive.

Clausewitz also recognized complexities now deemed to be 'post-modern.' Stateless forces were part of his world too, such as pirates, mercenaries or Russian Tartars. He argued that war is rarely final, and that popular uprisings may arise after the defeat of state militaries. He supported the idea of a guerrilla strategy against Napoleonic France, and believed the driving force of war was not the government of the state, but the nation, the people spontaneously mobilised. Clausewitz was both an advocate and student of 'people's wars.'[72] He wrote on the subject in Chapter 6 of *On War*, lectured on Small Wars at the Berliner Kriegsschule in 1811–12, and studied the insurgencies of his time, the Roman Catholic uprising in the Vendee against French Revolutionaries 1793–6, the Spanish guerrilla war from 1808, and the Tyrolean rebellion of 1809. He noticed that there was emerging the *Volkskrieg* ('people's war'), especially where populations defeated in the field refused to accept their leaders' formal surrender. Such uprisings were a symptom of the 'breaking down of barriers', which had been 'swept away in our lifetime by the elemental violence of war.'[73] While we cannot presume that he would have recognized the wars of our own time, we can certainly draw on his judgments to assist us.

Clausewitz was mindful that the external contexts and conditions for strategy could change. His trinity allows for an endlessly shifting relationship between the different dimensions of war, whether as a policy instrument, as a struggle transformed by popular passions, or as a chaotic conflict subject to friction. Because it accommodates variations in the context and purpose of war, Clausewitz's matrix can apply to sectarian fighting in Baghdad or European cabinet wars of the nineteenth century. *Politik*, as Clausewitz understood it, was not confined to limited goals, such as modest territorial aims. Warfare was political in nature even if its exponents pursued ambitious goals with few geographic limitations, such as a restored Islamic Caliphate, Al Qaeda's objective today.

With this in mind, we return to America's misadventure in Mogadishu in 1993. Shultz and Dew treat that episode as an example of the West's inability to understand sub-state tribal war in limited, 'Clausewitzian' terms. But it can actually be understood with the help of Clausewitz's trinity. The facts suggest that if the Somali factions fought a primal blood feud, it was also a highly instrumental political struggle, if politics is a pattern of relationships entailing power, rule and authority. The competing groups may not have been Westphalian nation-states, but as their military behaviour proved, they competed to seize state power. Control of the capital was the Somalis' central goal. Mogadishu was the seat of sovereignty and authority, of organised command of the armed forces, and the source of taxation machinery. This explains why they developed regular forces as well as guerrillas, in order to capture and hold territory. And whatever primitive 'social-psychological' desires Schultz and Dew would attribute to him, warlord

Mohammed Aidid directed organised violence for political aims. He waged a deliberate campaign to undermine a weakened regime, extort money from foreign relief groups, and to expel a UN-US intervention. Alongside the cultural 'Otherness' of clan warfare, Aidid had been schooled in Rome, had served in the Italian colonial police, had a son in the US marines, called himself the 'Eisenhower of Somalia', and drew his declared ideology not from native ethno-cultural traditions, but from American futurologist Alvin Toffler's theories on postindustrial democracy. He then returned to Somalia to mobilize religious, tribal and anti-colonial sentiment.[74] In turn, ethnic identity and clan differences are a fluid force in Somali politics that cut across region and class, to be manipulated or forgotten as political needs require.[75] Part Western-educated colonialist, part anti-colonial demagogue, Aidid's hybrid career shows the artificiality of sharp distinctions between modern and traditional worlds, instrumental Westerners and cultural Easterners.

The other elements of Clausewitz's trinity, passion or hatred, were clearly present. It was manifest in the hostility generated among Somalis against US forces by famine, civil war and invasion. It culminated in locals dragging corpses of American troops through the streets. The conflict was also affected by friction, in the tactical reverses such the crash of a helicopter and delays caused by miscommunication between troops, leading to the Americans being trapped in a bloody street battle.[76] No doubt our understanding of wars in Africa could be enhanced by examining cultural contexts. But we would be ill-served by Schultz and Dew's view of African wars as exotic, pre-Clausewitzian rituals.

Eastern Wisdom? Texts and Contexts

Are there Eastern and Western ways of war? The idea remains seductive. For political scientist Paul Bracken, Eastern war is 'embodied by the stealthy archer,' while the Westerner is a swordsman 'charging forward, seeking a decisive showdown, eager to administer the blow that will obliterate the enemy.'[77] Some regard the classic thinkers on strategy, such as Sun Tzu and Clausewitz, as spokesmen for different Eastern and Western traditions. At its most sweeping, this approach can be crude. In one corner, there are the children of Clausewitz, blundering and guileless Western forces obsessed with decisive combat and wielding the blunt instrument of overwhelming force. In the other corner, there are Sun Tzu's Oriental acolytes, weaker but mystical foes, who prefer deception and the 'indirect approach,' and who avoid the excessive slaughters on display at Verdun and Stalingrad. But as Jeremy Black shows, the concept of overarching pan-cultural traditions is insensitive to the variety of traditions among Arab militaries such as the Egyptians, Syrians and Iraqis.[78] And John Lynn argues against a continuous 'Western' military tradition, showing that in ancient China in the Warring States period, potentates mobilised large conscript infantry armies, equipped them on a scale comparable to Western states, for a direct form of combat.

The hypothesis of culturally determined war ignores too many contrary cases that cut across its neat frontiers. The longest conventional war of the twentieth century was fought between Arabs and Persians, the Iraq-Iran war of 1980–1988. It featured ruinous economic and human costs, and the fighting was reminiscent of the Western front: positional combat over entrenched positions, the use of poison gas, and continual waves of young men charging to their deaths, driven by ideologies of martyrdom. Conversely, one of the most elaborate pieces of deception in history was executed by a Western alliance in 1944, 'Operation Bodyguard' to mask the D-Day Normandy Landings. The Allies misled German spies, built dummies, false radio transmissions and newspaper reports, used double bluff, to such effect that the Germans continued to believe the Normandy landings were a feint. [MD1] It was an example used by Edward Luttwak to describe manoeuvre, 'paradoxical action that seeks to circumvent the greater strengths of the enemy and to exploit his weaknesses.'[79] This illustrated that deception and overwhelming force are not mutually exclusive absolutes, but relative parts of a spectrum. This was a point grasped by the Duke of Wellington and the Spanish irregulars in the Peninsular war (1808–1814). Many elements that some might classify as 'Oriental' were harnessed in this decidedly Western struggle. These included strategies of diversion and concealment, effective light infantry, and a popular uprising urged on by local clerics. Such operations culminated in major battles against a demoralised enemy. The 'metacultural' vision of war as a symptom of intrinsic differences between civilizations does a bad job of explaining actual historical behaviour.

And it also tells us little about the history of ideas. Sun Tzu's concepts were not peculiar to Eastern traditions. He may have stressed the value of intelligence and deception, praised the ideal of the bloodless victory, and stressed the economical logic of finding non-military ways to prevail. So did the Florentine diplomat and philosopher Niccolo Machiavelli, whose *Art of War* was one of the most prominent authorities on strategy before Clausewitz.[80] Like Sun Tzu in the 'Warring States' period, Machiavelli lived in a fragile, multi-polar and predatory political environment, of competing city-states, ever-shifting alliances and meddling foreign powers. Costly mercenary armies and multiple fronts of conflict made war a particularly risky and expensive business. His environment, more than cultural stereotypes, may explain why he asserted that 'He who overcomes the enemy by fraud is as much to be praised as he who does so by force.'[81] Moreover, Machiavelli argued for a synthesis of the 'sledgehammer' power of Roman citizen-armies and the 'sneaky' gambits of manoeuvre, surprise and deception, practised by the Parthian horsemen of antiquity.[82] He resolved the opposition between both modes of warfare pragmatically. Depending on the context, sometimes the caution and indirectness of the Parthians worked better, at other times the bold Roman approach made sense. Machiavelli bridged principles often thought to be opposite, and saw past the limitations of narrow traditions. So Sun Tzu's concepts were not so culturally-specific.

As well as overlooking the richness of strategic texts, cultural essentialism runs the risk of being politically naïve when it comes to the issue of *reception*, or understanding the arbitrariness of how traditions are read and used. Rather than just being influenced by great texts of strategy, commanders and rulers use them to justify different and conflicting policies. So the Clausewitz of the nineteenth century was invoked by Prussian generals to justify the pursuit of decisive battles to destroy the enemy's forces, to preach the inevitability of heavy casualties and the central value of morale, even to urge civilian government to stand aside as they prosecuted the war. By contrast, decision-makers in the twentieth century appealed to Clausewitz to argue different and even opposite principles, such as the assertion that the military should be subordinate to political direction and political ends. Such concepts inspired the US Weinberger-Powell doctrine, which codified the principles of prudent statecraft, the controlled application of force for achievable goals, concrete national interests and a clear exit strategy.[83]

A similar pattern of selective appeals to tradition can be found in medieval Chinese history. As Alistair Johnston has shown in his study of the Ming dynasty (1368–1644), Chinese rulers over centuries were happy to appeal to their supposed strategic culture when it suited them.[84] According to its mythical self-image, Chinese statecraft was inspired by a Confucian-Mencian skepticism about the utility of force, and was non-expansionist, non-aggressive, and preoccupied with internal order. Chinese rulers who pursued policies of conciliation and compromise often appealed to this supposed tradition, claiming that they were in tune with ancestral wisdom. But this they happily abandoned when they saw opportunities to go on the offensive. Ming rulers did so with great frequency, externally against Vietnamese, Koreans, Uighers, Mongols, and Tibetans.

To justify a more aggressive posture, they could appeal to an alternative tradition which was also to be found in their strategic texts—a philosophy of watchful aggressiveness. In this tradition, offensive force was desirable, to be mediated by sensitivity to the enemy's relative capabilities. Force could be used when the time was ripe. Strategic traditions did matter, but often only so far as they accorded with the hard-headed calculations of elites. This kind of opportunism was and is possible precisely because the notion of a clear, homogenous and unanimous culture is artificial. The same country can entertain multiple conflicting or overlapping strategic cultures, with rival interpretations of past experience. Cultural context can play a vital role in this area, but rather than approaching actors as the by-products of intellectual traditions, it will aid our understanding by explaining why culture is so politically fraught, tracing the dialectical, non-linear relationship between texts and behaviour.

This also touches debates in the US over how to define an American 'way of war' on which to build policy. For politicians and decision-makers, history is both ambivalent and politically potent as a way to legitimize policy. Russell Weigley's classic account of the 'American Way of War' argued that ever since the Civil War, the US armed forces favoured decisive battles and wars of annihilation with clear objectives through the heavy use of firepower, with a narrow view of strategy that neglected the non-military consequences of their action. But the same history can be quarried to show that the US military was long preoccupied by coastal and continental defence, that in wartime practice there was a preference for pragmatic improvisations and willingness to use attritional strategies, and that policy-makers had often been willing to wage 'small wars', deterrence and wars for limited aims.'[85] Concepts of a 'British way of war' are also necessarily partial.[86]

On one of the most fundamental questions, when to resort to war, culture offers no clear grid for policy, but throws up clashing lessons and analogies from the past. In 2002–3, the debate over Iraq exposed the fissures in American strategic culture. Some supporters of war in Iraq invoked Chamberlain, Hitler and Munich in 1938, arguing that against dangerous tyrants, an aggressive strategy was a winning strategy. Opponents raised Vietnam or even the July Crisis of 1914, warning that an ill-conceived invasion would lead to disastrous war with unintended consequences.[87] Where some warned against appeasement and Nazi Germany, others spoke of quagmire and Indochina. To support his vision of fighting expeditionary wars to protect America's interests, Max Boot appeals to the neglected history of America's 'savage wars' against insurgencies abroad.[88] But James Kurth, an opponent of peripheral military adventures, argues that they violate core tenets of America's strategic history.[89] Disputants choose the history that aligned with their policy preferences, making a weapon out of the past.

Strength and Weakness

So much for the use and abuse of strategic texts and traditions. The 'East v. West' view of war is powerful because it is a deeply political interpretation of military history. It uses the polarizing concepts of Orient and Occident, Eastern and Western strategic tradition, in order to distinguish not only the warfare of East and West, but also their cultural life[MD2]. War, and especially combat, become a commentary on the worth and value of the societies that wage it. Hence the portrayal of 'Oriental cunning', evasion or subtlety, against Western 'openness' or desire for decisive battle. After 9/11, the military historian Sir John Keegan claimed the war launched on 9/11 was part of an 'older conflict between settled, creative productive Westerners and predatory, destructive Orientals.' Whereas Westerners fight honourably 'in stand-up battle' with 'rules of honour', Orientals liked 'ambush, treachery and deceit.'[90] Cultures in this view are hermetically sealed boxes, separate and distinct. What are China and Turkey to make of this, for centuries productive, settled and creative cultures with well-drilled armies? Keegan's sentimental view of strictly upright, face-to-face Western warfare seems odd at a time when its militaries have stopped worrying and learnt to love long-range missiles, unmanned aerial vehicles and white phosphorous. But Keegan articulated cultural war to embolden the West with a vision of future victory. He reduced military history to a morality play, showcasing Western virtues and

Oriental vices. Alternatively, some military thinkers who urge reform of their armed forces argue that Western war culture should seek inspiration in 'Eastern wisdom', assuming that indirect methods of war mostly lie outside their own culture. As one asserts, 'The Eastern warrior, a master of stealth, deception, and flexibility...and his tactics, are worthy of study and possible emulation.'[91]

As a matter of self-definition, Westerners have often thought of their desire for pitched battle as a reflection of their integrity. As Col. Harry Summers said to Col. Tu in Hanoi in 1975 as North Vietnam's guerrilla strategy was paying dividends, 'you never defeated us on the battlefield.'[92] If war is the ultimate political act, it is also tempting to see it as the ultimate expression of one's political values. And it may be that, because they have relied for evidence partly on Westerners' statements about themselves, culturalists have reproduced this self-image. We might also have a nostalgia for set-piece battles in open fields, in a world when combats with such clarity are denied to conventional forces, and where war is dominated by a 'dismal globalised continuum' of urban terror, long-range bombing and massacres of unarmed civilians. Americans, Israelis or Britons might yearn for a time when their enemies shared their preference for a fair fight.[93]

But if we examine the record of actual behaviour, we can see a more textured picture. In fact, strategies of avoidance and indirection have a rich pedigree in Western military practice. In 1944, British Lt-General William Slim urged his Fourteenth Army to counter Japanese ruses with its own. His wartime guide to Japanese trickery quoted confederate General Thomas 'Stonewall' Jackson's advice: 'Always mystify and mislead the enemy.'[94] Jackson and other Confederate generals of the American Civil War had found themselves in a situation where duplicity was attractive as a way of offsetting material deficiencies and the disparity in forces.[95] Before that, George Washington kept his Continental Army out of the grasp of the British, who seized vital real estate in a vain attempt to bring him to open battle. Washington's evasion was given the name 'Fabian', which comes from the Roman consul and commander Fabius Cunctator ('Delayer'), who skilfully evaded Hannibal's forces after the Carthaginian invader had defeated Roman armies at Trebia and Lake Trasimene, and whose once-unpopular strategy was revived after Hannibal's annihilation of Roman legions at Cannae. The more formidable the enemy and the more undesirable a decisive showdown, the more acceptable indirect methods seem, whether against a determined Japan in the Burma jungles, a Hannibal emerging from the slaughter at Cannae, or the northern Union with its industrial might. As Clausewitz observed, 'the weaker the forces that are at the disposal of the supreme commander, the more appealing the use of cunning becomes.'[96]

Even ancient Greek hoplites, whose open and frontal combat between phalanxes some regard as the epitome of direct battle in broad daylight, also practised deception when it suited them. In the 7th and 6th centuries BC, Greek city-states (*poleis*) waged agonistic warfare against similar states, limiting it with agreed laws and conventions. Political rhetoric glorified the archaic hoplite's love of honourable, prearranged pitched battles that were bloody but decisive.[97] Herodotus, Thucydides and Polybios all included speeches against deception, and made their speechmakers claim that the Greeks' ancestors waged strictly non-devious warfare. But this was exaggerated self-celebration. Commanders used ruses, night ambushes, and raids when they believed they would work. Duplicitous moves included pretending to be friendly, pretending to be done for the day, sending false information, feigning flight, making a misleading agreement, and seizing undefended cities. Sparta trained boys to steal food, stay awake at night, lay ambushes and prepare spies. The military ethics of an Odysseus, avoiding pitched battle and embracing indirect means, competed with an 'Achilles ethos' of open battle, for the mind of Greek commanders. The Spartan Brasidas rubbished barbarians who avoided set battles, yet praised opportunism over open attack.[98] Athenians and Spartans denounced their enemies' stratagems but carried out their own. Greek strategic culture could also sustain conflicting ideas about grand strategy. It shifted between Achillean 'traditionalists' who saw the world as an anarchic place where only power could ensure security, and Odyssean 'modernists' who stressed multilateralism and cooperation.[99] This dualism anticipates the contested nature of strategic culture today, especially rifts within the West about unilateralism, power, and the role of force in international affairs.[100]

Like Greeks, Romans indulged in flattering mythmaking. Polybios repeated the claim of 'old senators' that their ancestral way of war was upright battle. Other propagandists contrasted Roman valour against foreigners' dishonour. Their forbears fought 'not through ambushes and nocturnal battles, nor through feigned flight', refusing to put 'cunning' above 'true courage.' They declared war first and announced the location of battle in advance. This contrasted them with 'Punic tricks and Greek craftiness.' But like Greeks, Roman history shows discrepancies between rhetoric and action. Roman writers used a stratagemic vocabulary to value Roman deception, while using the same language pejoratively to deprecate their enemies' cunning. Caesar despised the trickery of Germanic and Gallic chieftains while praising his own. Historian and moralist Valerius treated Roman stratagems as psychologically beneficial means of attacking the enemies' mind, but regarded Hannibal's manoeuvres at Cannae as unfair and abhorrent.[101]

In Greek wars against non-Greeks, Asiatic enemies did not have a monopoly on stratagem. Troy in the mythic story was finally stormed because of the Trojan horse. And historically, the survival of Athenian civilisation owed its survival partly to a trick. At the naval clash at Salamis, the navalist Themistocles lured the Persians to attack the Athenian fleet in narrow straits that would bottleneck the faster, lighter and more numerous Persian ships, neutralise their numerical advantage, and multiply the strengths of Athens' heavier ships. By sending a message to fool Xerxes that the Athenians were fleeing, Themistocles tempted him into one of the decisive battles of history. It made possible the life, cultural renaissance and empire of fifth-century Athens.[102] The democratic West, birthed in ancient Athens and later revived, depended on cunning military command.

Because it is so tied to a quest for Western cultural identity, it is no accident that the overarching thesis of a 'Western way of war' can be selective and ahistorical. It bypasses the history of Western strategies of deception, evasion, and indirectness, in its desire to present strategic cultures as symptomatic of core societal values or societal pathologies. As well as doing violence to the range and richness of historical experience, this kind of East/West concept can be dangerously permissive. As Jonathan Mirsky argues, 'If we have "curious rules of honour" on one side, and ambush, treachery and surprise on the other, we give ourselves permission to do horrible things.'[103]

Take suicide methods, an important case for this debate. Some accounts interpret the method of suicide bombing as mainly a product of [MD3]alien culture, warped psychology or radical ideology, in a way that denies it any strategic logic or rational aim.[104] According to Larry Schweikart, suicidal methods from Imperial Japan to radical Islam reflect little but fanaticism: 'Bushido has been replaced with the ideology of jihad, Shintoist shame and honour repackaged in Islamic theological terms, exaggerated by the madrassas.' Schweikart attributes the rise of suicide attack methods between 1975 and 1990 to 'a new theological strain' of *jihad* preached by ideologues such as Sayyid Qutb, the leader of the Muslim Brotherhood.[105] Schweikart 'Orientalises' the suicide bomber to praise the West, asserting the enemy's fanaticism in order to show the singularity of America's humane way of war. To him, the suicide bomber is a figure of cultural nihilism, and serves as a contrast to America's rational humanism.

This approach fails to recognize that the enemy is a strategic actor, not merely a cultural being. It is undoubtedly true that culture can help prepare the ground; that to volunteer as a suicide bomber, an ideology of martyrdom is one precondition; and that belief in Paradise is a powerful motivation. Ideological intensity is part of the cognitive terrain and interior world of the would-be martyr. And ideas may themselves be drivers, rather than epiphenomenal byproducts of other forces. But it is hard to understand suicide bombing if it is divorced from a practical strategic context of relative power and weakness. Far from being a form of expressive violence for its own sake, it is an instrument of calculated psychological warfare. It is attractive to those combating overwhelming military or state power. Suicide bombing translates the impulse of martyrdom into a literal and lethal practice. It is relatively cheap, offers an optimal rate of return, attracts attention, serves as a basis for recruitment, requires no escape plan, and is difficult to combat. Behind every individual zealous bomber is usually a collective organisation—indeed, it is an 'organisational phenomenon.'[106] This does not mean it is always used skilfully, or that the calculations behind it are reasonable. Suicide bombing can be counterproductive to a political cause. But we will struggle to understand it until it is demystified, so that apart from framing it is a fanatic act rooted in deranged ideology, we also see it as a tool of strategic coercion, used with a dark rationality.

Its high utility helps explain why it has been deployed by movements of many ideologies, secular and spiritual, including secular Tamil Tigers, Russian anarchists, Syrian nationalist-socialists, Lebanese Christians and Communists, and the Marxist-Nationalist Kurdistan Worker's Party.[107] Cultural quirks cannot explain the fact that many different cultures have adopted the technique when coming up against a heavily armed opponent. Orchestrators of suicide bombing themselves identify *utility* as the reason they make it their weapon of choice.

As Ramadan Shalah, secretary-general of Palestinian Islamic Jihad said, against an enemy with 'the most sophisticated weapons in the world' with a professional army, they had nothing but the 'weapon of martyrdom. It is easy and costs us only our lives...human bombs cannot be defeated, not even by nuclear bombs.'[108] Similarly, Imperial Japan did not deploy officially sanctioned suicide missions, through *kamikaze* attacks or human torpedoes, until October 1944, when the material imbalance of forces against them was vast, such as the disparity in air combat capability. Fleet Admiral Prince Hiroyasu Fushimi noted at a conference in June 1944 that 'In matters such as radar, our enemy is superior to us qualitatively and quantitatively', hence the need for 'special weapons.'[109]

The West should have no difficulty recognizing the impulse for wartime martyrdom. It has its own heritage of valorizing suicide, down to the present day where the US Marine Corps awards the Medal of Honour automatically for throwing oneself on a grenade to save one's comrades. The prospect of Western suicide flights was even raised by British Air Vice Marshal David Walker, in extreme cases where pilots whose planes suffer weapons failure could use their jets to down a hijacked plane or attack an enemy stronghold.[110] Historically, the idiom of self-sacrifice ranges from Irish political prisoners on hunger strike, to the young volunteer officers willing to be maimed or slaughtered on the battlefront of World War One. One does not have to be 'Eastern' to practice asymmetric methods. At the risk of stating the obvious, weaker sides of any culture, whether secular or religious, nationalist or Marxist, Arab or Asian, must face the grim arithmetic when on the wrong end of a disparity in 'hard' power, that they must be resourceful and flexible and avoid or postpone massed confrontation. No culture enjoys a monopoly over this logic. Being Vietnamese, Islamic, or 'Oriental' was probably not the main driving force behind the asymmetric strategies of the Viet Cong or Al Qaeda, any more than being Spanish or American was the main driving force behind the indirect methods of those who fought Napoleon or the British Empire.[111] Westerners are also capable of actual suicidal missions under duress, and can draw on their own traditions to do so. This was symbolized by the nickname of the suicide squadron Hitler employed to destroy bridges in the last days of the Reich: *Leonidas*.[112]

By widening our perspective in time as well as space, we can see the ruptures and discontinuities within traditions. A frequent practice in

European medieval war, for example, was battle avoidance. Regardless of their elite warrior cultures, medieval commanders were often wary of the dangers of pitched battle, and were constrained by problems of supply, hygiene, and of survival itself in expeditionary wars. Defenders also had an advantage. Defensive strongholds enabled one side to refuse battle. Between 1071 and 1328 in Flanders, often invaded, there were only eleven battles of note.[113] [MD4]And the weak did not have to be reared in Eastern traditions to find alternative ways to combat the strong. When they calculated that they could not resist English invasion through direct combat, Welsh and Scots defenders chose defensive strategies that eastern guerrillas would be proud of, such as scorched earth retreats, cutting off supply lines, punitive raids and the exploitation of terrain.[MD5]

Just as we should doubt the archetype of the 'direct' Westerner, we should be wary of the Eastern evader. The claim that 'Easterners' are distinctive for avoiding 'excess' or mindless loss of life misunderstands their strategic vision. From Ho Chi Minh to Osama Bin Laden, weaker sides have announced their will to sacrifice without limit. It is precisely this which they contend gives them the advantage against the stronger enemy, with its nervous politicians and civilian population reluctant to spend endless blood and treasure. As demonstrated by more than a million dead communists in the North's ultimate victory in Vietnam, or in the wave after wave of direct attacks made by the Vietnamese at Dien Bien Phu or by Chinese forces during the Korean War, bloodless methods and being economical with casualties were not always their war-winning strategies.

The dogma of cultural essentialism, then, often fails to deal with many of the complexities of military performance. It misses out the pragmatism and wiliness of both states and non-state actors at war. And its empirical and conceptual shortcomings reflect a more fundamental problem. It sees what it wants to see in history, making facts fit a theory to confirm its urgent contemporary agenda, which is to alert today's militaries and decision-makers to cultural differences. But however well-intentioned the theory, tradition and legacies are only part of the context in which strategic decisions are made, one variable in a matrix of negotiated interests along with material circumstances, power imbalances and individuals.[114] Cultural legacies are part of the process of decision-making and behaviour, but neither exhaustive of it nor a static element within it.

Culture and War: Rethinking the Relationship

There are different versions of the relationship between war and culture. Here I have argued that we should abandon some widespread conceptions of it. But in strategic affairs, there is still clearly an observable relationship between behaviour and culture, and if some theories are ahistorical and inadequate, we are obliged to suggest alternatives. To help this rethinking, we can turn to three sources. They are not explicitly about war, but their implications can enrich the subject. The first is Karl Marx's 1852 essay on the nature of political struggle and its relationship with the past, the *18*th *Brumaire of Louis Napoleon*. Marx described how revolutionaries invoked the dead of history, defining their cause in terms of heightened historical precedent:

> The tradition of all dead generations weighs like a nightmare on the brains of the living. And just as they seem to be occupied with revolutionizing themselves and things, creating something that did not exist before, precisely in such epochs of revolutionary crisis they anxiously conjure up the spirits of the past to their service, borrowing from them names, battle slogans, and costumes in order to present this new scene in world history in time-honored disguise and borrowed language. Thus Luther put on the mask of the Apostle Paul, the Revolution of 1789–1814 draped itself alternately in the guise of the Roman Republic and the Roman Empire, and the Revolution of 1848 knew nothing better to do than to parody, now 1789, now the revolutionary tradition of 1793–95.[115]

With theatrical metaphors, Marx shows how people make their own history within and through the power of the past, observing the elusive distinction between the outer form of conflict and its substance. Actors mobilize and invoke the pageantry of history to comprehend their struggle. We should recognize that the symbols have cultural resonance, even while being wary of their message, that the present conflict is a continuum from history. Ancient grievances and communal identity may form the rhetoric of conflicts from Belgrade to Baghdad, but we are not obliged to accept these claims at face value.

This points to a second source, sociologist Ann Swidler. She argues that culture is significant because it supplies resources with which people construct strategies of action. Swidler argues that culture is an instrumental 'tool-kit' 'with many parts from which people pick and choosein order to organise activity. 'A realistic cultural theory should lead us to expect not passive "cultural dopes" but rather the active, sometimes skilled users of culture whom we actually observe.'[116] The more unsettled the situation, the more malleable culture becomes. Marx and Swidler can help refine our conception of culture, not as a unified, objectively known fact, but as a loose, discordant set of memories, values, symbols, metaphors, interpreted experience, principles and 'lessons.' Consider the debate within Hamas or al Qaeda over two taboos, the adoption of suicide bombing and recruiting women. This shows movements internally debating their norms of war, changing their stance to justify methods that would be effective against their enemies' overwhelming military force, then justifying it by reworking interpretations of sacred text.

The third source is Indian economist and philosopher Amartya Sen. As he warns, culture becomes an impoverished concept when it is treated as homogenous and insular. Such an attitude ignores the multiple identities that people are capable of choosing among, and creates a dangerously self-fulfilling notion that we are bound to be separate and hostile collectivities. 'When a hazy perception of culture is combined with fatalism about the dominating power of culture, we are, in effect, asked to be imaginary slaves of an illusory force.'[117] Sen reminds us that it is people who mutually make culture. The strategic environment is more than a realm 'out there' to be understood, but a reciprocal space that is remade by those entering it. Soldiers patrolling a foreign city seeking intelligence, negotiating with locals or pursing opponents effectively constitute as well as interpret a shared culture, changing the very terrain they try to understand.[118]

All three of these perspectives can help us to understand events in Iraq, which demonstrates the volatility of the relationship between warmakers and their world. After the rout of Saddam's forces in 2003, Sunni Arabs did not behave as some triumphalists predicted, as people easily cowed by the 'shock and awe' of a stronger power. Neither did they behave, as some theorists argued, as a people made militarily inferior by an honour/shame culture. Instead, they proved to be resilient and innovative guerillas.[119] Once the Iraqi insurgency was underway, the US mistakenly treated it through Vietnam, its grid for Oriental uprisings. But the classic Maoist insurgencies in Vietnam, Malaya and the Philippines during the 1960s were homogenous, top-down and unified. Thus they were differently structured from the fragmented nature of today's global guerrillas.[120]

Iraq illustrated the problems of any culture-centric approaches that are divorced from a dynamic political context. Some argue that Iraq should return to its tribal cultural essence, and trisect into three permanently feuding parts, like Caesar's Gaul. But like Gaul, Iraq's internal divisions are proving more subtle and more unstable. Sunni insurgents, for example, have turned against their former allies Al Qaeda in Iraq, for the moment realigning with the US in the 'Anbar awakening.' Shia forces are factionalised and divided, while in Baghdad, Iraqis defy stereotypes, forming their own combined Sunni-Shia neighbourhood security groups.[121] The second difficulty with the partitionist argument is that it assumes Iraq is historically doomed to fragment into sectarian statelets. But the entities being proposed, such as Shiistan and Sunnistan, have little historical precedent, and territorial unity is as much a theme in Iraqi history as fragmentation, and either could be in its future.[122] We may be tempted to miniaturize people into predictable beings, whose loyalties, behaviour and fighting power are predetermined by history and bounded by indigenous tradition, but they may not cooperate.

In order to understand the war/culture relationship, we need not only observe cultures at war, but observe the observers, and grasp the impulses that have driven their fascination. The following chapter examines a moment that prompted a wave of cultural speculation, the Russo-Japanese war of 1904–5, when a supposedly inferior Asian nation defeated a great power, and got the West's attention.

3

WATCHING THE RISING SUN

OBSERVING JAPAN AT WAR

When Japan defeated Russia in the war of 1904–5, the world was watching.[1] In Asia, newspapers were read aloud in schools, barbershops and village assemblies. Muslim clerics predicted the downfall of infidel empires. Crowds cheered in Indian cinemas at the newsreels of Russian defeats. American President Theodore Roosevelt even took *Ju-jitsu* classes. Japan's triumphs inspired James Joyce's vision, in *Ulysses*, of the eclipse of British world power. And despite fears that Japan's victory might incite anti-colonial uprisings, Europe sent eighty-three international observers from fifteen countries, including British military officers and war correspondents. Their own nations, they claimed, could learn from Japan. The image of Japan became a rhetorical device they could use to criticise their own society. Intelligence scholars have already demonstrated the impact of political preconceptions on 'image', the way negative stereotypes about race or class can affect military assessments. But this is a case where criticism of one's own society, and the predisposition to idealise rather than dismiss the Oriental, could also shape perception.[2] This was Orientalism of a transformational where the example of the Orient held out the promise of regeneration and change. [3]

This chapter divides into three parts. First, it explores how British observers tried to explain Japan's victory and extract 'lessons' from it, making cultural judgements that varied in their sophistication and accuracy. British observers saw Japan's strategic outlook and societal values reflected in many areas. They ranged from the values of the military (such as Japanese combatants' attitudes towards death, and towards both military and state authority); to the conduct of war (in Japan's use of deception, surprise and intelligence); to wider society (in institutions such as war commemoration and education, and in the capacity of Japanese society to tolerate the human and material costs of war). Second, these perceptions are contrasted with the more complex realities of Japanese society during the war. Finally, it argues that British observers were especially influenced by their domestic political context, especially their anxieties about the state of Edwardian society and its capacity to accept the human and material costs of war. Japan appealed to them because it fitted with their belief in the potential benefits of state-driven social engineering, where state policies could prepare and strengthen a population for war. This political agenda shaped their perceptions, and misperceptions, of Japanese strategic culture.

Why did Japan win? There exists a rich literature examining how observers—who have discerned many, interlocking reasons for Japan's victory—interpreted the strategic, operational, and tactical 'lessons' of the war.[4] Japan enjoyed geostrategic advantages over the Czar's forces, not least because Russia divided its army between the Far East and western Russia, thereby blocking it from applying the same weight of force in the Asiatic region as Japan. The difficulty of transporting men and material across Siberia was compounded by inadequate roads and railway. The Czarist regime was also politically more constrained. It had hoped that a short victory might bolster its faltering legitimacy at home but it was soon threatened by revolution in its major cities. Japan was highly organised, closely attending to its logistics and supply.[5] Alongside these material factors, British observers also discerned more profound causes.

To fathom Japan's success, they turned to its culture. Arguably, the war could have gone either way, and its outcome was highly contingent. For British observers, the war was decided not only by the pulse of the battlefield or immediate events; they saw it as an audit of two warring cultures, an arbiter of their contrasting values and viability. Japan's victory, Britons argued, showed the superiority of its strategic culture over Russia's. The Japanese prevailed because they translated their social and political cohesion into military supremacy. Japan was deemed superior in several vital areas: in its social *mores*, in the relationship between its citizen and the state, its approach to the utility of force and its understanding of the nature of war. This victory would remain one high standard against which Japan's subsequent military capacity would be judged.[6] British observers did not just make these observations in a spirit of detached curiosity. Just as Japan had ascended to 'great power' status through imitation and innovation, so too could Britain.

At first glance, when it comes to the historical relationship between Japan and the Anglosphere many histories stress the themes of the hostility and perceived difference between warring cultures. But there is another current running through this history, of 'sameness', curiosity and admiration. Even before it was forced into greater contact with the wider world by Commodore Matthew Perry in 1854, Japan had developed institutions, social structures and national myths that Europeans found recognisable. A feudal warrior elite with its own warrior code of *Bushido*, for example, seemed to parallel the tradition of chivalry. Even though the Pacific war was presented as a war between alien cultures, the Allies ultimately were able to perceive their enemies more accurately, and to benefit from their insights. And half a century earlier, British officers and journalists wrote admiringly of Japan's victory over Russia.

For British observers during the Russo-Japanese war, it seemed that the event had world-historical importance, altering, as it did, the balance of power in the East. A small upstart Asian nation, once resource-poor and technophobic, only recently unified, defeated one of Europe's great powers. Britons' interest in Japan was magnified by the fear that they might face a comparable situation. If Russia could mobilise, assemble and maintain a large army miles from Europe by means of a single-line railway within months, it could also potentially do this on the Afghan frontier. Decades of exchange and mutual influence encouraged identification with Japan. Japan's army and navy were developed and trained by European advisors, while elites studied abroad in each other's country. And given the new strategic alignment, with the British-Japanese alliance of 1902, it was natural to search for affinities with their new partner, particularly as Japan was seen as a counterweight to Russian influence in the region. Yet their efforts to present Japan not only as a robust military power, but also as an ideal society, suggests a deeper attraction.

British analysts in 1904–5 were strongly influenced by their own preconceptions, namely their fear that cultures like Japan were better able to summon the political will to wage and endure war. There was a psychological element in Japan's victory that intrigued Britons, namely Japan's willingness to endure heavy losses. Why had Japanese combatants been willing to die in their hundreds of thousands? Commentators gave explanations of varying degrees of sophistication. A few commentators saw its roots in antiquity, admiring Japan's historic code of *Bushido*, or their perceived Asiatic Buddhist state of inner serenity. F.J. Norman, a British cavalryman who instructed in Japan's military colleges, gave a geographical and racial explanation, attributing the 'fighting and sea-faring instincts of the Japanese' to their Malay and Mongolian blood, and to the 'climactic conditions.'[7] The *Daily Mail* correspondent who was present at the siege of Port Arthur saw Japanese discipline as inborn, fostered by centuries of living 'as an inferior caste under the sway of the Samurais', their bravery coming from 'their fatalism, their faith in their officers, and their reverence for their god-Emperor.'[8]

While most observers agreed that there were traces of Japan's feudal past in its contemporary military performance, and that its culture of sacrifice was vaguely in its bloodstream or genetic makeup, they were not content to medievalise Japan's victories only as a result of an ancestral Samurai purity. They claimed, instead, in different formulations, that Japan had reworked a medieval warrior culture, giving a modern expression to ancient military and social values. Japan, it seemed, had achieved a marriage of *Bushido* and modernity, and its fighting spirit was mainly inculcated and developed by modern institutions and state policies. They admired Japan's adaptation to the modern world and its emergence through the transformations of the revolution under Emperor Meiji (1868–1912).

How these observers explained Japan's martial resilience tells us much about themselves. This was a period of empire which was built on racial hierarchy. Yet, strikingly, there was a lack of racialist determinism in the core assumptions of most officers. Consider the views of Sir Ian Hamilton, one of the most prominent 'Japanophiles' among the military observers. For him, the question was an existential one. In his own worldview, the British empire faced a strategic crisis similar to the late western Roman empire. A tired, emasculated power was in danger of being overwhelmed by simpler, tougher and 'untamed' warrior cultures. Left unchecked, Abyssinia and Afghanistan would become vectors of dangerous fanaticism and expansion, while 'India is Gaul, Central Asia is Germany.'[9] Hamilton himself had commanded Gurkhas in mountain operations, and argued that their abilities 'could shake to their foundations the artificial societies of the West.'[10] The Japanese example he held up as a way of countering these dangers:

In their schoolrooms are portraits of heroes and pictures of Great Battles. The Japanese have behind them the moral character produced by mothers and fathers, who again are the products of generations of mothers and fathers nurtured in ideals of self-sacrifice and loyalty. But they do not on this account trust entirely to heredity to produce them an army. If they wish to have every man in the nation a potential fighter they know they must begin at the beginning, and put the right ideas into the babies as soon as they begin to toddle. The parade march of the 5th German Army Corps impressed me far less than the little Japanese boys and girls I saw marching in their companies to say good-bye to the soldiers.'[11]

As Hamilton claimed, Japan's determined fighting population was the creation of deliberate policies of social engineering, not just an inherited 'national character.' State policies and processes of socialisation, especially through childhood education, were critical to Hamilton's conception of the rise and fall of civilisations. As soon as the Japanese boy was able to walk, another observer agreed, his military education began. Every family owned a lantern or national flag, children flocked to marching regiments, and village schools supplied guards of honour at railway stations. Patriotism became intuitive through constant programming of the 'boyish imagination.' National spirit, discipline and loyalty to Emperor were an 'indigenous growth' that had been midwifed by the trinity of the Government, Nation and Army.[12] Differences in military discipline or performance among the masses were due not to inherent racial characteristics but to the quality of the elite governing and commanding them.[13] This was a view that Hamilton also imbibed from his Japanese hero. General Nogi, who to Hamilton was an almost divine figure of 'superhuman unselfishness' and the 'finest flower of Japanese chivalry', had himself identified parental upbringing as the source of *Bushido*.[14]

In this hagiography of Japanese warrior values, Hamilton's conception of Japan's rise was formed in relation to his view of British decline. The Japanese had similar psychological strengths, but they represented qualities the British were in danger of losing. In his diary he wrote that 'Japs have exactly our ideas of calm and reserve—only our long success has made us careless—their feeling of being new and looked down upon makes them intensely the reverse.'[15] Japan embodied Britain in its infancy before growing power spread complacency, and Japan's hunger for world power in turn reflected Hamilton's fear of societal decay. In this view, his visions of Britain and Japan created and reinforced one another.

Hamilton's tendency to idealise Japan may have led him to overlook the heterogeneity and complexity of Japanese society, but it also led him to prescient observations. As the Anglo-Japanese alliance unravelled, he forewarned in November 1921 that the Japanese would not be scared away from expansionism by the prestige of British or American power; that they could seize the Philippines or Hong Kong, and that it would take five years for the world to subdue them and roll back their conquests. Like General Yamagata Aritomo who swam out with his sword to attack an American ironclad, the Japanese would not be easily frightened.[16] Awed by Japan's capacity to defy and challenge western powers, Hamilton's frame of reference led him into insight as well as error.

British observers often depicted Japan's combatants as the products of a better social and political order, and always in a dialogic comparison with their judgements over Britain. Major J. Somerville, for example, represented Japanese military strength as the manifestation of an 'ancient, fighting, feudal spirit' and contempt for money and luxury. This was facilitated, he believed, by the structure of Japanese society, by a cult of the emperor that was propounded in schools, the Emperor's public charisma, and a memorial culture of ancestor-worship that revered military service. Unlike British combatants, whose *espirit de corps* was focussed on regimental traditions and rivalry, Japanese combatants were driven by an exclusive loyalty to the Emperor, a civil religion 'more potent' than the religions 'of the more highly civilised European powers.'[17]

Japan seemed sufficiently comparable to Britain to be presented not as a barbaric threat but as an example of how to reconcile the advancements of modern civilisation with the supposed values of antiquity. Colonel Repington, the *Times* correspondent and the most important military journalist of the time, saw in the superior morale of the Japanese combatant and the European-trained army, the 'spiritual successors of Moltke and Roon in the high command.'[18] *Bushido*, a medieval code that had once been the monopoly of an elite military caste, had now become popularised into a value system for the nation as a whole. Although *Bushido* was intellectually aristocratic, anyone could become a *bushi* 'by conduct in peace and by valour in war…neither birth nor wealth is required, only personal worth and conduct.' *Bushido*, Repington argued, represented the negation of the flaws in British society. Its virtues included anti-materialism, self-sacrifice, the primacy of the state above the individual or family, submission to authority, and discipline.[19]

Hamilton, Somerville and Repington reflected a broad consensus of opinion among the representatives of Britain's military establishment and media. These military observers represented an Edwardian class of officers, educated at public schools, many of whom had taken part in imperial expeditionary campaigns from South Africa to India. For their part, war correspondents such as Repington manifested similar anxieties. There were also nine *language officers* present to observe the war, as well as keen life-long 'Japanists' such as Yate, Kennedy and Piggott. Though they might differ over the precise military lessons, both war correspondents and officers assumed that the war was to be interpreted in the light of a crisis in the ability of the British Empire to police itself. The war was also seen as foreshadowing the pattern of future major wars between great powers. It featured armies of millions, artillery duels, the domination of firepower, protracted battles, and entrenched positional warfare with lines of trenches protected by land mines, barbed wire and machine gun redoubts. The fighting was done by night as well as day. It was co-ordinated by field telephones and supplied by railway. Nine of the twenty-nine British army officers present would be killed in the First World War.[20]

Both journalists and officers repeated the myth that Japanese soldiers were 'human bullets' whose code of self-sacrifice and honour underpinned Japanese doctrine and was the decisive element in Japanese victory. Implicit or explicit in this theme was the corollary, of an unflattering contrast with the British. German military critic Major Wilhelm Balck, whose writing was reported in Britain, contrasted the Japanese, who supposedly fought like Mongols, against the British, with their reluctance to press home frontal attacks in the South African war and their over-carefulness with men's lives.[21]

But the more perceptive observers noted that the concept of a timeless *Bushido*, an unbroken traditional warrior culture, was ahistorical. Captain P.W. North, for example, stressed that Japan's 'splendid warlike spirit' was socially constructed by two modern instruments, conscription and mass education. He noted that warfare in premodern Japan was a specialised activity that had traditionally been the speciality of a small elite class, and that Japan had largely enjoyed peace for three centuries before the Meiji era, two conditions that were not conducive to militarising an entire population.

North drew these conclusions from conversations with older Japanese, who told him that a popular 'fighting spirit' was a recent innovation, which began only after the arrival of Commander Perry, and that military service was not seen as honourable until the Sino-Japanese war of 1894–5.[22] It was modern schools in particular that elevated the status of the military, by holding drills, parades and training, by promoting the military above other professions such as scientists, lawyers or politicians, by teaching patriotic songs, and by venerating alumni killed in active service. Whatever the factuality of North's claims, it is significant that he and others argued that the reasons for Japan's supposed psychological supremacy on the battlefield were systemic, and could be copied with a constellation of the right institutions in national life, such as infant instruction, schooling, war commemoration, and a system of government.

Even some accounts which stressed 'Oriental' racial features still often concluded that Japan's way of war could be applied across cultures. In a lecture delivered about Japan's system of intelligence in 1909, Colonel J.A.L. Haldane did some cultural typecasting, but claimed Britain could adapt Japan's intelligence system. Japan's wide-reaching, almost panoptic, surveillance system, he argued, was possible partly because of its 'natural aptitude for spying', a medieval 'inheritance' from intrigue among rival warlords and the Shogunate, and general 'Oriental cunning, self-control' and a 'reticence' that was less developed among westerners. Spying, he stated, seemed 'an unsavoury trade.' But he then advised officers to cultivate powers of observation, accuracy in reporting, and self-control, or in other words, develop qualities that were lacking outside the East.[23] Although he depicted Japan's intelligence system as symptomatic of a traditional cultural personality, Haldane also implied that Britons must become more Oriental in their intelligence capability.

For Britons keen to hold up Japan as a model, the most problematic aspect of Japan's 'way of war' was its use of stealth, deception and surprise. There was a seeming contrast between Russia's guileless and artless way of war and Japan's use of deception. The war had begun with a surprise attack, as Japan torpedoed Russia's Pacific Fleet at Port Arthur in February 1904, in a foretaste of their assault on Pearl

Harbor in 1941. Colonel Charles Ross would write in 1912 that the success of this sudden, unannounced strike proved the naivety and obsolescence of notions of 'gentlemanly' warfare. Assuming that deception was not peculiar to Asian war cultures, he cited Prussia's own use of deception in the Wars of Unification. 'Those who preach platitudes, clap-trap, as to "playing cricket" to the enemy, do but small service to their country. They would do well to study war and to look at realities...In the modern wars of 1866, 1870, and 1904 the defeated were mislead and brought to the verge of defeat by the victory before ever a shot was fired and in the midst of profound peace.'[24]

To prepare for war, Japan had deliberately concealed the strength of its forces, shielding information from foreign military attaches, thus enabling Russia to underestimate them.[25] Japan also skilfully managed media exposure, which was contrasted against both Russia's habit of allowing European newspapers to forecast its moves, and with Britain's lax censorship during the Anglo-Boer war, 'who published to the world our intention of attacking Spion Kop five days before we actually did so.'[26] Japan also exploited ruses, secrecy and concealment at the operational and tactical level. Britons were impressed with the effects of night attacks and feints and the discipline not to reveal information when captured.[27] While its sailors and soldiers were a nation of knights who could fling themselves heroically against devastating firepower, they could also be subtle and wrong-foot their opponent. Ian Hamilton commented on Japan's use of dummy bridges and fortifications, as diversions to draw fire. 'In the British Army I have known generals who would consider such a ruse de guerre...as highly irregular and undignified.' But they 'come quite naturally to the Japanese.'[28] Observing officers often feared that significant parts of Britain's supposed code of 'fair play' or chivalry were becoming outmoded in their contemporary security environment. By assuming lessons could be learned from this, they assumed that aspects of Japanese deception operations could be copied.

This view, that Japan's military culture was not unique or peculiar, but deliberately developed by the state, gave utility to the study of Japan. If societies were malleable and could ape one another's policies and social structures, then this gave greater value to close study. Japan itself demonstrated the value of being an imitative culture. It had studied European methods and learnt from the enemy, while Russia in its contemptuous attitude blinded itself to Japan's 'fighting efficiency' and courted disaster.[29] Before the war, Russian military attaches and the officer corps generally had mischaracterised Japan's military potential on almost every level, reporting that the Japanese lacked initiative and imagination, had copied European methods but not its spirit, that its infantry was indifferent and afraid of bayonet and night operations, unable to march or stand strain of war, its artillery slow and ignorant, its cavalry worthless, generals mediocre, and its army unfit to meet European troops.[30] Russia's misperception of Japan's capabilities, against Japan's more sober and open inquiry, had demonstrated the value of being receptive to foreign strategic cultures. Japan's subsequent victory was treated as a caution against dismissive estimates of foreign military power, and a lesson in the need to learn lessons.

Indeed, the war erupted precisely at a moment in Britain when the exercise of 'learning' lessons through the scientific study of wars was being institutionalised as an official, state-endorsed process. The Committee of Imperial Defence, which had been created a few months earlier to review imperial strategy, organised an historical section, which eventually produced the *Official History of the Russo-Japanese War*. It was formed partly in response to the disappointment with British failures in the Anglo-Boer war of 1899–1902. The management of *The Times*, too, believed it was necessary to print regular criticisms of military developments and to 'stimulate thought concerning the art of war.' Colonel Repington asserted the need to study the 'lessons' of the war, lest the British 'remain ignorant of all the lessons of the past, and then [be forced] to learn them over again, with each succeeding war, at huge and needless cost.'[31] The foundations of Japan's victory could be emulated by other nations as their militaries tried to forecast the conditions and demands of future war.

As Philip Towle notes, over time the Edwardian military establishment grew less enthusiastic about the usefulness of the Russo-Japanese war as an example, on the basis that Japanese infantry tactics, marksmanship, training, manoeuvres and horsemanship were deemed inferior, and that Japanese culture was wrongly thought to be 'purely imitative.'[32] Those who had not observed the Japanese army in action in Manchuria, but who watched only manoeuvres, reached disparaging conclusions. Estimates of Japanese military strength grew more dismissive and warped by racial condescension as Anglo-British relations soured. A Royal Navy analysis of Japanese naval efficiency would conclude, for example, that the Japanese lacked initiative and imagination, and had 'slow brains.'[33] There was a continuing respect for the physical endurance and discipline of Japanese troops, and officers who had watched the war of 1904–5 continued to assert that it was a lesson in the relationship between the citizen and the state. Japan had triumphed, it was claimed, partly because of the nature of its political ideas, its institutions and its concept of citizenship.

Despite their scientific confidence in the possibility of learning concrete and enduring lessons from the war, and although they were attentive to the complexities of Japanese history and the very modern roots of the institutions that helped its military success, they also idealised wartime Japan, both its society and in its prosecution of the war at the front. What did they admire about Japan's conduct of the war? First, there were the sheer massed assaults and limitless sacrifice and high morale, which they saw as the summit of what European ways of war could be. There was the organisational skill and hygiene. The apparent sobriety of Japanese combatants, with its implicit contrast with Britons, struck Britain's assistant military attaché at the embarkation of the Japanese 8th Division at Osaka, who noted the 'complete absence of any noise, shouting, or confusion', and the lack of drunkenness.[34] Some commentators singled out the rhetoric and ritual which marked Japanese national life, such as the ceremonial commemoration of the war dead. Other admirers praised Japan for its social cohesion and unity during the war and the spirit of self-sacrifice among its population. When the war was concluded by the Treaty of Portsmouth in September 1905, a number of journalists praised Japan's magnanimity and moderation in victory. They argued that the settlement's leniency and limited terms were due to the enlightened attitudes of *Bushido* and Japan's ultimately non-threatening, non-expansionist nature.[35]

As several historians have demonstrated, these views of Japan at war were overdrawn. The concept that the war effort revealed the anti-materialist spirit of Japan as a contrast with the commercial 'west' was problematic in itself.[36] Japan's war was financed and made possible by American capitalism, with loans from US bankers, including Jewish creditors in New York such as Jacob H. Schiff, opposed to the Russian Czar's anti-Semitic pogroms, the most recent of which had happened in 1903.[37] This helps also to explain the war's termination. Given its dependence on foreign credit in an expensive war, Japan had to accept the terms because of American fiscal and diplomatic pressure to end the conflict. Also misleading is the excited claim that the terms of victory in the final settlement illustrated Japanese magnanimity. In reality, the Japanese government and large parts of its population were disappointed with the outcome. There were in fact angry protests in Japan that they were not exacting greater financial penalties from defeated Russia.

Accounts of Japanese society in 1904–5 were at odds with the actual complexity and diversity of Japanese wartime society. Instead of being a monolithic and undifferentiated mass, Japan's population showed many examples of disunity, complaint, apathy and dissent. Despite claims that Japan was enlightened by patriotic education with a Confucian respect for the teacher, schools were underfunded and teachers frequently criticised for being 'lazy' or 'incompetent.' Against claims that strict Eastern morals reigned, erotic postcards became a popular wartime industry. Though both Japanese propagandists and foreign onlookers presented Japanese soldiers as austere heroes, there were complaints that the new *samurai* liked wearing fine silks and adventurous hairstyles. At a state level, while outsiders compared Japan to ancient Sparta, the government proved more flexible on issues of self-gratification. Strapped for money, the administration that had once discourage smoking and drinking now tried to raise tax revenue by promoting both habits.[38]

The notion that fanatical self-sacrifice was the result of Japanese combat doctrine and the decisive element in its victory is also misleading. The 'human bullet' mass assaults against fortified positions at the siege of Port Arthur (July to December 1904), for example, arguably resulted just as much from inadequate operational planning, logistical difficulties and intelligence failures. Heavy casualties happened often because of errors. The Second Army at Nanshan attacked before the arrival of its heavy artillery pieces, costing it thousands of casualties, while the siege at Port Arthur led to heavy losses partly because Imperial Headquarters underestimated the strength of Russian fortifications, and the artillery ammunition it would need. Japanese infantry manuals in the late 1890s had prioritised firepower rather than the cult of the bayonet. Limitless sacrifice and the centrality of morale were not necessarily the prevailing doctrines. Particularly in light of Japan's manpower limits in the war against Russia, and the time pressure to advance quickly before Russia could fully deploy its larger forces in the region, some generals complained that casualties from massed assaults were 'excessive.' In contrast to propagandist claims that they regarded death only as an absolute duty, officers did think about casualties on a calculus of cost and gain. Staff officer Iguchi reckoned that had an alternative position been attacked rather than the fortress, the Rising Sun would be unfurled over Port Arthur with 'no more than 10,000 casualties.'[39]

None of this is to suggest that British observers were entirely inaccurate in their assessments. Their view of a unified, self-sacrificing wartime Japan was overstated and influenced by both their own political preconceptions and by Japanese propaganda. But they were not wholly wrong to stress the impact of nationalist sentiment and social cohesion, generated partly by mass education, which underpinned the willingness of Japanese combatants to sustain high losses. Likewise, the value system of *Bushido* may have been a modern invention, but many Japanese combatants probably wanted to live up to it. One officer reported, for example, that there were numerous suicides in the Guards Division alone, over one thousand instances.[40] They were also accurate in identifying the relatively high standards of hygiene and logistical organisation in the Japanese forces, their interest in this aspect sparked by their experience of the Anglo-Boer war. Britons were struck by the meticulous standards of cleanliness, the comparative ratios of disease and wounds, the benefits of latrines, food preservation, the sterilisation of water, and sanitation rules.[41] And their general emphasis on the central role of state policy, in which social engineering and a malleable culture were the determining elements, showed a more sophisticated approach to interpreting Japanese society than some of their colleagues, who relied on lazier ideas of fixed ethnic characteristics.

However accurate, why were the British so predisposed towards idealised images of wartime Japan? Partly it was the impact of the censorship and propaganda of the Japanese state, which encouraged its admirers to collaborate in this myth of Japan. Observers were being directed by the Japanese government and military authorities. Many British officers were kept waiting for months before they were allowed to go near the battlefront. And Japan deliberately shaped global perceptions of its culture by cultivating the world-wide media. Its global audience was possible because the war was media intensive, as the advent of the electric telegraph, railway and mass literacy had a dramatic impact on the flow of information. European and American fascination with *Bushido* had already been encouraged by Nitobe Inazo's best-selling *Bushido: The Soul of Japan* of 1900. Inaz acted as a cultural bridge, an insider translating the Japanese samurai tradition for western audiences, linking it to familiar classical and medieval value-systems, and was reissued in 1905 to acclaim.[42] Then war inspired an unprecedented volume of visual representations, such as photos, posters, pictures and postcards.[43] Idealised soldiers and sailors were depicted on woodblocks, lithographs and in the print media. Japan encouraged outsiders to view the homeland as a dynamic martial civilisation, promoting the idea that Japan had graduated as a great power along European lines.[44] A whole network of information channels to the outside was developed by the state, which even westernised the facial features of Japanese combatants, encouraging western identification with Japanese soldiers and sailors. Japanese combatants were portrayed as both compassionate and formidable fighters. This played to a powerful theme in European discourses of war, namely the exemplary soldier with knightly virtues. And it was reinforced in 1907 by Tadayoshi Sakurai's *Human Bullets: A Soldier's Story of Port Arthur*, which portrayed Japanese soldiers unquestioningly laying their lives on the altar of the nation, received enthusiastically in Britain. The Japanese were not passive recipients of the west's perception of them, but active agents in making their own image.

British officers also valorised Japan because it was politically useful. Whatever the sophistication of their view of Japanese history and society, observers were often influenced by their domestic commitments and political context in their views of foreign reality. These Britons believed that they could use the example of Japan to vindicate their own explicitly illiberal views.

Several assumptions conditioned their image of Japan. These included Social Darwinism in international affairs; an empiricist confidence that observed wars had intrinsic meaning that could extracted and applied; a belief in the central importance of the psychological element and morale in modern war; authoritarian politics; and a new confidence in the potentiality of state intervention in society.

Social Darwinism, at least in their version, was a vulgarised application of Darwinian thought to human and interstate affairs, portraying the world as a predatory environment of competition, survival and extinction, and it seemed to make sense in the context of imperial rivalries and tensions.[45] Moreover, Japan's apparent insensitivity to high casualties, and its successful but bloody offensives, appealed to its view that psychological strength was the decisive element in industrial war. And they were drawn to Japan's authoritarian system of government, in which the Emperor wielded supreme executive power, with only minimal concessions to parliamentary representatives. Finally, the apparent role of Japanese state policies in its military success reinforced their growing confidence in the potential of state-driven social engineering to strengthen the nation for war.

All of these interlocking assumptions had been reinforced by the disappointments of the Anglo-Boer war. In the latter, a Boer insurgency tied down Britain's army of hundreds of thousands, costing 200 million pounds. Army doctors turned down between 40 and 60 percent of volunteers on medical grounds, and enteric fever swept through the British forces. This prompted inquests into the state of British military affairs, and Britain's capacity to police and defend its empire or repel an invasion. In a drive for 'national efficiency', the National Service League was founded to campaign for universal conscription in peacetime, along with the Inter-Departmental Committee on Physical Deterioration, which focused on the physical unfitness of the male population for military service.[46] The net effect of this movement was to bring many neglected areas of public welfare more strongly into the orbit of debate around imperial defence, such as health, hygiene, education, housing and material conditions of living. National decline, it assumed, could be averted by deliberate state policy, and modern Japan pointed the way. While this attraction to the Japanese model of militarised youth was held by officers whose political comments generally suggest rightist opinions, it was not necessarily symptomatic of the conservatism of the declining order of aristocratic privilege, land and established money. It echoed instead the British 'embryonic radical right' that was also represented by the military lobby in the House of Lords; it was driven by a fear of imperial decline, and the belief that it could be arrested only by state-sponsored measures.[47]

As their writing indicates, British observers were uneasy with the processes of industrialisation, urbanisation and economic growth, and the impact of these forces on the population's capacity to endure the strains and costs of war. Military minds feared that the coming of a materialistic, egalitarian and urban society would endanger traditional warrior values, such as physical and moral courage, discipline, and obedience. For example, the *Daily Mail* correspondent made revealing comments about an isolated episode of insubordination in the Japanese army. To explain the reluctance of a regiment to follow a major in a dangerous forward movement, the observer noted that the soldiers had been recruited from a relatively wealthy area.[48] Ian Hamilton warned that British 'city-bred dollar-hunters' had struggled against the Boer rebellion and that modern urbanised nations might 'go down before some more natural, less complex and less nervous type.'[49] By contrast, though not all of Japan's recruits were from agrarian areas, commentators claimed that most Japanese from rural or urban areas had retained a feudal sense of obedience.

The impact of urbanisation on a population's ability to field mass armies, sustain morale and make sacrifices is an old fear. The Roman satirist Juvenal complained that affluence changed noble Roman peasants into degenerate urbanites. German pessimists such as Friedrich Nietzsche believed that the human soul was damaged by radical egalitarianism and bourgeois leisure. Britain had urbanised more rapidly than any other modern nation, and this development, with its seemingly vast social impact, accentuated the anti-urbanism of Edwardian military commentators. In reviews of the Anglo-Boer war of 1899–1902, the poor health and questionable commitment of parts of the British military were explained as symptoms of the growth of towns.[50]

As well as worrying about the impact of urbanisation, British observers were particularly interested in the role of education in Japan's system of social militarism. Japan's resurgence was linked to its education system, and received more attention than the question of racial character. *The Times* cited the *Imperial Rescript on Education* of 1890 on moral instruction as the cornerstone of school curricula. The ideals of that speech had been 'instilled in the minds of teachers' when the generation who fought 'so valiantly' in the war of 1904–5 were at school.[51] Education had to be aligned with state interests to foster and enhance indigenous strengths. Lieutenant (and future Field Marshall) Archibald Wavell mused that 'if a sound national spirit is to be kept alive or engendered without the aid of disaster, the system of education must be with a view to national aims', as the Japanese had done by utilising traditional ancestor worship to assist national aims.[52]

Education was one of four institutions that interested British observers, also including military conscription, the cult of the Emperor, and war commemoration. Under the Meiji revolution, Japan's leaders had used education as a political tool, to create a national identity and inculcate national consciousness in place of older regional and feudal affiliations that dominated the earlier period of the Shogunate. Primary schools in particular were vehicles for this nationalist project. From 1894–5, the state-controlled education system became increasingly militarised, focussing on the Japanese armed forces as exemplary and heroic, and instructing students about dying in battle, making glorious military charges, and honouring one's family. This curriculum was then reinforced by indoctrination in military education and training.[53]

Consider attempts by British officers to learn from Japan's education system. In 1906, the British War Office commissioned a confidential report into the Japanese system of military education and training. Its envoy was Colonel A.M. Murray, who visited Japanese secondary schools, cadet schools, war schools and staff colleges.[54] Murray's report regurgitated the opinions of the Japanese authorities whom he interviewed. Their portrayal of the Japanese military ethos was something that he wanted to hear. Japan's robust military, he argued, was forged by a rigorous curriculum, the daily life at a military preparatory school conducted without 'relaxing of severity.'[55]

Murray's report relied on binary caricatures of modern Japan and the Occident. From the regimental mess to the classroom, Japan's system bred simplicity, discipline and patriotism. In his eyes, this contrasted with the individualistic, luxuried 'West.' The notion that the masses of the West were corrupted by opulence was a narrow caricature of British society, where excess material abundance was not a pressing issue for most of the population. This hyperbole was typical of cruder forms of Orientalism with its assumption that cultures were homogenous. But this artificial image of tough Japanese against decadent westerners was part of Murray's didactic purpose, invoking Japanese military education to draw attention to the perceived failings of British society. He also absorbed Japan's own propagandist claims about itself, even claiming that Japanese generals were devoid of jealous personal ambition, that Japanese officers were heedless of their own glory, whereas Russian generals were incapable of co-operation.[56]

All of this was intended to promote certain public polices back home. Murray believed that a nation could transform its military strength purely through artificial measures such as education and conscription, and that Japan's strategic culture could be transplanted across national borders. The Japanese conscript was the finest 'fighting material in the world, and this is due less to his natural characteristics than to the education which he receives in his youth.'[57] In a forum the following year about military education, he claimed that China with the same education system could become 'as great and as efficient and as up-to-date as Japan.'[58] The underlying, paradoxical fear within the culture of elite opinion over empire is here apparent—that within a period of expansion, there is the threat of societal decline.

Murray praised conscription, reporting that it nationalised Japan's army and opened it beyond the old clans to talent regardless of pedigree, raising merit above family interest. But alongside this egalitarian view, Murray railed against 'individualism', admiring the regimented conditions of the Japanese preparatory school. He assumed that liberalism, the political movement championing individual rights, was destructive of the political will and capacity to fight. This worldview, reinforced by his tour of Japan, showed a lack of awareness about the different forms of Japanese nationalism. There were more progressive or leftist forms of Japanese nationalism, which saw 'people power' in massed infantry assaults, and which saw the service of citizen-soldiers as emancipatory, justifying the extension of political rights and parliamentary power.[59] But regardless of his inaccuracies, Murray's praise of Japanese military schooling abroad was intimately tied to his unease with liberalism at home.

Another more sober report, about the Japanese Staff College, was prepared in March 1908. This too was written as a comparison against the perceived traits of the British system, with its strength of greater creativity but its weakness of amateurism. Mixed in its assessment of the Japanese officer 'character,' it judged that Japanese 'have insight and not imagination.' It praised Japanese intelligence and clarity of mind, and claimed that the Japanese officer was mentally developed from an earlier age and was committed more quickly to the 'serious business of life.' The national character archetypes are visible here—the improvising, unsystematic and creative British against the serious, systematic but unoriginal and uniform Japanese. This view was built primarily on the writer's experience of the staff tour, a severe exercise where the officers showed their endurance and methodical efficiency but few 'brilliant ideas', which were discouraged. As with British observations of the annual grand manoeuvres of the Imperial Japanese Army (IJA), this view was shaped by ethnocentric assumptions. The grand tour of Japan's staff college, like the Army's manoeuvres, was supposed to test staff work rather than individual initiative.[60] Like other assessments, this report identified racial features but gave great weight to education as the most decisive factor in differentiating Japan from others, reflecting an implicit view that Japan's attributes were the product of systemic policy.[61]

Such views made their way into internal debate amongst the military, as can be seen in a speech by Sir Alexander Bannerman in April 1910 at the Royal United Service Institute, Britain's defence think-tank.[62] Bannerman had acted as a language officer and military observer in the 1904–5 war. The speech was warmly endorsed in the discussion by the audience, which contained a number of 'Japanist' military officers. Bannerman attempted to de-racialise the explanation for Japanese victory, playing down the role of 'ancient traditions' in their recent triumph. He argued that Japan was not historically a nation of soldiers. Compared to Britain, he calculated from muster figures that many more Britons had been historically liable for military service than Japanese.[63] It was innovation, as much as tradition, that explained Japanese success. The samurai class had been defeated in 1877 by a modern conscript army, proving that 'a farmer made as good a soldier as any hereditary warrior.' Japan had reversed aspects of samurai culture, replacing clan armies with universal conscription, and the modern military was not a separate caste, but integrated into broader society.

Having rejected crude racial stereotypes, Bannerman ascribed Japan's victory to the 'national system of education' and patriotic instruction. He cited the *Imperial Rescript on Education* of 1890 with its ethos of 'identifying the children with the national existence.'[64] Victory, he explained, was not only due to the content of Japanese education. Suggesting an authoritarian attitude to governance and parliamentary oversight, he suggested that Japanese youth were successfully indoctrinated because education lay outside parliamentary control. Education was 'kept outside the range of party politics, and is under the control of a permanent department, as is the case with the Army and the Navy. The educational system is not determined by laws which have to pass through Parliament, but by Imperial Ordinances issued by the Emperor on the recommendation of the Cabinet after being submitted to the Privy Council...when it is a case of morals the Department of Education insists that no books shall be used except its own publications.'[65] His admiration of Japanese patriotism was closely allied with admiration of Japanese monarchism.

Bannerman's speech, and the discussion among the assembled officers, demonstrates that their attraction to Japanese *mores* was heightened by their reaction against the perceived dangers of British liberalism. Japan as a state that promoted civic duty and the authority of the Emperor was treated as the inversion of British liberalism's stress on individual rights. Alarmed at the effects of mass politics and broadening political participation, military elites were attracted to the Japanese model of civilian-state relations. Combatants, they insisted, should be apolitical and divorced from partisan public debate. They were drawn to the authoritarian ideas of Japan's *Imperial Rescript to Soldiers and Sailors* of 1882, that the armed services must be hermetically sealed from politics: 'Do not be beguiled by popular opinions, do not get involved in political activities, but singularly devote yourself to your most important obligation of loyalty to the emperor.' Japanese soldiers, another audience member Captain C.A.L. Yate had reported after the war, functioned like 'the legs and arms of a body' headed by 'His Imperial Majesty.' This attitude could be achieved through programmatic policies, through military instruction, fete days, readings of the Imperial Proclamation, and even through pressure on relatives not to send money.[66] Although Japanese propagandists claimed this was rooted in ancestral virtues, this ideology of state authority, chivalric duty and frugality, was a product not of ancient samurai values but of a struggle against the samurai. The *Rescript to Soldiers and Sailors* had been issued by the Japanese Emperor following the Satsuma Rebellion of samurai against the Imperial Japanese Army. This concept of an almost automaton military, divorced from politics and obedient to the state, was itself a highly political posture. Furthermore, it was not something British military elites were always prepared to follow in practice. This was shown in the later 'Curragh' incident of July 1914, where officers who opposed Irish Home Rule indicated that they would resist being ordered north against Ulster Protestants. Military officers of the right were capable of being highly politicised when they chose to be.

Nevertheless, Bannerman's speech provoked praise for Japan and unease over the state of Britain. The Japanese had a 'reverence for authority' and were marked out by their state of quiet calm, in a 'land of flowers and babies.' That 'babies are everywhere' illustrated the vitality of their culture, their regeneration from the war and the robust social conditions that supplied military manpower.[67] One audience member, Lieutenant Carlyon Bellairs, a parliamentarian and later a naval commander, had defected from the Liberals to the Unionists in

1909. Bellairs had no direct experience of Japan, but projected his politics onto the image of that country. He was distraught at the growth of 'disloyal and unpatriotic' sentiment in public life, at the hostility of certain Liberals to the naval budget, and to the use of the flag on Trafalgar Day, which was in marked contrast to the reverence towards Nelson of a visiting Japanese officer. Elaborating on the education issue, he cited Count Hirosawa, on the defects of British education, the absence of any provision for teaching the lower middle class 'their duties towards the State.' English education, warned the Count, 'instills discontent. They learn how to exact their rights, but there is apparently not a word or a line in any of the text books, or in the spirit of the education code, which teaches sacrifice for the country.'[68]

These anxieties echoed the belief among Britain's military lobby in the House of Lords that Liberals were 'soft on imperial defence and were prejudicing the safety of the empire.'[69] Even though the Anglo-Boer war had made them more receptive to social reform because it could be assimilated into the question of national defence, the Liberals as the architects of reform were still mistrusted on imperial security. Liberalism was also suspected of entailing other dangers. They feared that the national spirit might be eroded by the clamour for individual rights and the extension of the franchise. This was reinforced by the impact of the recent electoral victory of the British Liberals in January 1910, and their policy programme. In the officers' moral universe, the contrast of Japanese education with British education was symptomatic of a deeper struggle between the concept of a duties-based society against a rights-based society. Japanese children were taught 'filial piety, obedience to elders, affection and friendship, frugality, industry, modesty, fidelity and courage, and also in some of their duties towards society and the State.' The system was underpinned by the word 'duty', while the word 'rights' did not appear in the syllabus. 'Even when treating of the franchise, it is not spoken of as the 'Right to vote' but the 'Duty of voting.'[70]

As Bellairs' reliance on Count Hirosawa demonstrates, the rhetoric employed in Britain and Japan to frame the meaning of the 1904–5 war was very similar. In Japan, the concept of the fiercely courageous, self-sacrificing soldier was used as a standard against which nationalists criticised what they saw as the growing frivolity and corruption in Japanese society, particularly among youth.[71] British Japanists also invoked this kind of Japanese rhetoric, citing Japanese authorities to justify these criticisms of British society. Not only did the debate within the British military establishment parallel the rhetoric of Japanese military circles, it borrowed its terms from it. The discourse of Japanese and British commentators was mutually reinforcing.

The audience sought potential British parallels to Japanese institutions. Colonel J.H. Rosseter argued that the new Boy Scout movement would transmit values like *Bushido* to British youth.[72] Captain C.A.L. Yate agreed that there had been much 'nonsense' talked about *Bushido*, that the ancient feudal classes had degenerated in peacetime into 'lazy, bullying parasites', inferior to the 'new army raised by universal service.' He noted that the Japanese were just as reluctant to die as anyone else, and that they won because they overcame their natural feelings rather than because of some indifference to death. This bravery was encouraged through a memorial culture, which revered patriotic death: 'They are not obtuse savages, but highly civilised beings ... much is done in Japan to honour those who die in battle. Their pictures are hung up in the schools, and in the mess rooms of the regiments; their names are taught to the children and they are spoken of reverently, while the Grand Temple erected in their honour at Tokio is the scene of solemn and beautiful ceremonies at stated periods. What have we British soldiers to look forward to? We are thought stupid and looked upon as blunderers if we expose ourselves.'

Yate suggested universal conscription was the primary factor in Japan's resurgence. This issue divided observers more than other questions. Conscription attracted the support of some Japanists, like Yate, Repington and Bellairs, but the opposition of Hamilton. The National Service League, the conscriptionist pressure group, began to gather momentum during the Russo-Japanese war in January 1905, with influential supporters and a surging membership.[73] Nevertheless, it is striking that Yate was the only audience member to raise the issue, the rest focussing instead on Japanese education and social attitudes. This may be because by 1910, the issue had proven too divisive and electorally unpopular. The transferability of Japanese conscription might have seemed far more problematic in the context of a country with a tradition of mistrusting standing armies and a navalist 'blue water' defence policy. With conscription, they reached the limits of cross-cultural imitation.

There was, however, widespread agreement among military 'Japanists' that its memorial culture was enviable, one that was transmitted in Japanese schools. Greater reverence for the dead was needed in the school curriculum to strengthen combat motivation and improve the status of the British military. At this time, the concept of reverence for the war dead and patriotic sacrifice was actually becoming ubiquitous throughout British society, familiar in elite and popular culture, and would climax in the First World War, where the common soldier reached apotheosis in the Tomb of the Unknown Warrior.[74] The attraction to valorous warriordom was fed by many forces, including muscular evangelism, imperial competition, and anxiety about perceived decline, social change, waning religious belief, and racial survival in an urban and industrial age. But changes in warfare and politics, with the inception of revolutionary citizen armies of the eighteenth and nineteenth centuries, were happening faster on the continent, sweeping aside the feudal warrior elite's monopoly on military glory. This process, according to Yate, was not happening fast enough in Britain. He therefore recommended Japan's military culture, calling for a similar system of socialisation that validated the military profession.

Thus it would be mistaken to see the views of these military observers towards Japan as straightforward racialism, a view that ethnic groups have distinct moral and intellectual characteristics that are transmitted biologically from generation to generation. Though some may have harboured racialist opinion, this did not drive their obsession with Japan's war. Instead, Japan's military success suggested the potentiality of nations to reinvent themselves at a time of international competition, in the climate of self-examination that had been triggered by the South African war. That Japan, an ally, had triumphed seemingly on the back of state policy, high military morale, and authoritarian politics created a perfect 'fit' with the officers' preconceptions.

British perceptions of Japan can also be seen as part of a more wide-ranging conversation about the nature of strategic culture. The belief of British observers in the transferability of Japan's way of war points to an important theme in this intellectual tradition. This is the tension between two competing approaches to understanding 'Eastern' strategic cultures, what might be called the 'essentialist' and 'constructivist' views. The essentialist view sees differences between different ways of war as intrinsic or even permanent, rooted in fixed features of a culture or nation. They range from the positive to the derogatory. Ferdinand Foch, for example, argued that French soldiers were temperamentally suited only to the offensive.[75] 'Cultural discounting' led Hitler to underestimate the United States as a mongrel society incapable of operating a successful political or economic system.[76] The constructivist view, on display in this case study, is different. It sees strategic cultures as more fluid, open to being dismantled, remade, and copied. It appears particularly in writings that are prescriptive, or urging reform or conceptual rethinking. When it comes to military Orientalism, the foreign 'Other' can be treated as a superior model to inform self-examination.

In the analysis of British Japanists, the major misperceptions were not primarily of Japanese military ethos and society. Instead, it was their implicit criticisms of alternative kinds of societies that were most problematic. Because of the supposed frugality and simplicity of the Japanese soldier and sailor, they assumed that more urban, affluent societies would be unwilling to bear the costs of war. One officer judged that 'wealth and factory servitude' weakened military virtue, so that even Japanese valour might gradually unravel.[77]As others have already noted, this proved to be inaccurate. Many of Britain's privileged classes, Oxbridge undergraduates or sons of aristocratic elites, willingly volunteered for service, filled the British officer corps, and were slaughtered in great numbers at Ypres, the Somme, Passchendale and Gallipoli. British workers from industrial areas also defied the Japanists' predictions, enlisting and creating social pressure for others to enlist throughout the war. The BEF, which was the 'nation in arms' of the most industrialised and urbanised nation on earth, was also the only major military power not to suffer a widespread mutiny. It was in fact the more agrarian and authoritarian societies, such as the Austro-Hungarian and Russian empires, whose war efforts resulted in breakdown and revolution.

Finally, the Japanists wrongly assumed that liberalism was inimical to the spirit of military sacrifice. The falsity of this assumption was soon suggested by the popular appeal of the language of sacrifice and muscular liberalism in World War One. Strongest within the educated middle classes, such ideas also moved a broader penumbra of people. It was Liberal reformer David Lloyd George who articulated wartime paeans to sacrifice. This liberal 'holy war' would be reenergised by the entry of the United States under Woodrow Wilson, who declared another emancipatory war aim, to make the world 'safe for democracy.'[78] Liberalism as an ideology invested the war with messianic purpose, so that the rhetoric of the war went beyond tribal patriotism, and embraced one of the ultimate liberal causes: the end of war itself.

Conclusion

British observers were military Orientalists, but not in the sense that they depicted the Japanese in a derogatory way. They often saw Japan's way of war not as inferior and culturally specific, but as a superior strategic culture that could be copied. These perceptions of Japan are a reminder of the tension between different kinds of 'Orientalism': between the 'essentialist' view of strategic cultures being separated and determined by fixed ethnic characteristics, and an alternative 'constructivist' or 'transcultural' view, where ways of war transcend particular cultures and can be imitated.

British officers and war correspondents projected onto the war their own preconceived ideas. They were attracted to the Japanese model primarily because of their domestic political views. In particular, their fascination with Japan was spurred by their fear that British society was ill-prepared to defend its empire. Their views of Japan were shaped by several influences: authoritarian politics; Social Darwinism in international affairs; their belief in the central importance of morale and psychological strength in modern war; and the view that the state had a decisive role in guiding Britain's evolution in a predatory world. In Britain, their reading of the war gave added momentum to the Edwardian movement to prepare the nation for war and survival through social engineering, particularly through education. Their receptiveness to Japanese examples enabled them to rise above dismissive and racist attitudes. But the desire to idealise Japan could also prove misleading. They were inspired by Japan to assume that British liberalism could not endure future war. Therefore, their greatest misjudgement was not of Japan's strategic culture, but of their own.

4

THE GHOST OF GENGHIS

MONGOLS AND THE WESTERN IMAGINATION

...they left a desert behind them, and killed for killing's sake.

(Charles Oman, *The Art of War in the Middle Ages*, 1924, p.327)

...it would not be surprising for a modern-day military commander, when confronted by a tactical or strategic dilemma, to consider the question: What would Chinggis do?

(Timothy May, *The Mongol Art of War*, 2007, p.146)

Introduction

In April 1971, discharged officer and antiwar activist John Kerry appeared before the Senate Foreign Relations Committee to accuse US forces of war crimes. He alleged that American troops dismembered, raped, and murdered civilians, and 'razed villages in fashion reminiscent of Genghis Khan.'[1] At first glance, this is the simple reputation of the conqueror Chinggis Khan (1162–1227). In folk memory, he and the Mongols stand for a standard of barbarism without strategic purpose. Mongols rode for the pleasure of war itself, or in words apocryphally linked to Chinggis, he loved 'to defeat his enemies, to drive them before him, to take from them that which they possess, to see those whom they cherish in tears, to ride their horses, to hold their wives and daughters in his arms.' In his account of Allied atrocity and German victimhood in World War Two, Jörg Friedrich condemned the Allies' firebombing of German cities as a 'Mongol hurricane of devastation from the air.'[2] Westerners deploy the 'Mongol' analogy to condemn cruelties that offend their own norms of war.

For centuries, Arab, Persian, Turkish, Chinese and European cultures feared the Mongols as unstoppable aggressors. The horsemen from the steppes of Central Asia drove terror into the world's imagination.[3] They laid waste a continent, destroyed great cities, and built an empire from the Pacific to the Danube. Mongol conquest at its height was only blunted at the far edges of its vast contiguous land empire, by Egyptian Mamluks and Japanese Samurai. In Christian Europe, early rumours mistook Chinggis' tribal totem for a cross. Had Heaven sent a warrior to punish Muslims? But Mongols then came into conflict with European lands, and entered Christian demonology as agents of the apocalypse.[4] The English word 'horde', invoking the terror of inhuman and massed invaders, comes from the Mongol word for 'camp', *ordu*; 'mongoloid' signifies deformity; while the name Europeans gave to Mongols, 'Tartars', played on the Latin for hell, *Tarturus*. Chinggis skillfully practised 'psywar' and encouraged his enemies to fear him as the 'punishment of God.'[5] While some contemporaries carefully analysed Mongol warfare, others crudely identified it with the Scythians and the Huns, as just another wave of nomad plunderers rising from the steppes against sedentary civilizations. Edward Gibbon, for one, tried to balance the picture by stressing the religious toleration of Mongol rule and the *pax Mongolica*.[6] But their conquests still left the taste of ashes in the mouth, and their popular image as monstrous hordes lives on.[7]

Yet this was only part of the story. The Mongols in Western eyes also acquired a mystique. Studying them, and contemplating war with them or their successors, became part of Western internal debate and self-criticism. In the twentieth century, Mongols were seen by some as models of military excellence. Their systematic organisation and command structures, it was claimed, looked back to levels of Roman organization and looked forward to modern armies. Their ability to orchestrate forces separated by great distances attracted modern strategists, who themselves were trying to master the command and control of mass citizen-armies in age of population explosions and global war. Discipline and leadership meant that their forces could separate and converge, and their invasions were marked by well-coordinated and deep penetrating attacks followed by concentrated firepower against important targets. Most of all, their mobility drew attention. They would be acclaimed as the forerunners of the German theory of delegated and independent command (*Auftragstaktik*) and rapid penetration with mechanised forces (*Blitzkrieg*).[8] With tanks, aircraft and motorized transport, the instruments had arrived that could restore Chinggis Khan's principles to the modern battlefield. The Mongols were a medium through which Westerners debated the concepts of military transformation and, in the wake of modern warfare, the future of their civilisation.

This chapter examines one renaissance in Western enthusiasm for the Mongols, in the interwar period of the twentieth century. Mongols might be remembered as the predators that almost snuffed out European civilization. But, paradoxically, some believed after the First World War that the Mongol art of war might prove to be Europe's strategic salvation, and steer the West away from another disastrous war of attrition. One well-known western admirer of Mongol warfare was pundit Basil Liddell Hart (1895–1970), one of the most dynamic and exasperating strategic theorists of the twentieth century. The debate continues over Liddell Hart's proper status among strategists, his originality and integrity as a scholar.[9] But here, this chapter deals with something that has only had fleeting analysis, how Basil Liddell Hart used the example of the Mongols in his writings. Liddell Hart invoked the Mongols to promote mechanization and his main idea, the 'indirect approach.' I argue that he shoehorned the Mongols into a preconceived narrative in which boundless mobility, indirection, self-sufficiency and speed clashed with immobility, attrition, and direct battle. The Mongols at his hands became an ideal-type of warrior that reflected his ambitions for tanks and aircraft. This made his account of Mongol warfare selective and ahistorical. It overlooked aspects of Mongol warfare that often escape attention. Liddell Hart's concept of the Mongols is similar to misconceptions of the Huns, who were wrongly reputed in their enemies' rhetoric as pure nomads, even though they gradually unhorsed and fielded infantry forces as they expanded into country that could not sustain massed horse-power.[10] Above all, this reflected as much about the author and his anxieties as it did about Mongol warfare. Liddell Hart's treatment of the Mongols, like many others before and since, pressed Chinggis Khan's conquests into serving his own, contemporary interests.

Within Britain's Royal Tank Corps and in wider Anglo-American military circles for the rest of the century, Liddell Hart revived interest in Chinggis and his successors. His promotion of Mongol conquests as a military model influenced interwar debate surrounding mechanization and armour. His writings on the Mongols were incorporated into the teaching syllabus of Britain's 'Experimental Mechanised Brigade,' and he saw himself as the pioneer of the didactic study of the Mongol art of war.[11] To establish himself as the *fons et origo* of this line of study, Liddell Hart repeatedly (and unsuccessfully) tried to coax American General Douglas MacArthur into saying that he had been inspired by his writings on the Mongols.[12] In fact, he had not invented Western curiosity in the pedagogic value of Mongol warfare, but had revived it. He either did not know, or did not acknowledge, that he followed a long European and Russian tradition of fascination with Mongol warfare.[13] So it is worth recapitulating the range of claims made by Westerners down the centuries about the 'Devil's Horsemen.'

Monsters or Marvels?

The meaning and lessons of Mongol warfare have been continually reformulated to suit the preoccupations of each era. In the age of the tank and aircraft, Mongols were viewed as models for wars of manoeuvre, and were studied by luminaries such as Patton and Rommel. During the Cold War, predominantly American commentators saw them either as exemplars for fighting in strategic depth across the plains of Europe, or as the precursors to Soviet 'deep battle', the long-range thrust into an enemy's heartland, and Soviet operational art, which recalled the Mongols' ability 'to move in widely separated columns and then concentrate quickly, like the fingers on a hand.'[14] Alternatively, the Mongols could be the prototypes of America's Air-Land Battle and its operational concepts, with the twist that American airborne forces could now envelop the enemy from the sky.[15] Mongols might appear as a double warning against the enemy's agility and brutality. In 1984, the American film *Red Dawn*, about a communist invasion of the USA, depicted the Soviet Union as the heir of Mongols in both respects.

Today, Mongols are invoked to support visions of twenty-first century military transformation. In Gulf War II, pundits likened the sweeping invasion of Iraq by the 'coalition of the willing' with the Mongol conquest of Mesopotamia. The synchronized speed with which American tanks stormed Baghdad in 2003 recalled the Mongols' bloodier capture of the same city in 1258.[16] 'Shock and awe', psychological dislocation of the enemy, manoeuvrist warfare, swift crippling attacks all bore the footprints of Chinggis Khan. The American military now worries that modern weapons of mass destruction mean its forces must remain as dispersed for as long as possible before being symphonically concentrated into action. Accordingly, the RAND corporation portrays Mongols as masters of 'swarming' the battlespace, so that instead of massing large formations that would be vulnerable to WMD strikes, a range of assets would combine instantaneously for the attack, and then separate.[17] These appeals to Mongol warfare are modern versions of a medieval obsession.

Western opinion has waxed and waned over Mongol warfare ever since the thirteenth century, when Mongols were described by writers such as Franciscan monk and papal ambassador Giovanni di Plano Carpini, as well as the missionary William of Rubruck, the Dominican Simon of Saint-Quentin, the traveller Marco Polo, while in the fourteenth century there were over two dozen diplomatic missions from Europe to Mongol-ruled China. Because they left few written records other than the mythical narrative of *The Secret History of the Mongols* and the 'Great Yasa' law code, most representations of them come from outsiders. The latter were often, but not uniformly, hostile. And even hostile accounts were not always dismissive. To some, the armies of horse-born bowmen were brutes who succeeded because were merely parasitic on their enemies' weakness. To others, they were the product of a system of strategic and military thought that must be taken seriously.

Since first contact, Mongols have struck some observers as gruesome predators that relied on terror and sheer numbers to overwhelm their enemies. Especially chroniclers more distant from the Mongols often saw their onslaughts in millenarian terms, as signs of the end-times and of divine judgment.[18] Matthew Paris, in his *English History From the Year 1235–1273*, described the Mongols as a cannibalistic, demonic race, while a world map in Hereford Cathedral, the *Mappa Mundi*, depicts beyond the outer eastern perimeter of Christendom 'exceedingly truculent men, eating human flesh, drinking blood, cursed sons of Cain.'[19] After they defeated Hungarian and Polish armies in 1241, both superstition and embarrassment led some to claim that the Mongols triumphed because they were inhuman, or because they were agents of divine punishment against a sinful Christendom.[20]

Bleak and unflattering views of the Mongols endured into the modern world, albeit in more secular form. In 1898, Oxford historian

Charles Oman revived one medieval tradition, where Mongols represented not so much a brilliant war machine, but instead were agents of violent anarchy that would fill any power vacuum. They 'left deserts where there had been a civilized and thickly peopled group of states.' He attributed their success not to sophistication, but to the void of weak powers and divided principalities into which they plunged. Oman portrayed the Mongols as a force of nature, their violence directed to no political purpose. Like a flood, they were destructive and lacked rational goals, but were ultimately finite and confined to steppes, unable to break through major obstacles. In the end, it was topography that turned the Mongols back, as the barriers of forest swamps, mountains and fortified settlements beyond the plains of Europe were prohibitive to their horsemen.[21]

The Mongols' reputation for brutality across cultures probably reflects several things. There were the shock waves felt by their arrival. Previously, they had no place in the Western consciousness, so that they appeared as alien beings from 'some other world.'[22] Especially for Latin Christians, Mongols emerged out of mysterious and feared *terra incognita* beyond the boundaries of the familiar. Also, their image was created by the prejudices generated by wars fought across cultural frontiers, or 'transcultural war', where the fact that both sides fight by different rules and protocols creates a sense of mutual incomprehension or a perceived conflict in the ethos of war.[23] There was also the perennial antagonism felt by sedentary civilizations against the 'nomadic', even though the Mongols' pure self-sufficiency was a mythical construct, as the Mongol khanate with its commercial networks and economic interdependence with other societies became more of a hybrid.[24] And their reputation can also be attributed to the brute fact that some Mongol practices, even by the grim standards of the time, were notably cruel. The subjects of the Abbasid Caliphate, in what is now Iraq, could hardly forget the Mongols' destruction of their vital canal system. After Chinggis' beloved grandson was killed at the siege of Bamiyan in Afghanistan, every living thing was killed. And the inhabitants of besieged Urganj watched as the Mongols forced locals to die in their thousands in the moat, creating a human bridge upon which they built a ramp to storm the city.

But the Mongols' reputation for ferocity was more than the byproduct of their actions. It was also their own deliberate creation. They wanted to be reputed for their massacres, as a deterrent to resistance.

Through deception, they deliberately presented themselves as a gigantic 'horde', to fool their enemies into exaggerating their size. Before arriving, they sent advance agents forward with rumours about their vast numbers, used remounts with straw-dummies, placed captured enemy infantry on foot and civilian captives on horseback to swell their appearance. As Richard Gabriel shows, a Mongol 'touman', a unit of 10,000 men, could be disguised as a force of 50,000.[25] Their own propaganda in this sense dovetailed with the hostile propaganda of outsiders. Just as an image of merciless hordes was calculated to intimidate their enemies, a reputation for numerical supremacy was probably also a convenient alibi for medieval chroniclers who had to explain away the fact that Christian armies had been defeated by these strange aggressors. So for different reasons, the Mongols effectively conspired with their enemies to represent themselves as outsized brutes.

Another, more positive, tradition also grew to explain Mongol success. It saw Mongols as not just a 'horde', but strategists who carefully planned their campaigns, subordinating warfare to political objectives. It may be true that their enemies were often politically fragmented, but they were able to exploit this fragmentation precisely because they had dispersed old tribal groups into new integrated military formations, forming a cohesive whole. In fact, they were often at a numerical disadvantage when engaging the enemy, so they must have compensated by exploiting an economy of force, applying their strength at the decisive point. One great admirer was Giovanni de Plano Carpini, who had first-hand contact with the Mongol court as emissary (and spy) of Pope Innocent IV between 1245–7. He viewed them with a mix of fear and high regard. Unlike the purely diabolic explanation of the Mongols as a punishment sent from God, Carpini gave a worldly explanation for their strengths. He presented the 'barbarians' as dangerous and yet a viable model for emulation. And in this dossier, he set out a strategy for resisting them. He urged political unity and a coordinated effort, as the Mongols adroitly divided their enemies. On more tactical levels, he warned also against the Mongols' duplicity, as they 'like devils, are always watching and devising how to practice mischief.'[26] European forces, he wrote, should avoid premature demobilization and be wary of the Mongols habit of feigning retreats. He also implored Europeans to adopt the methods and strengths of these enemies, creating a higher standard of discipline, sending out scouts, keeping their generals in reserve rather than the confusing thick of combat, and imposing orderly organisation on their troops, instead of the rudimentary formations of feudal retinues. In chapter 16, entitled 'How they may be resisted', Carpini's various recommendations were persistently followed by the comments 'according to the Tartars' custom' or 'as it has already been said of the Tartars.' Effectively, he advised Christian military forces to become more like the barbaric enemy in order to combat them.[27] The enemy was also the exemplar.

As well as recommending that Latin Christendom adopt Mongol methods, Carpini also tried to demythologize them. Mongols were not invincible, which Carpini tried to support by identifying the peoples who had successfully battled them. Apart from the fact that he also mentioned a prophecy that the Mongols only had eighteen years left before defeat, Carpini traced Mongol supremacy not primarily to supernatural forces, but to their organisation, structure, material culture, weaponry, intelligence acquisition and deception operations. His analysis was deliberately symbiotic, stressing the interaction between Mongol strengths and their enemies' weaknesses, something that could be changed. This secular explanation stood in contrast with those who saw Mongol military might as a reflection of Christian sinful failure.

Carpini wrote during the era of Mongol expansion, when its outcome was unknown. He appreciated Mongol strengths, while assuming that they could be resisted only by the human agency of others. But other forms of Mongol-admiration, periodically revived in the last century, sees them as almost unstoppable. Some modern commentators, looking back, argue that the Mongols were only halted by themselves. Their flair for brilliant manoeuvre warfare meant that only the contingency of a khan's death, and the internal splintering that followed, prevented them from overrunning the West. Richard Gabriel, recent biographer of Chinggis' celebrated general Subotai the Valiant (1175–1248), claimed that without the distraction of the Great Khan's death, 'there is every likelihood that Subotai would have destroyed Europe itself!'[28]

Europe may hypothetically have been overrun. But Russia was. The Russian perspective was based partly on the historical fact that vast stretches of Russia and Siberia had actually been subjugated and ruled by the 'Golden Horde', as the Chaghatayid khanate became known. Popular western accounts of Russia's strategic culture, such as Peter Hopkirk's *The Great Game*, trace back to this event Russia's fear of encirclement and love of operational thinking.[29] Fear of Asian hordes, as a demonic pestilence of a force that could out-breed, out-number and overwhelm civilization, resonated in Russian literature. During the Sino-Japanese war of 1895, Vladimir Solov'ev feared the East, 'Innumerable and insatiable/As locusts/preserved by an otherworldly force/The tribes march northward.'[30] Yet the admiring study of Chinggis' campaigns had also been a tradition in Russian military education. Russia's conquest of Central Asia in the nineteenth century renewed Russian interest, and Lieutenant General Mikhail Ivanin (1801–74) wrote *The Art of War of the Mongols and the Central Asian Peoples*, a text incorporated into Russia's staff colleges.

As these different examples suggest, the Mongols haunt military-strategic thought in paradoxical ways, as foreign warlords regard them with fear and envy. At the extremes, Adolf Hitler intended to destroy the modern Mongols by using the aggression of their medieval forbears, using Mongol methods of enslavement and extermination to solve the contemporary 'Mongol problem.'[31] This pull between admiration of the Eastern model and dread of the Easterner was present in the rhetoric of American General Douglas MacArthur. As supreme commander in the South West Pacific and military proconsul presiding over post-war Japan, he was one of the twentieth century's most powerful military Orientalists. In his final Report as Chief of Staff of the US Army in 1935, MacArthur urged the armed forces to plunder Mongol history for the fundamental principles of war. He was so awed by their discipline and training of subordinate commanders, the speed and secrecy of their movement, their ability to overwhelm larger armies, that 'winnowed from the chaff of medieval custom' their history showed 'kernels of eternal truth, as applicable today in our efforts to produce an efficient army as they were... seven centuries ago.' For MacArthur, the modern soldier must separate Chinggis' military doctrine, methods and organisation from the 'ghastly practices of his butcheries, his barbarism, and his ruthlessness.'[32] Yet fifteen years later, in the Korean war, he called for brutalization of America's war effort. Testifying to the US Senate Hearings in 1951, he claimed to know the 'pattern of Oriental psychology,' seeing the formerly docile Chinese as lustful imperialists.[33] In the Orient, only strength prevailed. He insisted that expanding the war from the Korean peninsula into China would impress Asians, with air and naval bombardment of industrial centres, and possibly the use of atomic weapons.[34] America must heighten aggression to subdue and resist Orientals who threatened them with slavery and atheism. Macarthur loathed Oriental terror and called for counter-terror against it.

The Mongol analogy is also reworked through the question of empire. This is a vexed issue for the American superpower. Its armies are charged with a mission of democratic liberation, but struggle to exert power in some of the same geographic spots as the Mongols did. Americans often think of America as non-imperialist and non-annexationist, yet its elites are conscious that America exerts a hegemony in the footsteps of empires past, and should seek define itself against and draw lessons from them. So in Robert Kaplan's account of American expeditionary forces, a traveller's view of the imperial frontiers written in 2005, the Mongols are both barbarians and enlightened rulers. Kaplan recalls the terrifying sight of 'a Mongol cavalry, in all its stench and ugliness, girding the horizon' moving silently and then charging 'with diabolical shrieks and yells.' But then he surveys their great imperial achievements, pondering Chinggis' words, 'Conquering a country while mounted is easy...dismounting and building a nation is difficult.' Eight hundred years later, America too has dismounted, and it has inherited the Mongol's site of imperial ambition and nation-building in the Tigris Euphrates Valley. The Mongols turn from stinking predators on the horizon to kindred empire-builders, so Kaplan shifts from horror to empathy.[35]

But Western fascination to the Mongol way of war was revived most flamboyantly after World War One by Liddell Hart, to whose writing we now turn.

Unveiling the Captains

Liddell Hart was many things, a former British army captain and war veteran; a defence correspondent; a prolific writer on military affairs; and a controversialist who courted publicity, not to mention an enthusiast for tennis and women's fashion. Whatever else is said of him, Liddell Hart was one of a group of interwar visionaries who foresaw the importance of mechanization. For him, history was a weapon to be used to promote military reforms and affect a revolution in warfare. He was as much a polemicist as a scholar. His portrayal of the Mongols, in many ways elegant and sophisticated, was also convenient, done not in a contemplative scholarly spirit but explicitly to promote a particular policy agenda. He used the Mongols to inflame public consciousness by proposing a radical alternative to the war his contemporaries knew. Over time, his view of Mongol warfare and Oriental military genius also evolved, to suit his changing views. His treatment of the Mongols became part of his later desire to protect his reputation as the intellectual father of *Blitzkrieg*.

Liddell Hart's interest in the Mongols was linked to his own ceaseless quest to formulate an approach to warfare that would rescue the West from the 'mechanical butchery' of the trenches. He himself had been gassed at the front in 1916, so wrote as a survivor of the murderous battle of the Somme. He, and others, pointed to Mongol warfare with its mounted archers to show that it was possible to reunite the two forces—firepower and movement—that had been tragically divorced in the meatgrinder of the western front, resulting in the bloodlettings at Passchendale and Verdun. He presented the Mongols as exemplars of mobility, simplicity and indirection. He also attempted to warn about, and learn from, the potentialities of 'Oriental' warfare, in an almost undifferentiated view of a pan-Asian civilisation. Yet his homogenous view of Asia was not dismissive. Great captains, he warned, could emerge unexpected from outside the West. The Mongols hit the warrior aristocracies of Europe like a bolt from the blue, and Liddell Hart was prescient in warning that modern Japan, underestimated in some quarters, could surprise the world again.

Liddell Hart believed that there were 'lessons' and normative principles of warfare that were global and trans-historical, and could be applied across the boundaries of civilization and over time and space. Such wisdom could be revealed by studying the 'great captains' of history. He valued concepts and abstract doctrines more highly than material conditions or changing contexts, and viewed military success and failure as primarily a matter of inspired generalship almost in isolation. When it came to the Mongols, his main purpose was not to prepare the West rhetorically for conquest over the 'East', but to reform Western military practice. As a man who saw himself as re-educating the military and public, Liddell Hart was drawn to Mongol warfare because it held out the promise of change.

In March 1965, the same year that he published his *Memoirs*, Basil Liddell Hart wrote a short letter to American Sinologist Owen Lattimore, who had just penned an article about the Mongols in the *Scientific American*:

In my forthcoming Memoirs I have related how, in a study I did of the Mongol campaigns of the early 1920s, I came to visualise them as the prototype of future mobile operations by mechanised force—and in particular how much that study influenced my development of the concept of deep strategic penetration, which was applied by Guderian and the other panzer generals in the early campaigns of World War II. Douglas MacArthur also took up the idea and recommended a study of the Mongol campaigns and methods in his final report of 1935 as Chief of Staff of the U.S. Army.[36]

Here, in a nutshell, is how Liddell Hart presented this intellectual history as he wanted the world to remember it. He had spotted the genius of Mongol warfare and related it now to a futuristic vision of war. More controversially, he claimed that he passed it on to the German generals who became the accomplished practitioners of wars of movement, such as Heinz Guderian, the designer of the *Panzertruppen*, and Erwin Rommel.[37] According to Liddell Hart, Nazi Germany's rapid conquest of France realized the promise of Mongol-style warfare, and vindicated his argument that the principles of 'indirect approach' and rapid mobility were the essence of military strategy, principles that were shared by history's 'great captains.' Liddell Hart saw himself, and wanted others to see him, as the leading visionary of this revolution. In a private note, he retrospectively sketched this out:

This is my original definition of the method, which the Germans called Blitzkrieg—a definition with which General Guderian wrote that he 'entirely agreed.' He epitomised it as a combination of 'Mobility, Velocity, Indirect Approach.'

I deduced the potentialities and practicability of this deep penetration method, for mechanised forces, mainly from the Mongol drives of the 13th century together with a comparative analysis of Sherman's 'marches' and Forrest's hamstringing raids in 1864–5 campaigns of the American Civil War. I developed its theory by a strategic adaptation of the tactical 'expanding torrent' method of attack which I had worked out in 1920.[38]

Like British officers admiring Imperial Japan, he believed that military wisdom could transcend cultural traditions. It could also apply across the ages. But the transmission of that wisdom across cultural boundaries and time could only happen with the help of prophets like him.

Liddell Hart was claiming in the mid 1960's an influence that he traced to his writing four decades earlier about Chinggis Khan, and his celebrated general Subotai (1172–1245), along with other military dynamos from the past, from the Frenchman Marechal de Saxe (1696–1750) to the Briton James Wolfe (1727–1759). In 1927, he presented a study of these and other figures in *Great Captains Unveiled*. These men, ranging from the medieval to modern eras were, he claimed, the architects of what he would later call the 'indirect approach' to warfare. According to Liddell Hart, there was a set of principles that united these individuals and their campaigns, from the Khan's blaze through the Asian steppes to Sherman's march through the heartland of the southern Confederacy. In later studies, he further these developed claims about other figures, particularly in his study of the marches of American Civil War General, Willem Tecumseh Sherman, and Forrest's 'hamstringing raids' in the American Civil War.'[39] In this line of argument, Liddell Hart was strongly influenced by the military theorist, and fascist, Brigadier-General J.F.C. Fuller, but it was Liddell Hart who turned to the Mongols to fortify his vision of the 'indirect approach.'

Liddell Hart's evolving conception of the 'indirect approach' had a core philosophy. Instead of trying to destroy the enemy's military forces in head-on battles of annihilation and exhaustion, it was better to bypass an enemy's strengths, and dislocate the foe psychologically and unhinge it physically through attacks on its strategic vitals, through surprise and deception, aimed at alternative targets such as critical infrastructure, or civilian populations.[40] The 'indirect approach', first fully expressed in 1929 in *The Decisive Wars of History*, was the antithesis to what he saw as the witless, attritional 'direct' approach, formulated by the Prussian philosopher Carl von Clausewitz in his interpretation of Napoleon's campaigns, and put into practice with such disastrous results by the generals of the First World War. Like the Chinese sage Sun Tzu, Liddell Hart preached the message that war was a matter of defeating the enemy's will to fight rather than its physical forces, and the acme of skill was to unarm the enemy without fighting at all.[41] This 'indirect' approach, Liddell Hart argued, would ultimately be the swifter, more effective, and more decisive approach, and would foster a better state of peace as a result. The intellectual path of Liddell Hart is quite a varied one, however, as what he meant by the 'indirect approach' continued to evolve. By 1932, he would alter the policy implications of the 'indirect approach', arguing that instead of sweeping expeditionary invasions, it must entail another concept, the 'British Way in Warfare', which meant finding a way to defeat continental enemies without engaging their armies, applying maritime power and economic pressure.

Liddell Hart wrote as part historian, part strategist, part commentator on current events. He also wrote with an artistic temperament, believing that his creative appeals to history could render innovation in armoured warfare plausible and possible when it otherwise might have seemed fanciful to less adventurous minds. The Mongol analogy, he later claimed, 'stirred the imagination and threw light on the wider potentialities of the tank. Save for the influence of these analogies it would probably have remained merely a piece of specialised equipment, associated with 1914–1918 trench-warfare—and been discarded after that war.'[42] We might doubt Liddell Hart's hyperbolic claim that his historic analogies were the decisive element in giving tanks a future. But his method is clear. To him, a prophetic imagination was the critical tool in making a brighter future, and the East was the site of his prophecy. Fuller had come to similar conclusions from practical service, 'My approach to the problem of future warfare was from a different angle, and although I quickly came to the same conclusion, that armoured forces would be the dominant factor, my conviction came through imagination operating from a basis of reason, not of service with tanks.'[43] With the Mongols, Liddell Hart found an example that was both exotic yet vaguely familiar, the ideal combination for getting others to imagine the possibility of revolutionary change, but change rooted in historical precedent. In this way, Orientalism intruded on debate within the Occident.

Liddell Hart's study of Chinggis Khan and Subotai covered both the invasion of the Muslim empire of Khwarizm (1219–24) and the assault on Russia and the West (1237–42). He had three arguments. First, that the ability of both was 'matched only by Napoleon.' Second, their campaigns offered lessons for the present. And third, the West should heed the lessons. On the very first page, Liddell Hart's military 'Orient' is a subject of both wisdom and danger. The study of Mongol campaigns 'may convince us that we do wrong to dismiss lightly the military potentialities of the Orient.'[44] The Mongols, in other words, underscore the potential might of modern-day Japan. He noted that in the Russo-Japanese war, the Japanese had reminded the West that the Orient could produce 'courageous and disciplined' troops, while the Mongol campaigns revealed that Asia had birthed some of the most consummate war leaders in history. The Orient had excelled militarily before and could do so again. It is evident from the text that Liddell Hart identified a continuous 'Oriental' tradition, in that the 'Turco-

Mongol race' in the plains of Hungary and the steppes of Russia remained essentially a 'warlike' race, averse to the 'arts of peace.' But Liddell Hart meant 'warlike' in the most advanced sense, presenting the Mongols not vaguely as a brutal horde but as superb military practitioners, whose history bore lessons that were universally applicable.

To highlight these lessons, he vividly retold the story of Chinggis' and Subotai's campaigns, highlighting in particular their ability to outmanoeuvre the enemy and attack its rear, their logistic self-sufficiency and extreme mobility. At Liddell Hart's hands, the Mongol invasion of the Karismian Empire (1218–22) in modern-day Persia, Turkestan and Pakistan was a masterpiece of eternal principles of war. The Shah's forces had superior numbers, but they were dispersed in a cordon system. The Mongol invading army captured the city of Otrar on the Syr Darya river, and then with high-speed tempo and co-ordination, split into five divisions, each menacing different targets and thereby preventing the enemy from concentrating its large numbers.[45] Such 'brilliantly conceived and harmoniously executed operations' according to Liddell Hart, showcased the value of 'direction, mobility, security, concentration, and surprise—woven into a Nemesis-like web in which are trapped the doomed armies of the Shah.'[46] His writing on Chinggis was premised on the notion that the Mongols were far more than rapacious hordes, and he tried to correct the fallacy of some medieval chroniclers that numbers explained Mongol success in the Polish and Hungarian campaigns.

To illustrate the Mongols' grasp of the essentials of strategy, Liddell Hart described one of their bold manoeuvres, which typified a gambit most loved by enthusiasts of manoeuvrist warfare, the unexpected march through difficult terrain, which would surprise and psychologically stun the enemy. In 1220, one of his generals Chépé launched a diversionary attack on the Shah's right flank towards the vital centres of Samarkand and Bokhara, leading the Shah to reinforce this region. Two other armies, led by Chinggis' sons, were converging on Chépé's force on the Syr Daria. While these princes' armies fixed the attention of the Shah, Chinggis had crossed desert country and reappeared at the rear of the Shah, threatening Bokhara. Encircled and knocked off balance, the Shah's communications were cut off with his western states, and he fled. Chinggis had overpowered a numerically superior opponent by creating a deception, striking where least expected, and destroying its will. Numerical superiority could be negated by a differently-formulated 'weight', of 'weapon-power *multiplied* by its mobility.'

Liddell Hart went on to illustrate similar patterns in the clash of Mongol and European warfare. Confronted with the Europeans' heavy cavalry, the Mongols would avoid a premature direct collision, disperse and rally, repeatedly weakening and disorganizing the enemy with continual fire from their mounted archers. The Mongols had demonstrated the antithesis of the sterile and futile strategy of the First World War. According to Liddell Hart, the light tank and the future aeroplane were the 'natural heir[s]' of the Mongol horsemen, and the Mongol conception of warfare revealed the unsoundness of modern-day prejudices against 'a new and mobile arm.' In fact, the Mongols had torn up the rule-book of modern as well as medieval European warfare; or, in his words, they disproved 'the canons on which European armies, of the present equally with the past, have based their systems.'[47]

Intertwined with Liddell Hart's stress on Mongol mobility was another feature: simplicity. Liddell Hart emphasized in *Great Captains* that the Mongols had triumphed partly because they disowned the notion of 'combined arms' that Europeans had cherished. At one point, he mentioned in passing that the Mongols had excelled at 'artillery preparation.' But his dominant message in the chapter, which contradicted this, was that the Mongols epitomized the potential of the single arm of combat. Writing with an eye on future armoured warfare, he argued that the Mongols were able to out-manoeuvre their enemies because of their 'well-armed, highly mobile cavalry army', which was evidence that 'a combined force of infantry, cavalry, and artillery is not necessary.' It is worth quoting his position in full, because in later circumstances he would try to rewrite his own perception of the Mongols to fit later events:

> Although cavalry was the decisive arm alike of Alexander and Hannibal, it formed merely the mobile wings hinged on an essentially protective infantry centre, which was the pivot on which it manoeuvred. The prime feature of the Mongol military system was therefore its simplicity, due to the use of a single arm, in contrast to the inevitably complex organisation of a combination of several arms which has always characterised European armies. In this way the Mongols solved the ever-difficult problem of co-operation between arms which have radically different qualities and limitations. The single arm they used was that which possessed the highest degree of mobility, and in this lay the secret of their unbroken run of victory. At such local points where greater loco-mo-

bility was needed than mounted troops could achieve, a proportion of the troops were temporarily dismounted and fought on foot.[48]

To Liddell Hart, this asymmetry between combined arms and single arms was what advantaged the Mongols over the Shah's forces and European men-at-arms alike, and the fact that European armies in the First World War relied on a 'multiplicity of arms', and tied their mobile arms to their less mobile, was the weakness that generated the prolonged stalemate of the western front in World War One.

The Mongols Romanticised

Liddell Hart's writing is filled with binary oppositions, real or imagined. Whether it was the conflict of Napoleonic and Clausewitzian principles against those of de Saxe and himself, or the reactionary interwar British generals against German visionaries, or the contrast of Mongol sophistication with their enemies' immobility, Liddell Hart throughout his writings returns again and again to a core drama. There were those who unimaginatively approached war as an attritional struggle of direct battle where the costs outstripped the gains, and those who would appear on the right side of history, favouring swiftly paralyzing strokes to the enemy's Achilles heel, a concept that would accelerate, limit and civilize warfare. He saw the history of the clash between the Mongol way of war, and their enemies' inferior versions, as part of a universal contest between mutually hostile philosophies. He often changed his mind on how this essence of military strategy could be successfully operationalised. But it was a master narrative that he frequently revisited. Liddell Hart's idea of this clash between indirect and direct approaches had a long-term intellectual influence on analysis of the Mongols in military circles, as evident in the title of one article written during the Cold War, 'Clausewitz or Khan?'[49]

At the time he analysed the Mongols, Liddell Hart's writing sprang not from an obsession with fighting Oriental nations; he showed little interest throughout the 1930s in the rise of Imperial Japan. Over his work hung the shadow of the Western Front, where the West had turned on itself. To be sure, the war was not only a Eurocentric tragedy, as it mobilized imperial armies from the world over, while the propagandists of the Kaiserreich framed the war against Czarist Russia as a struggle against Asiatic barbarism, and resulted in European expansionism. But the war was felt also as a holocaust within white

European civilisation and a fratricidal war between Anglo-Saxon societies, especially in the theatre where Liddell Hart fought. His postwar writing on the Mongols was informed by an argument convulsing Europe, about the military implications of that war. In that sense, it was not so much an 'east *v* west' world view, where differences were culturally defined or even fixed and racially or biologically determined, but a struggle within and for the soul of military strategy everywhere. His intellectual orbit, however, was mostly West European. If there was an alien 'other' that Liddell Hart 'demonised,' it was one of Western parentage, the incubus of 'total war' created by the Corsican conqueror Napoleon and elevated into a philosophy by the Prussian Clausewitz.

Liddell Hart's approach to the conflict between different approaches to war paid far more attention to abstract intellectual concepts than to material context. While an enthusiast for technological innovation, he did not often allow for the material constraints when judging military performance. He rarely considered that military circumstances, as much as brilliance, may have enabled Scipio Africanus or Chinggis Khan to envelop and suddenly surround their enemies in ways that were harder for the generals of the Western Front, who had to grapple with a difficult and complex environment where demographic trends, industrial power and geographic limits made possible vast citizen armies that were difficult to coordinate in a very crowded and lethal environment. For Liddell Hart, the nightmare of the First World War was at root the product of an intellectual failure, the disregard for mobility and the intoxication of generals with the dogmas of annihilation and attritional offensives.

Liddell Hart was attempting to use history to influence policy in the present, to encourage specific technological and operational innovations, and to challenge what he saw as the stultifying and reactionary attitudes of the contemporary military establishment that he had once admired. The fact that he was ransacking the past to provide ammunition to support his preconceived opinions about modern problems meant that his writing contained an urgent relevance. His portrayal of Mongol warfare was suffused with his own contact with British military exercises. As General Sir Ivor Maxse remarked, 'I enjoyed Jenghiz Khan, and especially the masterly infiltration into it of our platoon training effort!'[50] Liddell Hart captured the imagination of a public anxious to find an alternative to the calamity of the Great War, and anxious to believe that war could be conceptualized and waged very differently. But because *Great Captains* was fundamentally written as a dialectical study of competing modes of war to reform the West, Liddell Hart cherry-picked the aspects of Mongol war that fitted this project. This meant that his treatment of Mongol warfare, and other case studies, tells us as much about him as it does about the Mongols.

Take the author's central contention, that Mongol warfare was based on powerful mobility rather than what he criticized elsewhere as 'The Napoleonic Fallacy', or witless Clausewitzian strategies of annihilation. It would be hard to deny that mobility was often central to Mongol success, which Liddell Hart demonstrated vividly. The difficulty with his stress on Mongol mobility is in the rigid dichotomy he creates between mobility and annihilation. Mobility and the annihilation of enemy field armies were certainly arch-enemies in Liddell Hart's vision. But historically they were not necessarily antagonistic goals. Precisely because they often were numerically limited, Mongol campaigns also had a logic of annihilation. They could not afford to divert manpower to maintain strong garrisons, nor to leave behind them unruly populations. Contrary to Charles Oman's claims that Mongol atrocities were little more than raw aggression, massacres arguably took place also for calculated reasons.[51] To prevent defeated or fleeing enemy armies regrouping at their rear and menacing their long supply lines, the Mongols frequently hunted them down and wiped them out to a man, something they also did during the Karismian and European campaigns that Liddell Hart celebrated. In 1299 after prevailing in the battle of Salamiyet, Mongol units were recorded pursing defeated Egyptian Mamlukes for 300 miles to Gaza.[52] Mobility served rather than contradicted annihilation.

Mongol warfare was in this sense more determinedly annihilationist than Clausewitz. In *On War*, Clausewitz stressed that war was about subordinating the enemy's will to one's own, rather than destroying the enemy physically. This would often entail the defeat—but not necessarily the absolute destruction—of its military forces. In battle, Clausewitz argued that the loss of moral force is the 'major decisive factor', and by 'moral' in this context he meant 'order, courage, confidence, cohesion and plan.'[53] Clausewitz went beyond the crude 'body count' approach and observed that often victor and vanquished in battle suffered comparable losses, and that the most severe losses only happened to the vanquished once it retreated with its will broken.[54] Heavy casualties could often be a symptom rather than a cause of the destruction of the enemy's will. At the higher strategic level, on the relationship between levels of physical destruction, the 'centre of gravity' and the attempt to make the enemy cease fighting, Clausewitz's observations were not obsessively related to casualties, but were also highly measured and qualified, both as to the location of the centre of gravity, and the degree of force needed to attack it.[55] For the Mongols, by contrast, it was often treated as an unacceptable risk to leave behind them a broken enemy that might regroup. If there was a 'Mahdi of Mass', as Liddell Hart derisively described Clausewitz,[56] Chinggis Khan and his successors with their commitment to literal physical obliteration were better candidates than the Prussian.

Chinggis discovered also that Mongols could not always fight precisely as they chose, that is, on horseback and living off the land. During and after the campaigns against the Chin, Mongol warfare was forced to adapt and became more attuned to military situations where mobility was constrained by factors beyond their control. In particular, Liddell Hart's account says very little about Mongol sieges. In Liddell Hart's retelling of the story, these are described quickly and appear as little more than 'mopping up' operations, sideshows and foregone conclusions after the important business of ingenious stratagems. This can be seen as part of an overarching bipolar vision, of the contrast between rapid, indirect and paralyzing offensives on one hand, and attritional pitched battles on the other.

A similar dichotomy can be found in the public and private statements of Colonel George Lindsay, a senior officer of the Royal Tank Corps who helped direct the Corp's evolution and doctrine, and Major Percy Hobart, who had just joined the Corps.[57] Lindsay's lectures cite Liddell Hart's earlier essay on the Mongols, representing Chinggis' forces as embodying a perfect balance of the four necessary principles of war from 'time immemorial':

Firepower (weapons to destroy your enemy)
Mobility (the power of manoeuvring the weapons)
Protection (of the men USING the weapons)
Moral (confidence of the men in themselves, i.e. In their weapons and training)[58]

Lindsay's interpretation of Mongol warfare had one important difference. Whereas Liddell Hart was self-contradictory about what lessons Chinggis' forces offered to the issue of combined arms, Lindsay clearly stated that Mongols 'combined mounted assault troops, mounted archers, and mobile mechanical fire-power. Therefore they, and not the Knights, were organized on the idea on which we must organize our Mobile Mechanical Force of the future.'[59]

Their correspondence made explicit something that was implicit in Liddell Hart's writing, that the model of Mongol warfare was appealing not only because of its example of deep mobility and logistical self-sufficiency, but because they expected modern Mongolian-style wars would be short wars that would suit a democratic era where populations were reluctant to bear protracted struggles, and unlikely to mobilize behind war aims that arouse total commitment:

Foch said—'There's only one thing certain: the next war will be utterly unlike the last'

Well—is it certain that the 'Mongolian' idea is dead? Extreme mobility—go for nerve-centres. Live on the country. You'll only need petrol, oil and v. little food (personnel comparatively small) all of which are endemic in any (even semi-civilised) country these days.

You see–

And—iron ration—supply by air...

But against highly civilized countries, with v. sensitive nerve-centres. Why limit ourselves to 3000x—4000x advance. The distance gunners can reach without moving. This Artillery obsession...

Why piddle about with porridge-making of the Third-Ypres type?...

Wars have to be democratic nowadays:...the nations have to be stampeded into them by Press, propaganda, etc...Still 'you can't bluff all the people all the time', and we've lost our capacity for fanaticism either about religion or dynasty.

There will no doubt come a time in national arguments, when appeal to force is the only way of settling certain points.

But both sides will want quick settlement.

And the points at issue are unlikely to be capable ever again of firing an enduring determination never to yield (to a reasonable foe—who will have a sense to gild the frill)—useless unless it comes to a fundamental racial question, I mean White v Yellow or +Black.[60]

In response, Lindsay agreed that 'The Mongol idea of extreme mobility, combined with great fire-power, is not dead, but lives.' Moreover, modern war could enhance the Mongolian model, where the enemy's nerve centres could be crippled with gas and tanks in combination.[61] In the same year that *Great Captains* appeared, the chief of the Imperial General Staff, Sir George Milne, in his Tidworth address on 8 September, appealed to the great cavalry assaults of history, clearly influenced by Liddell Hart's narrative of Mongol mobility with the sieges left out:

> It is the great cavalry raids by people like the Mongols and Parthians, where there was nothing to stop the action of cavalry, that want your consideration. There you have cavalry living on the country and travelling long distances. You have the absolute acme of strategic mobility in the theatres of operations and that is the sort of mobility I want you to study...what I am aiming at is a mobile armoured force that can go long distances and carry out big operations and big turning movements.[62]

Big operations and big turning movements, with logistically independent forces in deep strategic penetrations that quickly decided wars, was an appealing story to radical armour theorists. These comments indicate that Liddell Hart's binary vision was being picked up and developed among practitioners.

But it was blind to context. There were whole dimensions to Mongol warfare that the armour prophets omitted. Mongol wars could be very protracted, just as wars of swift technology could be. Historically, sieges of fortified positions and urban populations were a bloody, attritional form of conflict that dominated much of medieval warfare. The Mongols themselves had incorporated Muslim and Chinese siegecraft, by trial and error developing the capabilities, with Chinese siege engineers included in their ranks. Four years before Chinggis invaded the Karismian Empire, he had overseen the siege of Zhongdu (near modern Beijing) the capital of the Chin Empire of northern China. This siege lasted almost a year. The Mongols' subsequent campaign in the Karismian lands involved the five month siege of Urganj. In Liddell Hart's own lifetime, sieges such as the assault on Leningrad would rival the destructiveness and length of major battles. In contrast to the forecasts of interwar theorists like Liddell Hart who believed that the 'indirect approach' was a more economical and civilized approach, striking at the enemy's rear could be nasty, brutish and very long.[63]

On this point, there is an intriguing silence from Liddell Hart. He does not discuss, or even mention, the issue of Mongol treatment of civilians. His narrative of the Mongol campaigns is highly sanitized. He clearly was aware of this aspect of their warfare, as his own papers contain one document with transcriptions from various historical works about Mongol atrocities against civilians.[64] The document relates terror tactics that include massacres, rape, torture, the destruction of crops and herds, looting, the annihilation of cities, as well as Chinggis' supposed statements about the necessity of inclemency. To be sure, some of these claims may have been exaggerated or propagandistic, but the issue of Mongolian predations does not make it into his account of the Mongol campaigns. It is difficult to interpret what significance, if any, this omission has. Does it reflect Liddell Hart's interest in the search for alternative civilian targets instead of military forces, something that was central to his 'indirect approach' and part of his fascination with Sherman as the ravager of the South? Or does the omission of this grisly material suggest that it disturbed his view that the 'indirect approach' to warfare was ultimately cheaper and quicker, more rationally geared to restoring a better state of peace? Or is it because he feared that including the most notorious aspects of Mongol warfare would undermine his attempt to present them as exemplars to be followed? Or was he just interested in Mongolian military operations with the atrocities left out?

On this slim evidence, we cannot explain his side-stepping of this issue. But Liddell Hart's broader view should be tested. He suggested that it was more efficient and even humane to dislocate an enemy by bypassing its military forces in the main theatre and striking at alternative targets such as civilian populations. While he was not always consistent on this point, he did generally assume in this period that a strike on civilian targets was less attritional than a direct strike on the enemy's military force. What would be simplistic for the future was also ahistorical when it came to the Mongols. In reality, there was not a stark choice between a long, bloody campaign in pursuit of decisive battle and a short, paralyzing campaign of indirection. The alternative to front-on battles of attrition could be more attritional, even when allowing for the Mongols' well-executed manoeuvres.

This all points to a second historical problem with Liddell Hart's treatment of the Mongols, which has already been raised with other case studies. He set up a false polarity, where indirect methods are exclusive or antagonistic to direct ones. When it came to the American Civil War, Liddell Hart presented Sherman and Grant's contrasting approaches as conflicting, so that Sherman is praised as the general whose operations in the west and south, his attacks on the Confederacy's infrastructure, agriculture, railways, slave system and civilian centres really won the war, in contrast to Grant's costly frontal assaults in Virginia.

But as historians Spencer Wilkinson, Michael Howard and Azar Gat all contended in the case of the American Civil War, and as could be argued in the case of the Mongols, the 'indirect' and 'direct' models were often complementary and interdependent. Sherman's campaign could not have succeeded before the North had developed its material superiority over the South, and could hardly have taken place had Grant and the Union armies not been pinning down and 'fixing' the main Southern forces before Richmond.[65] A similar dynamic could be discerned in the Mongol campaign of 1218–22. Chinggis' successful surprise attack from the rear itself depended on two Mongol armies pinning down the Khoresmian forces at the river crossing. In turn, the success of Mongol warfare was not based purely on mobility. Instead, it depended partly on the ability to switch from mobile to immobile methods, from rapid to protracted operations, to exchange the mounted archer for the siege weapon (such as the catapult and battering ram) and to occupy ground in a stationary way to create opportunities for envelopment and surprise elsewhere.

In turn, this leads to another problem in Liddell Hart's approach to strategy and the Mongol analogy, namely his quest for universal principles and great generals that led him to disregard the material (and topographical) context in which war was fought. In an attempt to temper Liddell Hart's overemphasis on abstract ideas, Spencer Wilkinson argued that there were very good circumstantial reasons why many eighteenth-century commanders only rarely engaged in pitched battle. These included the difficulties of movement and reconnaissance, of finding and fixing the enemy in the first place, even if they wanted to. It was not just a case of doctrine and intellectual attitudes.[66] Or, as Brian Bond noted, the reasons why warfare produced 'decisive results' in one era and not in another might have comparatively little to do with generalship', so that the American Civil War became attritional even with the presence of talented generals.[67] Similarly, Mongol 'swarming' tactics may have worked well in certain terrain, where envelopment was possible, but it was less effective outside it, where their forces could be bottlenecked, such as in mountain passes. Liddell Hart confined the story to the optimum environments in which Mongols succeeded, but left out the moments when it might struggle, such as their defeat by the Polish-Czech army in the Silesian passes in 1241, or indeed as Charles Oman argued, the Mongols' decision not to raid Great Novgorod, because it was protected by woods, marshes and lakes.[68] Liddell Hart's dogma in the late 1920s was mobility, but this led him to disregard the conditions and situations where brilliant, sustained enveloping manoeuvres were impossible, whether in the mountains of Dalmatia in the thirteenth century or Germany's defensive zone on the western front in 1916, six to eight miles deep, and with no flank to turn.

As the statements of the tank theorists suggest, another hope of interwar armour prophets was that armoured forces might emulate the Mongols' logistic independence, their ability to live off the land and be sustained purely by the improvised exploitation of local resources. But this notion of the Mongols' logistical self-sufficiency, and indeed of future armoured forces, was based on myth. While on the move, Mongol flying columns surged ahead while the main army might be accompanied by long baggage trains. When laying siege, the Mongols needed supply lines for materials such as siege equipment, additional horses, weapons, and everyday items. They also pressed into service foreign craftsmen and artisans to maintain their weapons and armour, whole coercing local populations to work as forced labour during sieges, and obtained the submission of adjoining regions to obtain tribute, food and pastureland.[69] And armoured forces depend on a logistical chain to operate. The Mongols had not historically been able purely to live off the land, and neither, it turned out, could tanks.

The doctrine of extreme mobility would run into limitations in the twentieth as well as the thirteenth century. Liddell Hart's focus, in his advocacy of tanks and in retrospect, was what he saw as the climactic moment for armoured warfare, the Nazi defeat of British, French and Polish armies in 1939–40, which he believed unlocked the secrets of warfare that the Mongols had mastered. Or, to put it another way, he 'stopped the clock' in mid-1940. But it was precisely after this phase that one of the limitations and drawbacks of *Blitzkrieg*, and Liddell Hart's view of the Mongols, became apparent. Once the Germans invaded the Soviet Union, despite spectacular successes and deep penetration, they failed to solve the problem of adequately supplying their forces across the vast territories of Belarus and the Ukraine, over muddy roads or in freezing temperatures, so that only a fraction of needed material arrived.[70] An army 'designed, trained, and equipped for short campaigns in central and western Europe, with a highly developed infrastructure and a well-manicured road network', ultimately failed to translate the doctrine of rapid mobility and 'expanding torrent' invasion into a logistics-dominated winter war in the heart of Russia.[71]

British tank theorists, therefore, were only invoking certain parts of the history of Mongol war. They were making history fit a futuristic vision, where mechanised warfare with self-sufficient forces accelerated and cheapened conflict. Their accounts of the relationship between Mongol and modern warfare read like the German Army's triumphalist narrative of its victory over France in 1870–1. Despite the warnings of some far-sighted officers, the German army after 1871 celebrated the conventional phase of that war, with the story climaxing in the battle of Sedan, and played down the second phase of 'people's war' or *Volkskrieg*. The siege of Paris and the Commune, French civilian mobilization and the strain suffered by both sides, were all written out in order to fit the ideal of the quick and decisive victory in the field.[72] To be fair to the tank enthusiasts, they embraced a one-dimensional history of the Mongols partly because they had not read extensively on Mongol warfare other than Liddell Hart's writings. As Percy Hobart complained to Lindsay, it was 'V. difficult to get much hard fact to bite on. I've written home for some books and to a few people for information. Have you found out anything more? Can you put me on to any literature?'[73] Lacking extensive information, they filled the void with their preconceptions about the warfare of the steppe nomads, and their desires for future military transformation. In this way, their misreading of history, with its omissions, reinforced and was reinforced by a misreading of the present.

Another controversial analogy Liddell Hart drew in *Great Captains* was the Mongols' simple 'single arm' force. This, he wrote, demonstrated the enduring need for similarly unified armies in the future. Liddell Hart was not alone in the interwar period in over-estimating the extent to which future armoured warfare could or would be conducted primarily as a single-arm phenomenon. But he was the one who most prominently attached the vision of a fully integrated mobile force to the Mongols. Significantly, as armoured warfare evolved differently to how he imagined it, Liddell Hart would also alter his portrayal of the Mongols to fit the new circumstances. Consider his recollections from 1948:

> The 'Mongol Warfare' analogy, which I brought out in 1924, was of much help in showing the strategic potentialities of mechanised forces, and what great results might be achieved if they were organised to move self-contained

for supplies during a long-range drive. It also showed the general potentialities of an all-mobile army—in which the different arms, all being 'mounted', would acquire much of the versatility of a single arm.

Yet, because the Mongols had been popularly regarded as merely a horde of light horsemen, the analogy was sometimes taken superficially as an argument for having an armoured force entirely composed of light tanks—although I had brought out the fact that the Mongol army was really a combination of all arms, including artillery, on a common mobile basis.[74]

This may have been as Liddell Hart remembered it, but in truth, in 1927 his treatment of the issue of single versus combined arms had been agnostic. He had not clearly 'brought out the fact' that the Mongol army was a pure combined arms force. In *Great Captains*, he repeatedly described and praised the 'simplicity of a single mobile arm.' On the other hand, his vision of mechanisation did allow for an infantry role, albeit a minor one, 'employing the crews to act on foot [as the Mongols did] as land marines wherever the special loco-mobility of infantry is needed.'[75] This accorded with his view in the interwar period, that wholly armoured divisions should dominate, supplemented with only a small element of offensive infantry or 'tank marines.'[76] And at one point he mentioned the light artillery capabilities of the Mongols that could be readily transported. Yet the main thrust and chief rhetorical emphasis in his representation of the Mongols in *Great Captains* was that of a radically simplified military force.

This was a contradiction that *Great Captains* did not resolve. And it reflected a tension and uncertainty in armoured warfare theory in general that could only be clarified by war itself. In his other writings around the same time, Liddell Hart like Fuller leant strongly but not decisively towards the prediction of exclusively tank battles in the future. Liddell Hart's shifting views of how exactly Mongol warfare bore on the debate about interwar armoured warfare can be explained historically. In the interwar period, there were two competing visions of armoured warfare, the view that tanks should be massed all but independently, in all-tank or tank-dominant formations, and the other view that armour should be one component of a more integrated combined-arms force.[77] Over time, and after *Great Captains* was published, the latter view was more widely accepted in principle, and the German panzer divisions would contain all arms. So in *Great Captains*, the Mongols appear as forerunners of a more radical vision of armoured warfare, but in retrospect in 1948, Liddell Hart recast them as the forerunners of the more conservative combined-arms vision, the vision that prevailed militarily and intellectually.

In any event, Liddell Hart's vision of Mongol warfare in the 1920s, and the actual subsequent development of *Blitzkrieg*, would contrast more than he realised when looking back decades later. He may have drawn a straight line from his account of the Mongols to the Nazi conquest of Poland and France, but only a small part of the German force in 1939–40 was mechanised. In the invasion of Poland, many vehicles actually broke down on the plains, while most of the *Wehrmacht* moved on foot, and supplies were often transported in horse-drawn wagons. In the invasion of France in 1940, most German combatants walked to the front. Of one hundred German divisions, only ten were tank divisions and another ten were motorised. Almost in anticipation of this, some German armour strategists in the interwar period had been more skeptical about whether tanks could succeed autonomously, as they could become vulnerable to artillery or even infantry with grenades. Liddell Hart had upheld the Mongols for being exemplars of pure mobility. Yet the armoured units that waged *Blitzkrieg* and the great tank battles of the Second World War *would* in fact rely on infantry and artillery support. This was not a mechanised version of the Mongols. Rather, these invasion armies more closely resembled the very problematic forces of European history that Liddell Hart had complained about in the first place, those that untidily combined mobile with less mobile arms.[78] So when Percy Hobart praised Liddell Hart in 1948 for his vision, he regretted that '...You cast your bread upon the waters—unfortunately the only people who returned it at all adequately were the Germans in Poland and W. Europe in 1940. And the full idea was never put into practice as far as I know.'[79]

Blitzkrieg itself was not entirely the product of a revolutionary or even coherent doctrine devised in the interwar period. On the one hand, its core principles predated the debate of the 1920s, as they emerged from developments in the First World War. They grew out of German 'manoeuvrist' warfare and infantry tactics, using storm-troopers and infiltration, deep penetration, isolating strong points and paralyzing the enemy's brain. *Blitzkrieg* was an intellectual evolution from World War One assisted and accelerated by the arrival of tanks and mechanised infantry carriers, not a revolution where interwar theorists had discovered the secrets of modern warfare, or indeed of eternal warfare. On the other hand, *Blitzkrieg* did not even exist as a word before *Time* magazine coined it after the Nazi conquest of Poland in 1939, and even then the form of warfare it described was still being evolved by the German Army between 1931 and 1941. And the successes of *Blitzkrieg*, or *Bewegungskrieg* ('war of movement') as it had been known in Germany, was as much due to a series of accidents, improvised reactions and good luck as it was a distilled doctrine inspired by the theories of Liddell Hart and others.[80]

Over time, Liddell Hart emphasized different aspects of Mongol warfare to accord with the changing contours of military debate. In 1960, for example, he argued that the Mongols operated optimally when they combined light and heavy cavalry rather than deploying just one type.[81] But in *Great Captains* he had accorded almost no significance in the distinction between their light and heavy cavalry, one of the more marked differentiations within Mongol combat. This can be explained historically. His writing in 1960 was in a different strategic context, as Liddell Hart intervened in a debate about the composition of NATO land forces, so the distinction between light and heavy tanks, and the analogy with Mongol light and heavy cavalry, was far more significant an issue to him then than it had been in 1927.

It is difficult to understand Liddell Hart's changing view of Mongol warfare unless it is grasped that in his career there were many Liddell Harts, many incarnations of his attempts at innovative thought, and his 'indirect approach' proved to be an elastic idea. At the time he wrote *Great Captains*, he was stressing mechanisation and a far-sighted view of tanks and planes as the principle weapon, even if he lacked a clear idea of how to implement this concept and even if it owed a great deal to the influence of Fuller. But by the late 1920s, he distanced himself from the notion that the tank would restore mobility to the offensive, and began to switch his emphasis to the power of the defence. By 1932 he developed the concept of the 'British way in warfare', with its weapon of economic pressure and seaborne armies striking from the periphery. He then switched back to the potentiality of bombing civilian populations, as originally outlined in his earlier work *Paris, Or the Future of War*, where he had argued that air power could drop bombs and poison gas on major cities so devastatingly that they would destroy morale and bring victory cheaply and swiftly. In his more excitable moments in the 1920s, Liddell Hart had optimistically forecast that modern complex societies were so vulnerable to any disruption of their equilibrium that an air power campaign could cripple their will to fight within days or even hours.[82]

Mongols, by contrast with all of this, did not confine themselves to the periphery or the defensive, fought battles of annihilation, found that physical mobility was not always possible or desirable, and assaulted civilian populations in ways that were often expensive and protracted. Taken in its totality, Mongol warfare demonstrated that the 'indirect approach' could have attritional results; so far from limiting war's scope and costs, as Liddell Hart envisaged, it prolonged and intensified it. So our author, thinking more about policy and the present than about carefully weighed scholarship, used the 'Orient' instrumentally and ahistorically, to arouse a sleeping public and military establishment.

Conclusion: the West v. Itself

Ever since the Mongols were known, they have been alternatively demonized and valourised. The romantic view of Mongol genius sanitizes them, to make them attractive models for the West. The 'barbarian horde' view presents them as monsters without rational purpose. Both are inaccurate. Both utilize a selective vision of the East for purposes of strategic debate in the West. Down the centuries, and in Liddell Hart's own time, the Mongols represented a paradox. They stood, it seemed, for barbarism. But they also stood for strategic profundity. In the minds of Western observers, they had threatened civilization, but especially after the holocaust of the Great War, their example could also save it. For Liddell Hart, the main enemy was not the threat of Asian masses, but a misguided concept of warfare that had originated in Europe and worked such devastation in the Great War. Part of his answer was to search for alternatives in the pre-Napoleonic past. The other part was to search outside Europe. What better case study than one that was exotic, radically different from the western front, and staggeringly successful?

Little of the Mongols' history was known in detail by Liddell Hart and his contemporaries. So they projected onto the Mongols their own preconceptions of future war. Interwar futurists who championed the cause of mechanisation based their case on appeals to history, so that modern mechanised armies would be seen not as dangerous experiments, but as embodying the fundamental principles of war. Mongols could be invoked to show the possibilities of creative iconoclasm and change. Like the British officers who admired and at times romanticized

Japanese warfare in 1904–5, Liddell Hart recognized that philosophies, doctrines and practices in war could be diffused across cultural boundaries. But to help his attempts to influence the future, he also distorted history. He sanitized and simplified the Mongols, turning Chinggis' campaigns into a usable parable, and later, into a historic dress rehearsal for *Blitzkrieg*, without long sieges, terror tactics or balanced combined arms, without logistic difficulties and without the symbiotic relationship between direct and indirect warfare, and in the end, without acknowledgement of the difference between his utopian theories of the 1920s and the messy realities of the campaigns of 1939–45. As circumstances changed, and as he sought intellectual vindication, Liddell Hart's view of the Mongols adjusted. Mongol warfare became a mirror, reflecting back his evolving thought, his organizing ideas and his desired role as prophet of military revolution. As so often, his Orientalism was as much about the West as the East.

5

EXOTIC ENEMY?

AMERICA, THE TALIBAN AND THE FOG OF CULTURE

According to Thucydides, humans wage war out of 'honour, fear and interest.'[1] But in the ongoing war in Afghanistan, some Western analysts see honour as the enemies' prime impulse. This was shown in an incident in October 2005, which created outrage in Afghanistan and apprehension in US embassies. Ambushed by the Taliban, a US patrol killed two Taliban fighters and burnt their bodies after the local village refused to accept their corpses. Cremation is an affront to Islam. In their defence, the guilty soldiers claimed that concerns for hygiene had prompted their act. But an American psychological operations team (PSYOP) then tried to exploit the incident by shaming their enemies into fighting. Calling them 'ladyboys,' Sgt Jim Baker taunted through a loudspeaker, 'You allowed your fighters to be laid down facing West and burned. You are too scared to come down and retrieve their bodies.'[2] This dismayed an expert on psywar, who called this blasphemy a 'watershed cultural blunder.'[3] But Jim Baker and his critic had something in common. Both assumed that it is culture above all that makes Afghans tick.

The incident did not help win hearts and minds. But the view that it might determine the outcome of the war says more about Western observers than the nature of Afghan society. The wartime behaviour of Afghans suggests that their culturally-rooted beliefs and taboos are not decisively important. First, the Taliban did not come out and fight. In a tactical moment, self-preservation trumped religious sensitivity. More deeply, the idea that this scandal was the tipping point, or that ritual honour is the Afghans' political centre of gravity, contradicts other patterns of behaviour. It fails to explain why Afghans in embattled areas repeatedly change sides and defect to and from American-led forces. They do not like to be offended, but this hardly determines their allegiances. Likewise, it cannot answer why the Taliban's propaganda appeals to Afghans' survival instincts and practical fears as well as religious honour. And it fails to explain why some Afghans on both sides desecrate human remains, booby-trapping corpses or leaving them rotting on open ground.

And the idea that this incident reflected a distinctively Afghan or Islamic culture may also be overstated. Concern for the integrity of the dead, and outrage at profanity and the desecration of corpses, is a near-universal human pattern, famously explored in Sophocles' *Antigone*. The US Marine Corps, for example, takes it as an article of faith. In its credo, to retrieve the bodies of killed comrades intact is vital to honour and unit cohesion. Historically Marines have risked death in their efforts to evacuate the dead.[4] What some mistake as cultural quirks at play should in fact be a familiar motif, however much details vary with context.

The discussion this incident provoked was symptomatic of a broader tendency in popular and academic discourse, the urge to reduce people with multiple interests and identities into one-dimensional beings. This chapter explores how Westerners, particularly American observers, have perceived the Taliban, and shows why our preoccupation with the exotic may be misleading.[5] The Taliban operate as cultural realists, reinventing their cultural codes as they go. They are neither an invincible enemy beyond Western understanding, nor a primitive force of reaction destined to fail.

A War of Cultures

In the autumn of 2001, an American-led coalition overthrew Afghanistan's Taliban regime.[6] Observers saw the war as a clash of cultures that pitted a theocracy in a poor country against a rich, cosmopolitan society; turbaned *jihadis*, seemingly from a medieval era, against a hi-tech superpower of the Information Age. The American-Afghan alliance seemed a marriage of different species. Special Forces with night goggles, like insects from a science fiction film, teamed up with mounted tribesmen. The weapons of both cultures were the artefacts of different worlds—horses and cruise missiles, old Lee Enfield rifles and laser designators. For an American special forces Captain, it was 'the Flintstones meets the Jetsons.'[7] To American audiences, war revealed Afghan's strangeness. CNN analyst Maj.-General Donald Shepperd identified an 'Afghan way of war' which was 'bizarre' for its lack of centralised command and control.[8] War correspondent Anthony Davis saw a 'peculiarly Afghan culture of war.'[9] The Taliban also talked of a culturally-defined struggle, reinforcing the myth of the hardened warrior fighting a weak, materialist West. Mullah Omar, the Taliban leader, described the infidel Americans as 'simple-minded and arrogant. Strong with its warplanes, bombs and equipment but weak in its content,' boasting years later that his men would hunt them down like pigs.[10]

The Taliban in Western media often appear as archaic and zealous. Their visual image is one of bearded tribal warriors snarling for the camera. As America prepared for war in 2001, a journalist warned in classically Orientalist language about the Taliban's deadly exoticism, 'one of the world's most inscrutable regimes, fanatically loyal to one of the world's most mysterious leaders' in 'a land that has proved to be the graveyard of every previous foreign invader.'[11] They are often cast as a militant Pashtun movement supported by foreign Islamic volunteers. Historically, the Pashtuns' reputation for ferocity draws (and has drawn) mixed reactions, from contempt to romantic admiration.[12] In particular, observers claim that Pashtun tribes who form the bulk of the Taliban are bound to an honour code (*Pashtunwali*), which forces them to avenge their dead relatives. In this view, their warfare drives from blood ties, a thirst for vengeance (*Badal*), and ancient tribal lore. This image was also popular in nineteenth-century colonial minds, of the Pashtuns bound by their honour code regardless of rationality or material considerations.[13] In another twist on this narrative, others present the Taliban as mystical Muslims, fighting under the banner of a talismanic holy man. Analysts urge militaries to observe these traits as a way to predict behaviour.[14]

But the archetypal Pashtun-Taliban fighter, impelled more by visceral tribal instincts (or under the spell of a mystic leader) than by strategic calculation, is similar to stereotypes applied elsewhere about frontier warriors gripped by tradition and superstition. While their tribal codes and religious ideas can command great authority, under the pressures of war the Taliban constantly choose among and between taboos, survival, loyalties and success. What Fouad Ajami said of states, applies equally well to the Afghan insurgency: 'States avert their gaze from blood ties when they need to; they see brotherhood and faith and kin when it is in their interest to do so.'[15] This is crucial to knowing the enemy.

Busted Flush or Deathless Army?

The West's preoccupation with the exotic nature of the Taliban takes many forms, both triumphalist and defeatist. As they discussed the war from 2001, and forecast the outcome, people on both sides of the debate persistently fell back on culture to explain the conflict. Optimists claimed that the Afghan holy warriors were inferior and could not compete against the West. The Taliban were being tested against the technological muscle and political dynamism of the world's most powerful liberal democracy, and in less than ten weeks they were found wanting. Suffering only four combat deaths, the US had smashed them with a new way of war, combining air power, cash, Special Forces and Afghan troops as their spearhead.[16] A reactionary brand of militant Islam could not cut the mustard against an open, affluent civilisation. While the Taliban and their Al Qaeda allies were able to turn their enemies' innovations against them, from mobile phones to digitised capital, they were essentially backward foes whose days were numbered. Cultural difference was critical to victory and it would benefit the superpower and its allies.

Implicitly or explicitly, commanders, politicians and pundits depicted the Taliban as ultimately unviable, doomed to failure because of its backwardness. President George W. Bush identified the Taliban as part of a cosmic clash between 'freedom and fear, justice and cruelty', an ideological struggle in which victory for the just was 'certain.'[17] Secretary of Defence Donald Rumsfeld declared in May 2003 that the war in Afghanistan was in a 'cleanup' or 'mop up' phase.[18] The Taliban was a 'force in decline', said Major General Eric Olsen in March 2005, who had helmed the American campaign, pleased that the enemy were morally and psychologically reeling from successful free elections in 2004. The Taliban were a 'busted flush' according to a gushing article reporting his efforts.[19] Even with the Taliban resurgent in 2006, Secretary of State Condoleezza Rice claimed the Taliban's regressive nature ensured its ultimate defeat. 'They are not going to win. They don't have a positive agenda for anyone.'[20] In a post-script to his thesis about the supremacy of the 'Western way of war', Victor Hanson argued that the rapid defeat inflicted on the Taliban demonstrated the superior lethality of liberal democracies. Western society, with its strengths of shock battle, civic audit, citizen soldiers and technological innovation, was likely to succeed in this new war.[21]

These arguments seemed vindicated as the onslaught against the Taliban enabled political and civil progress. After the Taliban were removed from power, America and its Afghan allies could point to great achievements. Free elections were conducted successfully for a President and a National Assembly. In contrast to Taliban policy of gender apartheid, ninety-one women were elected to the new parliament, a higher proportion of female representatives than most Western democracies. And the gains of the post-Taliban order were not merely constitutional; they involved life and death. Thanks to improved access to medical care, approximately 40,000 fewer infants died annually.[22] Against the predictions that the war would create a mass refugee exodus, following the flight of the Taliban 4.6 million Afghan refugees came back to their native country, as the White House announced, 'one of the largest return movements in history.'[23] The economy doubled in size. Girls could go to school. Football stadiums hosted football matches, not executions. Despite the sufferings of war, by decisive margins Afghan opinion in late 2005 and again in late 2007 claimed that it rejected the Taliban, favoured their removal, and supported the foreign presence.[24] Had the American 'way of war' made possible a better Afghan way of life?

But from the moment 'Operation Enduring Freedom' began, sceptics disputed this sunny outlook.[25] Academic historians and military commentators repeated cautionary tales from the past, warning that America was blundering into an unmasterable country, a death trap for empires past, an impenetrable landscape of xenophobes it did not or could not understand.[26] Seven years on, the sceptics now believe they have been proven right. An enemy continually pronounced dead refuses to die. The international coalition struggles to translate the rapid victories of 2001 into enduring political success. The signs of trouble are many. They include periodic Taliban offensives, Afghan riots, civilian alienation (because of everything from food shortages, the deaths of innocents from NATO bombings, to government corruption), and the seemingly endless supply of Taliban recruits, (from Pashtun tribal areas, as well as Arab, Uzbek and Chechen volunteers).[27]

Scattered in 2001, the Taliban and their allies have found sanctuary for new recruitment and operations in Pakistan. And Western military credibility may be eroding. In the Afghan south, the heartland of the conflict, half of 17,000 men surveyed now say that the Taliban will defeat NATO forces.[28] The Taliban are able to threaten, strike and leave quickly. They kidnap or assassinate aid workers, travellers, teachers and members of particular ethnic groups. Hacking off the ears and noses of three Afghan drivers who delivered fuel to a US base in March 2007, they sent out a brutal physical reminder of the costs of collaborating with the new state or foreign occupiers. They wage an 'armed information operation' to appear as an 'unstoppable, growing insurgency.'[29]

Now, sceptics argue that we should not see the Afghan population as a people who can be politically 'won over' by the promise of a democratic alternative or by a linear process of armed social work and economic reconstruction projects. Indeed, it is delusional to view Afghans as biddable people who can be induced into clear-cut partisan allegiances to either side. Instead, from long experience, Afghans in embattled regions are survivalists. They prefer to 'hedge', either siding with the perceived overdog, or playing both sides and avoiding outright commitments from fear that aligning with the loser will lead to recrimination.[30] As well as asking who Afghans *want* to win, we need to ask who they *expect* will win. In their propaganda, the Taliban play on the simple view that time is on their side. In their 'night letters' of handwritten messages, face-to-face warnings and radio broadcasts, they remind Afghan communities that their enemies will run out of 'political time', and that the Taliban will be there long after demoralised foreigners leave.[31]

Even apparent success may be the sign of a premeditated 'waiting game.' Sceptics might argue that opinion polls reporting consent and support for NATO and the US are inherently distorted. Those questioned are by definition being surveyed in pacified areas outside Taliban strongholds, or that their claim to support NATO is unreliable, as they are wary of declaring their allegiance to the Taliban to foreign questioners.[32] In terms of operational tempo, it is difficult to define victory and measure progress. As an unclassified memorandum from an American Task Force noted in October 2005, the Taliban exploited 'the misconception that the insurgency was over' to regroup, restraining from violence during elections to tempt America into a premature withdrawal.[33] A massive spring offensive by the Taliban was expected in 2007, but barely happened. Is this inactivity a sign of Taliban weakness, or a calculated ploy to 'lie low'?

Whatever the answers, sceptics also often stress culture. But they do not draw comfort from cultural 'asymmetries' that differentiate America from the Taliban. Instead, they fear cultural difference is the West's weakness, not its strength. Most recently, commentators warned that the Taliban could only be understood in terms that were 'alien to Western thinking.'[34] Similarly, on the eve of the 2001 invasion, a Defence Intelligence Agency report warned that as America 'searched for the enemy's centre of gravity, the most serious danger lies in using Western points of reference and not the enemies'.' Westerners were preoccupied with the conventional fronts of material assets and state support, whereas the true front was in 'the minds of men.'[35] In this view, the West is hampered by its own culture of ethnocentrism, impatience and heavy-handedness.

But what if the underlying assumption is mistaken, that exotic tradition drives Taliban warfare? The case of the Taliban is not only important in terms of grasping the nature of this particular war; it also has a wider significance. It restages the debate about the relationship between war, strategy and culture. What happens when imperatives born of tradition clash with strategic imperatives?

The Taliban may represent a landscape and society that are vastly different from America's. But it is not so strange that it cannot be understood within familiar strategic ideas, or within familiar dynamics of insurgency. It operates primarily not according to rigid cultural codes, but to a strategic calculus about success and failure. It has proven to be pragmatic and innovative. When forced to choose in a trade-off between effective compromise and hard-line dogma, Taliban leaders often choose the former. It is not monolithic, but made up of a loose and shifting series of alliances with their own disagreements over issues including treatment of civilians, death in combat, and the use of technology. They are actors with agency, in other words, who try to make their own history.

The Taliban: Rise, Fall and Rise

The Taliban (from the Arabic *talib*, 'seeker') re-emerged in their modern form in a crucible of war, dislocation, and religious indoctrination.[36]

While their historical roots are deep, it was the Soviet Afghan war (1979–1989) that gave new vigour to militant Islam in the region and prepared the way for their dominance of Afghanistan. The invasion of an atheistic communist superpower created a generation of seasoned 'strugglers' (*mujahidin*). Military occupation drove millions of refugees over the Aghan-Pakistan border. Along this frontier, especially Peshawar and Quetta in Baluchistan, Gulf countries such as Saudi Arabia sponsored the creation of religious schools (*madrassah*) controlled by Islamic parties. Afghan refugees sent their children to be educated there, for free accommodation and a monthly salary. While the Afghan *mujahidin* actively recruited in the camps, students dislocated from their parents' native country were educated in the concepts of sacrifice and holy war (*shahadah*), and the Wahhabist strain of Islam. They also received military training, and were taught that they were obliged to continue a struggle that had killed many of the fathers and brothers.

With the withdrawal and collapse of the Soviet Union, the Taliban lead a revolt against parasitic warlords and rival factions, promising peace, security and the formation of a national assembly. Anarchic conflict, corruption and brigandage on the roads created a political space for them to flourish. They successfully established themselves as bringers of order out of chaos. More a loose coalition than a tightly ordered government, they exerted control with the authority of clerics as their core. Having overrun 80% of the country in a civil war, they imposed an unsmiling and draconian form of Sharia law on the population. In a country where puritanical Islam had rarely been dominant, the new order banned music and alcohol; it introduced punishments such as amputation and death by stoning; it led an orgy of iconoclasm, smashing thousands of pre-Islamic artefacts in the Kabul museum and blowing up ancient Buddhist statues; it carried out ethnic cleansing, massacring thousands of Hazaras at Mazar-i-Sharif; executed homosexuals and political dissidents; it banned girls' public education; and created a religious police force which beat women for offending the dress code. The Taliban also gave sanctuary to, and were propped up by, the Islamist movement of Al Qaeda ('the Base'), which was dedicated to taking armed struggle to the 'far enemy' of the United States and its allies, exporting the civil war in the Islamic world to inspire a global war, expelling the infidel from the Middle East, and restoring the lost Caliphate, climaxing in an apocalyptic struggle between believers and infidel.[37]

None of the Taliban's pathologies, or their dangerous guests, may have become defined as the prime security threat to America. But Al Qaeda's attacks on 9/11, and their evident ability to attack over vast distances, made their Taliban hosts hard to ignore. Bin Laden's network had already struck at American embassies, a warship and had made foiled attempts on airlines and major cities. Now with Afghanistan as a staging ground, it had exploited a shrinking world of rapid communications, capital flows and cheap travel to incinerate skyscrapers in Manhattan, strike the Pentagon—the nerve centre of American military power—and almost hit a major target in Washington. With a fraction of the resources, Al Qaeda had inflicted more damage and taken more lives than Imperial Japan at Pearl Harbor. Furthermore, the tremors of economic damage were global.[38]

How should we classify and understand this regime? Both optimists and pessimists have turned to Orientalist versions of culture to explain the enemy and the conflict. This has not always been helpful.

The Fog of Culture

To exoticise the Taliban is to reduce it to a timeless essence, thus divorcing it from the volatile, unpredictable and dynamic tendencies that war often creates. As an example of this problem, consider three recent arguments, two by scholars and one by a popular writer. The first theory comes from Thomas H. Johnson and M. Chris Mason. Drawing on the theory of Max Weber, they argue that the Taliban are a form of social mobilisation built around the authority of a 'charismatic leader' in the form of a 'mad mullah', in this case the one-eyed veteran and former village cleric Mullah Omar. They argue that the essence of the Taliban has been overlooked because it cannot be understood within traditional 'Western thinking':

> ...unlike most insurgencies, which are not centred in the personality of a single leader, the Taliban's centre of gravity, in Clausewitzian terms, is not Taliban foot soldiers or field commanders or even the senior clerics around Omar, but Omar himself. Because it is a charismatic movement socially, if Mullah Omar dies, the Taliban, at least in its current incarnation, will wither and die. The mystical charismatic power that came from wearing the Cloak of the Prophet is not something transferable to a second-in-command. Unfortunately, because this phenomenon is so alien to Western thinking, U.S. analysts generally interpret the Taliban in terms more compatible with Western logic.[39]

Moreover, they argue that the Taliban are sustained by Pashtun traditions of familial blood feud:

> ...the death in battle of a Pashtun guerrilla invokes an obligation of revenge among all his male relatives, making the killing of a Taliban guerrilla an act of insurgent multiplication, not subtraction. The Soviets learned this lesson as they killed nearly a million Pashtuns but only increased the number of Pashtun guerrillas by the end of the war. The Taliban centre of gravity is Mullah Omar, the charismatic cult leader, not teenage boys or mid-level commanders, and no amount of killing them will shut the insurgency down.[40]

This argument has several weaknesses. First, as an issue of fact, they may be exaggerating the extent to which Omar's charismatic authority binds the movement together. A number of Taliban figures such as Mullah Mohammed Khaqzar or former media operations chief Ishaq Nizami have left, become inactive or defected from the Taliban partly for pragmatic reasons, but partly because of Mullah Omar's authoritarian style, and partly out of opposition to the alliance between hardliners and al Qaeda.[41]

And as an account of the Taliban, Johnson and Mason's argument is undermined by its own self-contradictions. They claim that the Taliban have been misunderstood because they cannot be fathomed within 'Western logic' and 'Western thinking.' Yet ironically, they draw on nineteenth-century German theorists who are squarely within European intellectual traditions: Weber with his theory of charismatic leadership, and Carl von Clausewitz with his concept of the enemy's 'centre of gravity.' Arguing that the Taliban are so different that they operate outside Western frames of reference, fighting and dying by different rules and alien logic, Johnson and Mason end up relying on Western concepts to understand them.

Johnson and Mason's argument is also problematic in other ways. It is not entirely coherent to argue that the Taliban are driven by familial revenge and tribal customs, yet are bound together only by the mystique of one leader. If Pashtun traditions of revenge are as compelling as Johnson and Mason claim, if the obligation to avenge a family death multiplies the ranks of the Taliban with aggrieved men out to avenge their relatives, wouldn't this motivation continue even if Mullah Omar were killed or captured? With their leader gone, the Taliban would surely retain its sociological, tribal and ideological base. And if so, this would undermine the argument that the Taliban's centre of gravity is its charismatic leader. Alternatively, if the Taliban are in fact reliant on one figure for their life as a movement, then their fighters' tradition-based desire for vengeance can't be as compelling as the authors suggest. It is hard to see how the Taliban can be both unquenchably vengeful and yet a bullet away from psychological collapse.

It is also probably ahistorical to assume that the leader's charisma cannot be passed on, and that his death will destroy the movement. History suggests that charisma can be projected onto individuals, as well as radiating from them. In order to continue their feud, the Pashtun may be willing to discover charismatic leadership in another individual. To be sure, the death of a messianic leader can rob an insurgency of a leader's expertise and experience. But it can also energise rather than cripple a movement, by giving authority the added attraction of martyrdom. This can then translate the leader's authority into a posthumous cult. Consider one precedent that is not an exact parallel but nevertheless suggestive: the Mahdi of the Sudan. Having been able 'to inspire and inflame the masses' to prepare them for 'acts of sacrifice' in their uprising against the British Empire, he died of typhus shortly after the fall of Khartoum in 1885.[42] But his death did not result in the meltdown of the Sudanese Dervishes. Instead his legacy was carried on by Khalifa Abdullahi. Indeed, the movement grew under the Khalifa's leadership and the Mahdist state lived on until 1898–9. It was not ended by the demise of one iconic figure, but by an Anglo-Egyptian military campaign. Until then, the Mahdi's corpse had become a site of veneration that inspired his followers. So it is not obvious that blood-feuding Afghan tribesmen would shrug their shoulders and give up the struggle if their leader perished.

Johnson and Mason's argument, that the Taliban are an exotic enemy operating outside the 'Western' imagination, can be compared to other forms of exaggerated culturalism. For example, there is the pessimism of those who argue that Afghanistan is a *terra incognita*, where success for the invader is historically impossible. In the case of Afghanistan, this is an overstatement. True, the region has long been an attractive strategic chokepoint to the mouth of the Persian Gulf, the Asian sub-continent and the Indian Ocean that is hard to dominate. The passes of the eastern reaches of the Hindu Kush, and the plains of the Indus River valley are some of the most violently contested spaces in history. And at different times, Afghans repelled the most confident imperialist lunges, Britain's *Pax Britannica* in the 1840's, and Brezhnev's 'irreversible' Soviet socialist revolution in 1979. But Britain enjoyed partial success in the Anglo-Afghan war of 1878, enabling it to leave Afghanistan until 1919 as a buffer state and a counterweight to Russian influence, even winning another short war in 1919 before withdrawing. Before leaving to invade India, Alexander of Macedon dominated the region of Bactria through a dynastic marriage after overcoming almost unreachable mountain strongholds. Invaders have not always wanted to occupy or possess Afghanistan, but tame, control or exert distant control over it as an important artery to other places. Total conquest or permanent occupation may be rare, but it is not always the invader's aim.

There is a second, 'culturalist', argument, common within military circles and public discourse, that the Taliban insurgency is not essentially Islamic or charismatic, but essentially tribal or overwhelmingly ethnic. Public servant James Dobbins, former US envoy to Afghanistan, claims 'This is a Pashtun insurgency. I don't mean to suggest that all Pashtuns are insurgents, simply that all insurgents are Pashtuns.'[43] NATO's chief intelligence officer, Canadian Brigadier-General Jim Ferron, describes the Afghan insurgency as essentially 'tribal-based,'[44] compounded by material deprivation. Steven Pressfield, whose historical novels are bestsellers within America's armed forces, argues that tribalism characterises the 'East' throughout history. [45] The religious element of today's insurgencies is no more than tribalism articulated in another form. In classic binary and Orientalist terms, Pressfield depicts the West and East as 'polar antagonists.' 'The West is modern and rational; its constituent unit is the nation. The East is ancient and visceral; its constituent unit is the tribe.' This applies in urbanised Iraq and the Afghan hinterland. Pressfield does not account for the late development of the nation in Western politics, nor for the fact of non-Western nationalism. He concludes that there is no resolution to such a conflict but withdrawal, allowing the 'crazy' tribal enemy to save 'face.' The 'tribal mind' honours no agreements, respects no other principles outside the tribe, and has an irrational, instinctive mind of 'warrior pride, not of Enlightenment reason.' This essentialist argument informs his latest novel about Alexander of Macedon's Afghan campaign in 330–327BC, where a Western army with a secular and humanist code fights a 'proud Eastern warrior nation.'

But this is both empirically false and conceptually flawed. As a construct for understanding insurgencies, tribalism should be approached with caution. The urge to classify foreign peoples as neatly defined demographic or geographic units with fixed hierarchical structures can create an 'ethnographic fiction' of isolated and homogenous groups only mating with one another, descending from common ancestors and with a clear hierarchy. It is a hangover from nineteenth-century colonialism, when encroaching states imposed artificial and formal political structures on seemingly formless societies which had once had more 'casual social divisions.' White Americans assumed that the Lakota and Cheyenne tribes were ruled by an 'Old Man Chief' when in fact power structures were more fluid and boundaries more vague, and by giving commissions and support on war chiefs, older systems of consensus politics and shared power were diluted.[46] In reality, any political and collective group responds not only to genealogical affiliations but also to external political and economic stimuli.

The Afghan insurgency has an ethnic base among Pashtuns, but is not reducible to tribalism, or indeed to any single identity. Traditional tribal loyalties in Afghanistan, and their agricultural power base, were disrupted and altered by the emergence of *tanzims* (roughly 'political parties' or groupings) as well as the *qawm* system of sub-national loyalties that includes religious sects and practical alliances. The Taliban themselves do not just operate tribally. Their leadership has both Durrani and Ghilzai members. They include rival tribes in their movement, including marginalised Hazara groups in Ghazni. They contain many Tajik and Uzbek clerics allied to their cause. And they have established supply lines and communications in the west, north and northeast of Afghanistan, areas populated mostly by non-Pashtun ethnic minorities, and staged recruitment drives outside their traditional regions of control, in Lashkargah and Kandahar city.[47] The 'neo-Taliban' that has recently emerged is trying to expand its recruitment beyond its Pashtun base, by appealing to local grievances. As Antonio Giustozzi argues, the Taliban do not define their movement in tribal terms but actively try to transcend tribal limits. Ever since 2001, they were

> ready to accept anybody who shared their views and accepted their rules, regardless of ethnicity and tribe. Taliban teams were always mixing together individuals with different tribal backgrounds. Clearly, the Taliban did not want to present themselves as aligned with a particular tribe or community. This made it easier to move across tribal territories without antagonising the locals, but at the same time was also a way of advertising the Movement as above inter-community rivalry.[48]

The Taliban attract support from disparate layers of domestic society: individuals and communities angered by state corruption; displaced Afghans, whose abodes were destroyed by bombing, seeking refuge in camps; among mercenaries, young unemployed, bandits and criminals. They draw from material grievances, opportunities for organised crime, religious arguments, and the volatile but powerful influence of the battlefield itself, that tempts Afghans to think not only to act from cultural identity but to identify with the likely winner, or wait until one emerges.[49]

The Taliban also have an unstable relationship with Pashtun tribalism and tribal codes. *Pashtunwali*, for example, is a powerful but loose concept that can be applied differently on a situational basis. It does value blood vengeance, but can also value recompense, and prudence, and need not result in violence.[50] This is clear from the defections of Pashtuns who have gone over to a Tajik-dominated state and the international coalition, either as individuals, small groups or en masse.[51] That Pashtun loyalties and the code of *Pashtunwali* do not dictate choices is demonstrated in the defection in January 2008 by Mullah Abdul Salaam, leader of the Alizai, the largest Pashtun tribe in Helmand. With him, he brought one third of the Taliban fighters from Musa Qala, a district that had been through heavy fighting. For those fighters, some of whom must have had family killed by the enemy, the demands of tribe trumped the demands of familial revenge. Here is how Salaam addressed his followers on relations with fellow Taliban commander Mullah Abdul Bari:

> 'Abdul Bari is our brother,' he said. 'He can come and sit among us ... He is from this land. Speak with him. But don't let him be stupid. If he is not on the right path then don't let yourself be sacrificed for him. Tell him to take his jihad somewhere else.'[52]

This rhetoric suggests a leader prepared to abandon the writ of blood-brotherhood in the name of survival. A veteran of wars against the Soviet Union and the United States, Salaam knows when to wink at ancestral customs. And from below, Afghans on the frontier between warring sides may be Muslims or tribal loyalists, but they also have other pressing interests and identities, as people making practical choices about survival, their ideology based on forecasting who will prevail.[53]

Also odd is the idea that religion is merely an epiphenomenal texture to a local and tribal uprising, which fails to explain the role of international and religious volunteers. It also neglects the dynamic and the globalized aspects of the insurgency. The Taliban's resort to new al

Qaeda-style tactics, such as kidnapping, roadside explosives and the marginalization of tribal elders, suggests that the insurgency mutates from its 'original reason for being', a tribal brand of religious fundamentalism pursuing a Pashtunistan statelet in the south, into an umbrella movement of 'Muslims of all sects' based less on parochial structures and increasingly on opposition to occupation.[54]

A third version of culturalism focuses on the Taliban's 'irrationality.' Shah M. Tarzi claims that the lavish cultural difference between the US and the Taliban was shown in the failure of America's coercive diplomacy towards the regime before 9/11. The US was dealing not with a 'rational' state actor, but with people of 'deeply held fanatic, extremist fundamentalist belief system', impervious to persuasion because of their 'particular conception of messianic Jihadist and fatalistic struggle, the special role of Mullah Omar as *Amir-ul-Momineen* (defender of the faithful), and the Taliban ties to Bin Laden in combination of culture-bound code of honor of *Pushtunwali*.'[55] This is at odds with archival evidence that indicates the fluidity of Taliban statements about the issue, and the internal disagreement within the Taliban about its relationship with Bin Laden. In their private discussions with US envoys, Taliban officials were prepared to breach supposed strict rules of hospitality in pre-9/11 by entertaining the notion that Bin Laden be expelled. They also made contradictory claims about the relationship between Bin Ladin's network and Afghan society, saying either that the majority of Afghans and even 80% of officials disliked Osama Bin Laden and resented Mullah Omar's toleration of him, or that Pashtun traditions forbad Bin Ladin's expulsion and expelling Bin Laden would result in an uprising.[56] While this may indicate manipulative 'mixed messages', that in itself suggests that they were using cultural perception as a rhetorical tool, making different and contradictory claims about it as it suited them. This ambiguity undermines the argument that the Taliban are one-dimensional zealots, imprisoned within their culture of extremism and tribal honour. It also might reflect an internal policy debate, as one report stated: the Taliban Ambassador 'asked some questions as to how Bin Ladin would be treated should he be expelled to Saudi Arabia...it would appear that the Taliban are wrestling with the Bin Ladin issue and that their heretofore hard-line stance on this issue may be in some sort of flux.'[57] By focusing on the Taliban's supposed 'refusal' to surrender Bin Laden, Tarzi assumes that the Taliban in fact had the power to do so. The power relation between Bin Laden's forces and the Taliban was exactly the reverse—it was probably he who was propping them up, not the other way around. These nuances are lost with the narrow focus on extremist ideology.

Because of Afghanistan's forbidding geography, its recent history of Islamist warfare and its traditions of resistance to foreign rule, it is easy to overplay the Taliban's 'strangeness.' On the one hand, it is misleading to treat disparate 'Oriental' cultures as a family within an overarching, undifferentiated 'non-Western' way of war. Doing so might neglect the differences between them and the unpredictable and dynamic nature of war itself. At the same time, to mystify or mythologise the Oriental enemy as singular and almost beyond Western recognition can also be misleading. The Taliban have their idiosyncrasies, and the war has distinctive aspects. But if these are allowed for, the nature of the Taliban—and the conditions in which it can succeed or fail—can still be grasped historically within established strategic thinking about counter-insurgency.

The Taliban insurgency and the struggle against it are shaped by several dynamics that are arguably not peculiar, but widespread in insurgencies over time and space. Insurgency has been defined recently as 'a struggle for power (over a political space) between a state (or occupying power) and one or more organized, popularly based internal challengers.'[58] The generic elements of insurgency were noted by such theorists as French officer David Galula and British expert Robert Thompson. They include geographic conditions, support among the people at large, the direct or indirect aid of regular troops, longevity, military credibility, and the ability to develop an irregular force over time into a force that can capture and hold territory.[59] Historically, one of the critical elements in the survival and success of insurgencies is often external support. A survey of ninety-one insurgencies since 1945 by the RAND Corporation indicates a high correlation between external support and success.[60] Insurgencies sponsored from abroad, such as the Vietnamese Communists or Spanish guerrillas, have often been able to survive devastating losses. Those starved of external patronage, for example in Malaya and the Philippines, have not. In the case of the Taliban, sanctuary and a territorial base in Pakistan tribal areas have been fundamental in enabling it to survive continual military attrition and regroup. In addition, the Taliban benefit from America's reluctance to pursue them across the border, because of the destabilising impact of occupying the soil of a politically volatile ally.

The Taliban have also been able to replenish their manpower with what seems an inexhaustible supply of fresh recruits. This has been further supplemented by the flow of stateless transnational *jihadis* who offer expertise, money, weapons, and tactical innovation.

Several other, non-unique, historically recognisable developments have enabled the Taliban to fight back as a resurgent 'neo-Taliban.' First, there is the issue of economic welfare and civilian opinion. While substantial majorities of Afghans have continually expressed consent to the work of the international occupation, the war has inflicted enough economic distress to create a permanent supply of Taliban recruits. The anti-narcotics programme, in which the coalition is destroying opium fields, literally burns down Afghan livelihoods, and the Taliban promises to protect farmers from eradication campaigns, or coax them into illegal production and sale of opium.[61] Against dispossession and poverty, the Taliban offers a steady income. The narcotics dimension in this war also makes it comparable with past and present cases from Columbia to Kosovo to Lebanon where the drug trade has fuelled, financed and prolonged warfare, and complicated the counterinsurgents' pursuit of legitimacy.[62]

The Taliban are able to operate also because of the issue of sheer resources and their allocation, again with historical precedent. The Taliban's most powerful enemy, dedicating much of its manpower, spending and political capital to the war in Iraq, has not always given the Afghan war top priority. In June 2007, total American forces in Afghanistan were around 27,000, compared to a projected 155,000 in Iraq. Only six of thirty-seven NATO allies permit their troops to fight, and aid for reconstruction projects is relatively modest, amounting to US $57 per head compared to $679 in Bosnia.[63] This priority problem also has historic precedents. For example, the American revolutionaries in the War of Independence benefited from the fact that the British empire decided that the conflict was less important than its global war against the French and Spanish.

The Taliban, therefore, are partly explicable within the broad historic pattern of insurgencies. They also share some of the more contemporary features of today's breed of 'complex insurgency.' Now out of power, the Taliban operate as a 'coalition of the willing' with a loose command structure, a pluriform membership and small units. While this differentiates them from classic Maoist-style insurgencies with tighter control and top-down hierarchies, it suggests that they can be identified as part of a more generic, contemporary and fluid enemy coalescing around a body of ideas and a global deterritorialised network. This enemy continually improvises its techniques and forges new alliances in a 'bazaar of violence' and mobilizes around cyberspace as the new forum for rhetorical incitement and the electronic *levee en masse*.[64] Their struggle is part Afghan, conducted by locals for localized objectives, and part transnational, waged and shaped by foreign actors and forces.

So the Taliban and their war are explicable within familiar strategic concepts, both classical and more contemporary. And if we observe their behaviour in wartime, it is far less determined by culture than often assumed. As the following section argues, there is a pattern of cultural manoeuvrability in many of their operations.

Breakers of Tradition

The cultural differences between America and the Taliban could hardly seem starker. In government the Taliban preached and practised a *fossilised*, puritanical ideology. Yet when we observe the behaviour of the Taliban while at war, a different pattern emerges. As one American official wrote in 1985 of the *mujahidin* who fought the Soviets, they are 'not simply a group of xenophobic reactionaries engaged in a hopeless struggle.'[65] Their war is a practical war. They might cherish holy war as a struggle with a sacred meaning even in death and defeat, but their leadership also wants to win.

On a range of fronts, the Taliban have compromised their cultural codes for strategic success. Their stance on opium represents a significant shift. In 2000, Mullah Omar banned the production of opium and issued a *fatwa* against poppy cultivation. But because of the grievances and opportunities created by the American anti-narcotics programme, the Taliban have now repositioned themselves as defenders of the industry and the narco-state, thereby posing as the guardians of rural life. In Musa Qala, they relaxed restrictions on social behaviour to win the population over, rescinding their demands that men grow beards, and their ban on music and movies.[66]

Consider also one of the most violently contested issues that once divided the Taliban from their domestic and foreign opponents: public education. In power, the Taliban enforced rigid religious education for boys, and forbade girls' public education. Girls' schools only operated covertly. Thrown out of power, between 2001 and 2006, the Taliban targeted women's education in a campaign of terror. They threatened and assassinated teachers, and burnt or blew up schools. In 2006, they destroyed about 200 schools and killed 61 students and educators. Historically, the Taliban viewed education as a potential vehicle for subversive threats, such as women's emancipation, and a vehicle for liberal, secular and feminist influence.

Recently the Taliban have reversed their education policy. In reaction to their unpopularity in the south of Afghanistan, they have announced a new programme of school-building.[67] The Taliban announced on its website that it would open ten madrassa seminaries for boys in ten districts it controls in southern Afghanistan, and promised also to open schools for girls.[68] Instead of the narrow religious instruction that marked its years in power, the curriculum now includes geography, history, physics and chemistry. As the Taliban were renowned for their hostility to open scientific inquiry and liberal education, this suggests a willingness to sacrifice dogma for popularity.

This does not mean that the Taliban are ultimately sincere or committed in the long-term to changing their education policy. The textbooks they will use still assert Islamic fundamentalist principles, prescribing strict Sharia law. Neither does it mean that the offensive will necessarily succeed. Compared to the budget for the international education rebuilding programme, their initial fund of approximately $1 million is modest. But this new provision of a social service is an effort to win back Afghan support and reclaim legitimacy in those regions. And it places the Afghan government on the horns of a dilemma. Allowing the project to proceed will concede territory, influence and credibility to the Taliban. But attempting to shut down the Islamist schools as 'terrorist training centres' and attack them if they were opened, as the Education Minister Mohammed Hanif Atmar threatened to do, might harm the state's legitimacy. It might alienate the civilian population by recasting the state as the menace and denier of social services. Conversely, the Taliban positions itself as provider, not just predator.

Taliban rhetoric and official statements about the 'education offensive' are revealing. 'The Government controls the cities [in the targeted provinces] but we control the entire countryside, so there should be no problem running these schools,' said one spokesman.[69] In other words, the education offensive helps the Taliban project power and indicates the state's inability to control territory, especially in rural areas. It aims to establish the Taliban as localized patrons of social services, thereby challenging the federalist project of nation building. 'The Islamic Emirate of Afghanistan wishes to be prepared in all aspects for the defeat of its enemy.'[70] This statement points to a policy that is well known in the history of guerrilla warfare and insurgency, particularly in the history of wars of 'national liberation', of building up a parallel government, a virtual state with its own administrative apparatus and structure. Such a change in policy has a logic that would be identifiable in the recent US field manual on counterinsurgency, cultivating the population and working towards creating a political alternative to the existing state, a 'vision of a counterstate.'[71]

The Taliban's innovation in schooling parallels NATO's declared aims about how to conduct counterinsurgency. Just like its American-led enemies, the Taliban are trying to combine different lines of operation, political and economic policies with armed struggle, to achieve their strategic objectives. As Afghanistan expert Barnett Rubin notes, 'They recognize that Afghanistan has changed. The people desperately want their children to be educated, including girls in most cases, even in conservative tribal areas. The Taliban attacks on schools are very unpopular, and they are trying to win the hearts and minds of the people by showing they share their priorities.'[72] Because of the necessary compromises this entails, the Taliban's evolving strategy and shift in policy shows that it is responding the dynamics of an insurgency, rather than its own intrinsic cultural peculiarities.

Another stereotype which the Taliban themselves promote is that they are ultra-strict martyrs committed to death. 'We embraced death, we were willing to be martyrs' declared Ali Amjud, a veteran of the Soviet-Afghan war. And they do recruit zealots. But in wartime the Taliban are more subtle operators than their fanatic image suggests. They do not always behave as a death cult. It is symbolised by the story of Mullah Qahir, a Taliban commander who in November 2001 tried to avoid capture by trimming his beard, which had been a crime under the Taliban. Beards in their world symbolise masculinity. The Mullah's cultural identity as an Afghan fighter, literally growing from his face, proved less important than survival.[73] More broadly, the Taliban sometimes disagree with foreign fighters and their Arab allies about how to conduct combat and what 'rules of engagement' to follow. Consider the statement of 'Hamid', one *mujahid*, who believes that the value of martyrdom has its limits:

> Hamid said the Afghans and the Arabs have a common enemy, but don't necessarily like each other. He described the Arabs as firebrand Islamists who don't obey orders and are obsessed with martyrdom. 'They won't stop shooting even when they are told to. And they always write messages home before battle—they get ready to die. I know them well, and I don't like them; they just don't trust Afghans.'[74]

Ethnic tension, differences over authority and how to fight, and mutual distrust—the stuff of coalition warfare! There are also historic precedents where the Taliban have at times doubted the military effectiveness of foreign volunteers.[75] Before and during the invasion of 2001, the Taliban divided on critical questions. In the initial phases of 'Operation Enduring Freedom', the US government was highly aware of the fluidity of the Taliban/international jihadist alliance, as well as the actual and potential divisions both within the Taliban and between the Taliban and al Qaeda. As former Defence Secretary Donald Rumsfeld argued in his explanation for how to isolate al Qaeda, 'there are people in the Taliban who don't agree with Omar and they don't agree with...creating a hospitable environment for al Qaeda. And then there are people in [the Taliban] who do.'[76] Unfortunately, this political awareness of the differences within and among the Taliban has been overshadowed by more monolithic views.

The Taliban's internal debates and policy shifts indicate that their strategic culture is highly contested. In adapting to invasion, the Taliban have differed on both methods and values. Just as they once disagreed on whether to shelter Bin Laden, since 2001 they have debated whether to mount aggressive attacks or fight a 'war of the flea', bleeding the enemy over time.[77] And they have reshaped their view of suicide bombing, a method unknown to Afghanistan before 2001. Previously some Taliban argued that wearing an explosive vest was cowardly, as the insurgent should fight face-to-face, while others argued that it would alienate Afghan civilians. At one point, a Taliban faction placed an advertisement in a Kandahar newspaper promising to punish those responsible for a suicide bombing and blaming it on foreign fighters. But this has now changed, as the Taliban employ the more avowed *fedayeen* (those ready to sacrifice their lives) as suicide bombers, whom they call 'Mullah Omar's missiles.' This method of 'martyrdom operations' is a significant innovation. It violates the sentiments of Afghans, for whom suicide and suicide bombing are an affront to Islam. Taliban religious leaders developed a convenient re-interpretation of the Koran to justify this new tactic, bending sacred narratives to their will:

> Several of the insurgents said they couldn't remember the specific reference to Islamic holy texts used by their teachers to justify the idea, but some made reference to a story about a Muslim army that existed in the seventh century, during the lifetime of the prophet Mohammed.
>
> 'There is a story from the time of the prophet,' one insurgent said.
>
> 'There were two companions of the prophet, and...they were attacking a place [where] the walls were high, so they could not jump over the wall...One lifted the other over the wall and he died in the attack. He knew he would be killed, but it was his duty.'[78]

This is a classic instance of the mutability of culture. Mullahs act as authority figures, or keepers of strategic culture, find within their tradition a potent narrative, and instruct the mostly illiterate flock that the method befits Islamic martyrdom. And within the discourse of piety and tradition, there is a utilitarian justification: 'It is good to be used against the non-Muslims, because they are not afraid of fighting for five days against us but they are afraid of one bomber.'[79]

Like Hamas, Hizbolla and others, they turn to suicide bombing for strategic purposes. It is now possible to see patterns in Taliban-orchestrated suicide bombing from a recent Jamestown Foundation study.[80] Instead of being a liability in combat, these fighters are being directed towards a form of violence where their suicidal convictions are strategically more rewarding. 'I have come here for jihad, to drive the occupying U.S. and infidel forces from our Muslim country' declared one Pakistani from Peshawar. 'I want my body and bones to hit the U.S. Army.'[81] Suicide bombing, 'propaganda of the deed', is seen to deliver several benefits. It tempts international audiences to liken the war in Afghanistan with the invasion of Iraq. It deters reconstruction efforts. Domestically, as well as killing, it inflicts psychological distress at a disproportionate level, eroding Afghans' confidence in the government's ability to provide security and discrediting faith in the new state. And if carried out in Afghan cities, suicide bombing helps to separate the civilian population from military forces and their vehicles, who become preoccupied with force protection. It disrupts the military's ability to contact and cultivate the population by making them fear, warn and sometimes fire on civilians nearby. The Taliban's adoption of suicide bombing also demonstrates an openness to innovation flowing from the Iraq war. At the same time, while al-Qaeda style methods are increasingly apparent, some aims of the Taliban are different from Iraqi *jihadi* groups (such as Ansar al-Sunnah or 'Al Qaeda in Mesopotamia'), and they have customized these methods to suit their particular purposes. Iraqi groups aim to incite sectarian violence by inflicting indiscriminate carnage, attacking crowded markets or mosques. By contrast, the Taliban aims to discredit and demoralise the new Afghan state and the infidel occupiers while not losing 'hearts and minds', rather than create civil war among the population. Their bombers therefore target mostly 'hard' objectives, such as military convoys, government officials or police.

The pattern of their targets suggests that at least some Taliban leaders are aware of the potential strategic costs of collaterally killing civilians. In only eight out of 158 suicide attacks from 2001–2007 did civilians appear to be the direct targets, and in two of those incidents, the Taliban apologized for civilian casualties, while the others may have been unintended.[82] Taliban awareness of the political dangers of casualties among civilian bystanders has precedents among the *mujahidin* of the 1980's.[83] The dream of the suicide bomber may be paradise, but the intentions of the Taliban directing them are towards specific discriminate effects. To be sure, their evolving methods may prove ultimately counter-productive, as 84% of the victims have been civilians. But the evidence as a whole suggests that influential figures among the Taliban have been prepared to defy traditional 'culture' to adopt a new method, and have then sought to calibrate the method to suit their strategic objectives.

There are also other distinctions between the Taliban and foreign jihadists. The Taliban desire success primarily in their own particular localized war, whereas Al Qaeda supports a worldwide Islamic jihad with global objectives.[84] As their aims are not identical, there has been friction in the relationship between the two. For example, the Taliban had been split by bin Laden's declaration of war on the United States in August 1996, which some feared would turn a former ally into a powerful enemy.[85] More recently, the Taliban's relationship with elements of the Pakistan military-intelligence establishment has strained its relations with Al Qaeda. Al Qaeda reportedly will 'have nothing to do with the Islamabad government.' Al Qaeda sources now claim 'it is just a matter of time before the sides part physically as well.'[86]

Contrary to the one-dimensional image of the Taliban as single-minded martyrs, they are not just ideologues who fight. They orchestrate killings as well as participating in combat. They recruit people whose motivations are not always primarily ideological. A number of attacks against both coalition and Afghan forces have been carried out by hired civilian Pahstuns, economically needy people from unemployed youth to indebted farmers. Outside its core, it is not so much a fixed cabal of people but a political movement and coalition that expands and contracts. UK Regional Coordinator for Southern Afghanistan, Nick Kay, claims that 80% of the population of south Western Afghanistan are 'reconcilable' Taliban supporters, alienated by the government's inefficiency and corruption, as distinct from the 'ideologically committed' 20%.[87] The Taliban are better understood as a loose multilayered alliance, with an inner core of hardened believers, and broader concentric circles of foreign volunteers, then warlords, more flexible men who act as 'bargaining agents' between competing interests, and then an outer ring of economic recruits. The further from the inner ring, the more the movement fluctuates in size.

Because the Taliban operate as a 'coalition of the willing', they must struggle with the misbehaviour of some members, attempt to impose authority over subordinate commanders, and limit competition between Taliban groups. In late 2006, it emerged that the Taliban had issued a *Layeha*, a nine-page code of conduct, imposing twenty-nine rules on fighters' conduct. It forbids house raiding, theft of weapons, robbery of money or property. It bans 'vice' such as smoking and the participation of 'boys without beards' in the combat zone. It outlaws the ransoming of prisoners without authorization from a senior commander. And in an attempt to curb vigilante justice, it requires that spies only be punished after being tried in an Islamic court.[88]

This codex indicates that some combatants do not behave as strict Islamic warriors, as the Taliban would like. It also reflects the plurality of the Taliban, made up of fellow-travellers, criminals, opportunists and jihadists who succumb to the temptations of war. And it illustrates that as the Taliban and the US-coalition continue their war, they are responding in comparable ways to the logic of civilian alienation, by regulating the impact of operations on civilians, or in the Taliban's case, regulating the conduct of their soldiers. This should not be a surprise. It is reminiscent of a similar dynamic during the Afghan-Soviet war, where the predations of some groups and the participation of opportunists jeopardized the cause of the *mujahidin*, as one 1983 CIA agent reported.[89] As the US tries to refine its image, rules of engagement and relations with Afghans, so too do the Taliban.

But it is their evolving approach to technology that most reflects the Taliban's uneasy blend of traditionalism and improvisation. A movement renowned for its technophobia has evolved into one of the most media-savvy operators in modern warfare. In government, the Taliban both used and abhorred Western technology. Their religious police would search neighbourhoods to find and destroy radios, satellite dishes, computers and televisions, the instruments of depravity and unbelief. Paradoxically, they also developed their own website to preach their beliefs and advertise their regime.[90] At war, the Taliban have proven to be willing to break cultural taboos in the realm of the information battlespace. Thanks partly to the influence of one Taliban leader, Mullah Dadullah, the Taliban refined their policy. When this veteran military commander was killed in Helmand Province on 13 May 2007, the Taliban lost an innovator. The one-legged hero of the Taliban rank and file had fought against the Soviet invasion, then against the Northern Alliance, going on to become one of the most skilled and brutal Taliban commanders. He orchestrated kidnappings, suicide bombings and beheadings. But his main contribution to the Taliban cause was more profound. He was one of the first Taliban leaders to give interviews to the print and electronic media. With his satellite phone, he called journalists to pronounce on Taliban operations and threaten 'Afghan and foreign forces.' He also broke with the iconophobia of his comrades, consenting to be photographed when others refused for both spiritual and practical reasons.[91]

Following him, the Taliban have adjusted to the broadcasting power of modern media, developing a sophisticated ability to exploit information for strategic advantage. Within an hour of most incidents, they have prepared a statement about the event, indicating an agility that flies ahead of the multipolar international community, negotiating between the separate parties of the UN, Operation Enduring Freedom (OEF) and International Security Afghanistan (ISAF). While the Taliban make propagandist claims instantly, it takes weeks to complete independent verification of civilian losses.[92] Taliban information operations follow an annual cycle, the spring thaw that marks the new combat season, which brings an 'intelligence surge' by their enemies that the Taliban must counter. In late 2006 and early 2007, the Taliban escalated their 'information operations' into a media blitz. Mullah Dadullah appeared on a BBC interview, as did Ghul Agha Akhund and Mullah Hayatallah Khan, while the Taliban began recording executions of alleged 'spies' on video and posting them on the web. By late 2006, they had representatives in Iraq, to learn from Al Qaeda's video production arm, Al-Sahab.[93] Pakistani security officials claimed that by July 2005, a group of international *mujahedin* allied with the Taliban operated in Waziristan a 'sophisticated fully-computerised propaganda shop.'[94] Mimicking Western practices, by April 2007 they had an embedded journalist broadcasting a series for Al-Jazeera. From the vantage point of their faith, this is revolutionary, as the Taliban in government outlawed depictions of the human form, especially in modern media outlets, as evil. That the Taliban once abhorred 'image-making' as sinful is indicative that ancestral culture does not determine their strategy, or as Fred Burton argues, 'This is not your father's Taliban.'[95]

Equally ironic is the fact that this regime that once banned music and caused musicians to flee now enlists singers in its propaganda output, creating cassettes with songs praising the Taliban's martyrdom, denouncing infidels, and even taking on a style similar to American rap music.[96] This resort to music makes sense strategically, given that most of the Afghan population is illiterate. It is also helped by the expertise and experience flowing out of the propaganda war in Iraq. And it confirms not only that the Taliban are cultural entrepreneurs in wartime, but also that this technique is another case where a local conflict intersects with a globalised market of skills and styles. Simultaneously, in the Pakistani border areas, the Taliban have banned shaving and music. This suggests that they continue to avow a form of 'pure' Islamist politics where they believe it does not harm their strategic interests. But where taboos and strategy conflict, the dictates of the battlespace, including now the virtual battlespace, will shape the Taliban's decisions where they believe it will be to their advantage.

While often depicted as medieval, the Taliban's attitude to modernity and its instruments is actually ambivalent. Like modern fascism, it loathes modernity, but wants the benefits that its technology can deliver. Critical to this development is the distinction between 'Islamism' and 'fundamentalism,' charted by Olivier Roy. While the Pashtuns who were at the core of the Taliban in the 1990's were termed 'fundamentalists' for their attachment to custom and ritual, two forces are arguably transforming the 'neo-Taliban' from fundamentalists to Islamists: the Taliban-Al Qaeda alliance that bridges the two traditions, and the influx of young urbanised men from Pakistan for whom innovation and technology come naturally.[97] Paradoxically, an aggressively anti-modern movement exploits the tools of modernity.

At the same time, the evolving Taliban have found a global and receptive audience. One reason their propaganda operations can succeed is the willingness of the Western media to accept and broadcast Taliban claims. Not only do the Taliban harness media outlets, they also exploit audience perceptions and preconceptions. Put bluntly, they are prepared to spread misinformation and lies about civilian deaths and casualties, and their claims are often uncritically recycled. This reflects one of the more innocent versions of 'military Orientalism', where some Western observers who are ultra-sceptical of their own governments and militaries also see the eastern enemy and the eastern population as uniformly honest and simple. As Jonathan Foreman argues,

> It is one of the ironies of our time that members of the media are so hypersensitive to being used or manipulated by any official person from their own society—military officials, government spokesmen, etc—but can be as naïve as children when it comes to voices from other cultures...There is sometimes a strange, sentimental, inverted racism at work in this: Surely such simple, ardent, technologically unsophisticated people—like the mullah who speaks for the village, or the weeping mother who swears her slain son was a good boy and would *never* have shot at the soldiers—wouldn't tell *lies*? While there is no justification for reverting to Edwardian-era bigotry and assuming that all Orientals, especially South Asians, are compulsive liars, it would be equally wrong to assume the opposite or ignore the role of rumour and the likelihood of deceit in a place like Afghanistan.[98]

The image of the guileless enemy, unable to lie, is also rooted in some Western traditions of primitivism, which stress the original innocence of the 'noble savage.' The Taliban are not like this. They use human shields, occupy small towns to maximise the collateral civilian deaths caused by America and its allies, and rapidly contact the international media to blame civilian casualties on NATO. As Foreman argues, the Western media have at times credulously accepted Taliban claims about civilian deaths, without allowing for various Taliban methods of presenting all the dead as civilian innocents. These methods include threatening local civilians not to report their presence in an area, and 'sanitising' corpses by removing weapons from them so that they all appear as non-combatants. So in its more subtle forms, 'military Orientalism' could mean we lose sight of how the information we receive is filtered through Taliban manipulation. In an information war, this could help tilt the balance between success and failure.

Like the prospect of being hung at dawn, war focuses the mind, imposing a discipline of its own. Its pressures penalise culturally valued behaviour that does not deliver the goods, and drive even the most hardened reactionaries towards compromise and renegotiation with their own traditions.[99] In Clausewitz's metaphorical terms, war as a duel is competitive reciprocal activity where the stakes can be high. Like the international system, it demonstrates what behaviour fails or succeeds, showing that those who skilfully adapt to its demands generally do better than those who don't. Over time, the importance of 'internal differences across cultural boundaries' diminishes.[100]

Conclusion

The Taliban will be better understood once they are de-mystified. Agility, compromise and adaptation make them as rational as they are visceral. Their metamorphosis, from iconophobic puritans to drug-peddling media manipulators flirting with women's education, shows cultural realists at work. When America went to war against it, triumphalists and pessimists alike fell back on a broad cultural exoticism to fathom the conflict. But as they moved from government to war fighting, the Taliban turned out to be not so exotic after all. Though they were culturally rigid when in government, the discipline of war caused them to embrace pragmatism, strategically trading off and redefining their codes. This case study stands as a warning against turning culture from an influential variable into a dogma. If we do so, we risk forgetting the wildness of war, its ability to break loose from neat conceptual theories, and surprise us all over again.

6

THE DIVINE VICTORY

HIZBALLA, ISRAEL AND THE 2006 'JULY WAR'

When Heraclites claimed that 'war is the father of all things', he overstated his case. But in the history of Israel, war has been a major progenitor of its identity and that of its neighbours. The collective memory of fighting a war to defend one's existence can harden a sense of separateness. In turn, this can create delusions as well as wisdom. If a state feels surrounded by hostiles bent on its destruction, from Palestinian militants to Iranian theocrats, from Hamas to Hizballa, and if it believes rightly or wrongly that they are in league, and if it then believes that this is part of a global war, it runs the risk of misidentifying its enemies or confusing the warfare of one with the other. Shock can result. Most scholars would agree in the abstract that many ideas, leaders, and influences have shaped Arab warfare, and no singular military tradition or strategic culture unites people from Morocco to Syria. But within the Israel Defence Forces (IDF) in July 2006, there was a generic archetype of the 'Arab at war.' Instinctively, Israeli combatants had formed a strong set of expectations about how an Arab enemy would fight. And at higher levels of command and government, some key individuals were misled by a fictitious image of the enemy as a passive object, whose consciousness can be quickly altered by a show of force. In the July War of 2006, Israel discovered that these impressions were false. When Israel invaded Lebanon that summer to smash the paramilitary Shiite Hizballa movement, it met an enemy who fought differently and more effectively than expected. Caught off guard by the ground war, Israel also found that despite its military power, it could not shatter the enemy in an air war, and failed to dominate the propaganda war. Instead of being a helpless target discredited by Israel's onslaught, the enemy proved to be an active agent who adroitly exploited worldwide perception.

In this chapter, I examine these facets of the war. I argue that a generalised preconception of an Arab 'enemy' contributed to the problems that the IDF suffered. Israel's conflation of Palestinian with Hizballa warfare, and the notion of the enemy as a passive object, both cost Israel blood, treasure and prestige, from the broken terrain of southern Lebanon to the trial of global opinion. Those keen for polemics blaming one 'side' or the other will have to look elsewhere.[1] This chapter is not about blame, but about the capacity of the weak to surprise the strong, to overcome ethno-cultural fictions, and to fight back by crafting their own image.

The July War

If this was a 'small war', it had large ripples. It began on 12 July, when Israel invaded Lebanon after Hizballa kidnapped two IDF servicemen. Israel struck Lebanon with weeks of bombing and artillery barrages. Its invasion had the diplomatic and logistical backing of the United States and the UK. The munitions Israel rained down on Lebanon were from US suppliers, while Iran backed Hizballa with long-range rockets, missiles and possibly also personnel from the Iranian Islamic Revolutionary Guards Corps, and Russian anti-tank missiles from Syria.[2] Israeli air power failed to disarm or disable the guerrilla army. Even when hovering above launching areas and attacking targets daily, Israel's Air Force could not stop Hizballa's ability to fire rockets daily on northern Israel. Israel's cabinet then authorised an expanded ground invasion 25 kilometres into Lebanon on 9 August. After surprising levels of resistance, including at the border town and Hizballa stronghold of Bint Jbeil (known in the IDF as the 'terror capital'), the IDF attempted to control a narrow strip of land north of the Lebanon-Israel border. Military operations ended on 14 August, with United Nations Security Council Resolution 1701.

On the opening day of the war, Israeli chief of Staff Dan Halutz was full of confidence. After a squadron attacked Hizballa's long-range Zelzal rockets, he announced 'We've won the war' to Israeli Prime Minister Ehud Olmert. Halutz is an avowed believer in air power who had threatened to 'turn Lebanon's clock back twenty years.'[3] But this proved premature. A different kind of war unfolded over the following weeks. As the UN-brokered ceasefire began, it was clear that Israel's military actions had unintended political consequences. Hizballa's stealthy fighters had mounted a strong resistance to the Israeli army in southern Lebanon, and held off both a ferocious air campaign and a ground assault. Israeli infantry and armoured brigades invading southern Lebanon were surprised by the lethal performance of an enemy that was supposed to be wrecked within days. Despite the upbeat claim of the Israeli ambassador to Washington that Israel had made progress in destroying Hizballa's capabilities,[4] the war left the government of Israeli Prime Minister Ehud Olmert beleaguered. It shook Israel's security and pride in the region. Militants had fired constant rocket barrages into Israel and survived. Worse, they had forced an exodus of Israeli refugees.[5]

Intelligence failures were made by both parties. As will be shown in greater detail, Israel had underestimated its enemies' capacity to create an effective defence and shape the image of the war, even as its main ally the United States had recently overestimated the apocalyptic arsenal of Saddam Hussein. Hizballa's leader, the charismatic Shaikh Hassan Nasrallah, underestimated Israeli will. He confessed that he was surprised by Israel's invasion. Nevertheless, Hizballa claimed a 'Divine Victory.' That same slogan, as well as 'Victory from God', appeared on new billboards at Beirut International Airport. Nasrallah mocked Israel by flaunting the body parts of Israeli soldiers during a speech in Beirut.[6] Hizballa killed 116 Israeli soldiers and 43 civilians and was still firing rockets on northern Israeli settlements, towns and cities after the ceasefire began, on the final day launching a record 246 rockets against its hated neighbour.[7] As a result of Hizballa's survival, the war politically strengthened it, leaving its power and stature unbroken in Lebanon. It also weakened Lebanon's Siniora government. In late 2006, Lebanese Cabinet ministers were hiding in state buildings as protesters demanded a new government.[8] The war battered the mystique of Israel's military deterrent power, with large sections of the IDF looking mediocre. After the conflict, Syrian President Bashar al-Assad warned that he might retake the Golan Heights, and Iran threatened to fire ballistic missiles at Tel Aviv in response to any American attack. The war also impeded any chance of a settlement with the Palestinian Authority.

Both sides portrayed the other as the aggressor against the innocent. Israel successfully destroyed many of Hizballa's long-range missiles and claimed to kill 530 of its fighters, roughly a quarter. Israel also killed at least 1,000 Lebanese, mostly civilians.[9] Its bombing campaign against Hizballa's nerve centre and headquarters in the suburbs of southern Beirut left the wreckage of thousands of buildings and multi-storey tenements. This prompted demonstrations and condemnations throughout the world. While both sides had violated the principles of discrimination and proportionality, the balance of global opinion had tilted against Israel.

How had this happened? Israel's aims ranged from the local to the regional. Its core strategic objectives were to return two abducted soldiers to Israel, halt the firing of Katyusha rockets against Israeli communities, dismantle or distance Hizballa's rocket arsenal, to show the costs to the Lebanese government of allowing Hizballa to operate freely from its soil, to create a zone purged of Hizballa forces that Lebanese or international forces could then occupy, and to restore its flagging power of deterrence.[10] But government spokesmen quickly announced more ambitious war aims, including turning Lebanese mainstream opinion against the militants, the complete disarmament or destruction of Hizballa, to alter political conditions by creating a process that would give the Lebanese army a monopoly over force, or as Brigadier-General Shimon Naveh argues, to force Hizballa to abandon being a military organisation and become wholly 'political.'[11] From the beginning, Israel set down strategic aims that outstripped its military means. In response, Hizballa's Shaikh Hassan Nasrallah claimed that survival would be victory. He set a realistic goal, to pose as the vanguard of a Lebanese national resistance, who withstood Israel's coercion.

Israel's war has met sustained internal criticism. Majority opinion is disappointed with the outcome, from the general population to the forty inquiry teams appointed by the IDF Chief of Staff Lieutenant General Dan Halutz, who resigned in January 2007, to the Winograd Commission created by the government to investigate the war.[12] Israeli intelligence and the US Defence Intelligence Agency concur that Hizballa is re-armed and active.[13] Many reasons for Israel's failure have been identified, and most have little to do with debates about Orientalism and cultural perception.[14] At the strategic level, they include a lack of realistic objectives, a utopian and unrealistic vision of air power based on false inferences from the 1999 Kosovo war, a failure to integrate air and ground operations into a political strategy, a lopsided and failed civilian-military relationship, and too much or too little caution; at the operational and tactical levels, the lack of consistent orders and mission objectives, a labyrinthine, obscure and flawed military doctrine driven by retired Brigadier General Shimon Naveh; failure to orchestrate air and land forces, and a lack of concentrated effort, initiative and persistence; a failure to assign specific objectives, poor and insufficient equipment and logistical supplies, a reliance on ill-trained reservists, and the lack of a robust armour protection system. Defeat is an orphan.

The broad military 'lessons' of the war are debatable and still being contested, will be for some time, and are inflected by politics. While some argue that the war reveals the limitations of military force, hawks insist that Israel erred by over-limiting its war and missing an opportunity to strengthen its hand in the region and in Washington.[15] Putting this aside, it is argued that two specific assumptions contributed to the crisis: an undifferentiated view of Arab warfare, and a false confidence that through impressive force, Israel could control images, manipulate Lebanese and world opinion, and humiliate its opponent.

Israelis and Arabs at War

It would be arbitrary to classify this conflict, or indeed any war, as a simple 'East/West' clash. The cultural identities of Israel and Lebanon are complex. Lebanon has a sizeable Christian population and a strong association with the Roman Catholic Church. Israel was militarily birthed in an uprising against Britain, was formed partly on the premise that Jews are not safe in Christian Europe, and now has over a million Arab citizens and émigrés from all over the world. Its identity was shaped both by Mizrahi Jews and émigrés from Europe, Russia and North America. Israel still closely identifies with the West (however paradoxical that may seem from centuries of Christian persecution of Jews), and particularly with the US.

Despite this cultural complexity, the July War *restaged* the ideas of both Orientalism and Occidentalism, and reproduced the rhetoric of a bipolar cultural conflict between Israel and Hizballa as proxies for a cosmic struggle: between liberal civilization and religious extremism, between conventional armies and terrorist-insurgents, or between Western imperialism and national resistance. Israel and Lebanon cut across cultural arbitrary East/West boundaries. But Israel's war extended beyond Hizballa to Lebanon itself. Israel also escalated its confrontation with Palestinians in Gaza at the same time. As Hew Strachan notes, 'Two separable conflicts, waged at opposite ends of the Israeli state, were conflated into one existential crisis.'[16] Hizbulla's war was directed at Israeli civilians as well as its declared enemy, the Zionist regime. With Washington extending its support to Israel, and Tehran to Hizballa, the war had international dimensions that accentuated the rhetoric of 'culture clash.' Israel Opposition leader Benjamin Netanyahu framed the war as part of America's struggle against a global terror network.[17] An Israeli foreign ministry spokesman defined the war as a blow to 'all extremist jihadist forces in the region.' Speaking before the Knesset years later, President Bush identified Israel and America as amongst the most ardent defenders of liberty, and associated Hizballa with the eliminationist charter of Hamas and Bin Laden's call to kill Americans and Jews.[18] Iranian President Ahmadinejad defined the war as an American crusade via the Zionist regime to plunder the Middle East.[19] The rhetoric of the war was shot through with Occidentalist and Orientalist terms, from the grasping imperialist West to the barbaric East.

Indeed, the Arab-Israeli wars, like the July War, served as a focal point for the very debate over Israel's identity and legitimacy. Through Israel's wars, the state has been called everything from bulwark of liberal civilisation, to flawed democracy, to Zionist empire, ruling occupied territories as a police state, or as the tail, or dog, of American hegemony, the beacon of democracy in an autocratic region, or a doomed equivalent of a crusader state. As a society, its identity has derived from its collective memory of existential threat in wars with both Arab states and stateless Palestinians. Yom Kippur, in Israel the Day of Atonement and the most solemn occasion in the calendar, is also the anniversary of the 1973 war, a national holiday in Egypt and Syria. A 'frontier' state on the east of the Mediterranean, Israel's wars were and are a critical front in the rhetoric of the defence of the West.

Israel's wars with Arabs are also central to debates about the relationship between regime type and military performance. In war studies, a few scholarly observers even approach Arabs as a collective group. Historian, former CIA analyst and Middle East expert Kenneth Pollack argued in *Arabs at War* that common cultural traits explain the frequent operational failure of Arab armed forces in the modern age, particularly when they battle Israel. He claims that deference to authority, as well as a fixation with honour and shame, have created an inflexibility which is a handicap in the world of high tempo manoeuvre warfare, an ineptitude with weapons systems, and a tendency of frontline commanders lying to their superiors about ground realities in order to save face.[20] Pollack's is probably the most sophisticated of a range of metacultural approaches that argue for an 'Arab' strategic culture, and that link Arab military failure to its perceived cultural eccentricities.[21] The very concept of an Arab way of war or culture of repeated failure ('Why Arabs Lose Wars'), an idea still alive within strategic studies, needs further thinking. These recent studies focus narrowly on the fate of Arab states in the postcolonial period, whereas a more comprehensive coverage would include successful Arab guerrillas and insurgents, and might even start with the medieval Muslim conquests.

While the literature on Israeli military culture is rich and diverse, Israel is at the centre of questions about the relationship between democracy and military success. It is a prime case for democratic triumphalists, who insist that liberal democracies fight more effectively, and that regime type and cultural norms are critical to military performance.[22] Yigal Allon, commander of the Palmach, claimed that Israel's military proficiency was rooted in its democratic political culture:

> To be a political and social democracy in the midst of backwards, patriarchal, autocratic or dictatorial regimes was by itself an advantage.... The political history of the Middle East has shown that a genuine democracy such as Israel's could command the loyalty of its citizens as the regimes of the Arab countries had never been able to do. It guaranteed (to begin with) their fullest mobilization, both physical and moral, in times of national crisis; it enabled Israel to give arms to each and everyone of her citizens; and it ensured the qualitative superiority of her fighting forces, expressed in their fighting moral, in the qualities of leadership at all levels, and in the efficient use of military equipment. It was conducive to more stable government, and to a greater sense of unity and common purpose. It ensured a conspicuously higher level of government culture and education, of scientific and technological know-how, of basic physical health.[23]

The same fixation with regime type can also be interpreted negatively. Some 'democratic defeatists', elites and policymakers, argue that Israeli democracy leaves it vulnerable to casualty sensitivity, and that its societal strength and stamina have waned.[24] This belief that the population is exceptionally sensitive to loss has exerted a broad influence on governments from Bill Clinton to Ehud Olmert. Yet a body of empirical research in both Israel and the United States suggests this presumption of exceptional public sensitivity is false.

While this debate continues, it remains significant that powerful democracies still entertain anxieties about the relationship between political values and wartime resilience. Where such states suffer adversity and surprise in lesser wars against enemies presumed to be weak, they undergo fresh self-scrutiny. So a war that Israeli leaders launched to alter political realities in Lebanon instead revived familiar questions about Israel's own viability and existence. In the July War, Hizballa turned the logic of democratic triumphalism upside down. It surprised Israel with its tenacity, agility and modernity. As Mossad agent and strategist Yossi Alpher observed, Hizballa 'may be the best Arab troops we've ever faced.'[25] The statistics for its performance relative to others is impressive. Hizballa inflicted more Israeli casualties per Arab fighter than any of Israel's state opponents in the wars of 1982, 1973, 1967 or 1956.[26] This showed that the relationship between military effectiveness and political values is not straightforward. In many ways, Hizballa resists the binary divide between Western/Israeli/sophisticated and Eastern/Arab/primitive, and goes against popular but false antitheses. Hizballa, 'the Party of God', is a political movement and a Shiite social organisation, with 'Islamic Resistance' forming its military arm. It grew out of Israel's eighteen-year occupation of Lebanon, from 1982 to 2000. It has evolved into a hybrid movement, part welfare provider, part warfighting outfit. Branded simplistically as a 'guerrilla' force, it also has weapons normally associated with states. Organised in authoritarian fashion, it also participates in Lebanese parliamentary elections. Neither pure guerrilla nor conventional force, it can hide in the wilderness or among the civilian population, but also possesses territory and can select and hold urban ground. It combines rhetorical colourful-rhetoric[27] with cutting-edge military technology and expertise and an ability to operate as an agile force, organising its combatants in a complex 'network' structure, ordering its fighting forces into amorphous, decentralised units. As one observer notes, 'the organization's violence has often been considered to be random in nature, either against the West or against Israel. On the contrary, there are well-defined mechanisms and reasons why Hizballa turns on and off the violence, most often in alignment with changes in its environment or in alignment with carefully calibrated strategies.'[28] While in this instance Israel reacted more aggressively than Hizballa reckoned, Hizballa was still prepared to fight on its terms. Hizballa typify what may be a future trend, the return to a fusion of different modes of war.[29]

Does Israeli military excellence come from its cultural/political roots, as democratic triumphalists argue? This theory may have some validity, but it is highly contextual. It is based upon the selection of its conventional, short wars against coalitions of more numerous enemies. These are the wars of 1956, 1967 and 1973 which for Israel were struggles of survival. They sustained the population's motivation and consensus, and involved open direct battles where the IDF's famed initiative, aggression and speed could be lethally and effectively applied.[30] However, similar 'cherry-picking' of history could also make the case for particular Arab fighting effectiveness when it comes to unconventional wars of attrition over long periods, whether in the Arab Revolt against the Ottoman Turks (1916–1918), the Algerian insurgency between 1954 and 1962, or the 1982 Lebanon War. By widening the frame beyond state armies of the postcolonial era, and including historical moments of Arab fighting power, the picture changes significantly.

In diagnosing the war of 2006, some commentators blame Israel's inattention to culture as a reason for its failure. To Adam Garfinkle, Israeli leaders were blind to the idiosyncrasies of Muslim countries and to the tenacity of Hizballa fighters because 'they could not take seriously the possibility that an entire society in southern Lebanon could really assume the mentality of a death cult.'[31] Yet Lebanon's broader population did not respond to the invasion as a 'death cult', but like many other civilian peoples faced with an unexpected onslaught by air, land and sea; they united against the aggressor.

The problem for the IDF was not that it disregarded culture, but that it presumed the existence of a 'universal Arab' that it could bend to its will. Seeing warfare of disparate peoples in different times through the prism of an 'Arab way of war', Israeli forces shared the same mindset that confuses one Arab society for another. At a visceral level, it is one of the conceptual errors that led the IDF into a trap in 2006.

Great Expectations, Tough Surprises

For Israeli decision-makers, observers and fighters alike, the dominant experience of the July War was one of shock. The military operation did not have its desired effects and nor did the enemy behave according to the script. When Israel invaded in 1982, it took only two days to get within ten miles of Beirut. But in 2006, they were stalled, ambushed and surprised by a carefully prepared battlefield of 'kill zones', with booby traps, observation posts, fortified defenders, stockpiled arms and subterranean tunnels and bunkers.[32] By August, wounded soldiers reported that there would be tough fighting that could last weeks, in contrast to the 'swift and decisive victory many of them expected when the fighting began.'[33] As one anonymous soldier sardonically quipped, his enemies 'had never heard that an Arab soldier is supposed to run away after a short engagement with the Israelis.'[34] Political columnist Ari Shavit typified the anxiety that can be triggered when a dominant power is surprised by the calibre of a 'small death army' (though how this distinguishes Hizballa from any other effective army he did not explain):

> ...more than they surprised us in Summer 2006 with the strength of Hezbollah, they surprised us this summer with our own weakness. They surprised us with ourselves. They surprised us with the low level of national leadership. They surprised us with scandalous strategic bumbling. They surprised us with the lack of vision, lack of creativity and lack of determination on the part of the senior military command. They surprised us with faulty intelligence and a delusionary [sic] logistical network and improper preparedness for war. They surprised us with the fact that the Israeli war machine is not what it once was. While we were celebrating it became rusty...Israel tried with all its soul and all its might to be Athens. However in this place, in this era, there is no future for an Athens without a speck of Sparta. There is no hope for a society-of-life that does not know how to organize itself to deal with death.[35]

Here, military fear entails existential and moral fear, and forms a kind of pessimist Orientalism, where the enemy is a mere barometer of Israeli strength or weakness. But for the IDF, the main difficulty was not the lack of a 'Spartan' element, with the state's reliance on strength and contempt for the enemy. Rather, it was the lack of 'Athenian' judgement, with the capacity to discriminate and differentiate between enemies, which led to the shock. And by apportioning most blame to Israel, Shavit gives agency to Israel, presenting a passive *East* and giving the enemy little credit for the outcome. This approach primarily blames Israel for defeating itself, militarily and culturally, rather than according the enemy a leading role in inflicting defeat.

The IDF was surprised at Hizballa's level of preparation, technical expertise and operational sophistication. Intelligence failure happened at many levels. Hizballa had spent the six years after Israeli withdrawal dispersing about 12,000 rockets across southern Lebanon in a web of hidden caches, all divided into local zones with independent command. They accessed the weapons only at the moment of attack, before disappearing. This made forestalling their attacks difficult. Hizballa's capabilities in electronic warfare had also not been appreciated. Israel's General Staff officers believed that they had disrupted Hassan Nasrallah's communications system from his Beirut bunker to his frontline command posts. Yet despite Israel's interdiction strikes, Hizballa remained in contact with its ground commanders.[36] Hizballa's considerable propagandist victories and the mobilising speeches of Shaikh Hassan Nasrallah were also possible because of technical expertise, as its television station 'al-Manar' was able to continue broadcasting from hidden studios, even as Israeli blasted antennas and relay towers.

Hizballa also defied the stereotype of the classical guerrilla. It is often assumed that irregular, 'asymmetric' forces rely on dispersion, concealment, hit-and-run methods, are primitively armed, and use terrain to inflict casualties rather than to control it, and melt away when attacked by superior conventional forces. But as Stephen Biddle and Jeffrey Friedman show with their taxonomy of military behaviour, this can be a fictitious ideal-type on the fringe of the spectrum, and is an inaccurate portrait of Hizballa.[37] Like most actors, Hizballa fell somewhere between popular conceptions of conventional and guerrilla modes, between the extremes of the Viet Cong and the Maginot Line. It was a hybrid force that had mastered techniques of hedgehog defence, and fought to hold territory rather than purely population-centric methods. It put too much emphasis on holding ground and concentrated force to be a classical guerrilla army, and put too much emphasis on coercion and harassing fires to be conventional. And thanks to the globalized arms market, and thanks to the support of its armourer Iran, Hizballa had acquired technology that was once almost monopolised by the US military, such as global positioning devices and night-vision goggles, as well as unmanned aerial vehicles.[38] On 14 July, two days into the war, it almost sank an Israeli warship with a Chinese C-802 missile.

The under-estimation of Hizballa also occurred at ground level. As diverse statements suggest, many Israeli combatants expected that religious fanatics could not also be technically advanced. Despite foreknowledge higher up the chain of command, they had not been forewarned of intelligence about the underground network of caves and bunkers filled with missiles.[39] 'We expected a tent and three Kalashnikovs—that was the intelligence we were given. Instead, we found a hydraulic steel door leading to a well-equipped network of tunnels.'[40] Hizballa also gained intelligence from Israeli reservists talking on personal mobile phones. Hizballa had acquired a list of phone numbers of Israeli commanders. Despite strict orders not to divulge sensitive information over the phone, they talked anyway, possibly assuming Hizballa would never be sophisticated enough to intercept their calls. Using eavesdropping technology supplied by Iran, Hizballa guerrillas hacked into Israel's advanced radio communications system, overcoming its 'frequency hopping' and encryption defences. This gave them a picture of Israeli supply routes, movements and casualty reports, thereby enabling them to anticipate the approach of Israeli armour. It also allowed Hizballa to obtain and exploit reports of Israeli casualties, broadcasting these fatalities on Al-Manar TV almost immediately, thereby dominating the media war.[41] The complacency with which Israeli troops chatted publicly about the details of the war stood in great contrast to the strict secrecy observed by Hizballa.

The clear impression from this pattern is that without explicitly saying so, Israeli forces did not reckon on Hizballa ever being so sophisticated. Why?

Great Expectations

It would be unfair to accuse all Israeli observers of a complacent, Orientalist mentality. Ever since the IDF withdrew from South Lebanon in May 2000, its intelligence services had observed Hizballa's movements and preparations very closely. Its dossiers documented Hizballa's subterranean networks and bunkers. Israeli officials, and chiefs of staff Lt. Gen. Shaul Mofaz and Lt. Gen. Moshe Yaalon, increasingly regarded Hizballa as a strategic threat.[42] Israel as a state could not be accused of failing in its efforts to gather information and 'know the enemy.' But before and during the war, this information was not provided quickly enough to tactical commanders.[43] Thanks to this poor communication, the IDF entered the field mentally unprepared. Moreover, while Hizballa's missile capability and its threat to northern Israel were taken seriously, its capacity to mount a defensive war under invasion was not as strongly appreciated. This was due partly to high politics. Under the premiership of Ariel Sharon, who was blamed for the 1982 Lebanon war, there had been a reluctance to plan for operations inside Lebanon. From a systemic failure, errors of judgement flowed. Without sufficient information, the IDF fell back on its assumptions about how an Arab enemy would behave.

For the IDF of 2006 and those who filled its ranks, it was the fight against Palestinian irregulars and the policing of the Occupied Territories that was the most influential template for fighting Arab opponents. This had practical results, as it left many combatants without sufficient training to meet the kind of warfare they stumbled upon in 2006. As a reserve soldier explained, 'For the last six years we were engaged in stupid policing missions in the West Bank...Checkpoints, hunting stone-throwing Palestinian children, that kind of stuff. The result was that we were not ready to confront real fighters like Hizballa.' This combination of overconfidence, a narrow experience dominated by counter-insurgency, and false expectations was observed also by Brigadier Shimon Naveh: '...the IDF fell in love with what it was doing with the Palestinians. In fact it became addictive. You know when you fight a war against a rival who's by all means inferior to you, you may lose a guy here or there, but you're in total control. It's nice, you can pretend that you fight the war and yet it's not really a dangerous war.'[44] Debriefing teams have likewise concluded that combat in the West Bank made the IDF overconfident.[45] Because the typical mission for Israeli infantry troops from the south or from Palestinian territories between 2000 and 2006 was to seize a wanted Palestinian fighter or guard a checkpoint, one IDF general complained that 'they weren't trained...There was a big difference between the units who came from the south and those who came from the north.'[46] For example, as they occupied urban areas to combat Hizballa fighters, the IDF had not reckoned on the ability of Hizballa fighters to penetrate such shelters. As a senior IDF source observed, 'What is suitable when you are fighting a poorly equipped enemy like the Palestinians is clearly insufficient when facing a well-trained, well-equipped organisation like Hizballa.'[47] The false confidence drawn from combat with Palestinian fighters can also be traced back to the campaign against the PLO that Israel fought in 1982 in Lebanon, where Israeli intelligence had extensively penetrated its enemies' ranks, enabling Israeli forces to advance far more rapidly. According to Professor Fawaz Trabulsi, a veteran of the 1982 conflict, 'Israeli officers seemed to think they could duplicate that performance against Hizballa.'[48] The experience of fighting Palestinians thus had intellectual results. The recent bodyblows Israel inflicted on Hamas militants left an image of a dramatically weaker opponent who could be overwhelmed and who fought as a beleaguered guerrilla.

Psywar and Self-Portraits: the Propaganda War

This was a war about perception as well as concrete outcomes. Both Israeli Prime Minister Olmert and Shaikh Nasrallah enunciated a theory of victory, and both declared that they had triumphed. Because the results of this war were inconclusive, and because there was no neat outcome with a clear winner, the battle over image became central. In terms of material damage, Israel managed to destroy most of Hizballa's strategic missile arsenal and many rocket launcher sites. But for Hizballa, endurance enabled it to pose as a victor and liberator. A campaign waged to isolate and weaken the image of Hizballa ended up breathing new life into the movement, so that in the eyes of the world, Hizballa was identified with Lebanon's suffering. This is particularly significant, as Hizballa has never been purely a Lebanese movement. While it insists on its own independence, it has always been part of a wider Syrian-Iranian relationship, and looks to present itself within the confessional makeup of Lebanon as a national force.[49] The July War, therefore, gave it a rare opportunity to re-indigenise its image.

Israel did not only enter the war confident in its military capability. It also began hostilities convinced that it could predict and control the psychological and cognitive effects of force. With its supreme military power, it could 'send a message.' In this theory, air power could coerce, persuade and awe the Lebanese state into disowning Hizballa. Israel's attacks could pressure the Lebanese government to disarm Hizballa and secure the southern border. Even more ambitiously, as current and former army officers reported, the Israeli government and the IDF hoped that the experience of bombardment would turn the Lebanese people against Hizballa, generating a 'local political reaction to Hizballah's adventurism.'[50] This faith in psychologically-directed violence was central to Israeli doctrine. It had been developed by the IDF Institute for Campaign Doctrine Studies under the aegis of former Chief of Staff Lieutenant General Moshe Ya'alon. Instead of destroying the enemy, this 'effects-based' approach seeks primarily to inflict 'physical and cognitive' distress. Dan Halutz, Israel's chief of staff, had a particular faith in the capacity of strategic bombing and standoff fire, with ground forces only as a last resort, to shape the mentality not only of Hizballa, but the Lebanese population, while avoiding the need for a ground war. In 2001, he argued that 'we also have to part with the concept of a land battle...Victory is a matter of consciousness. Airpower affects the adversary's consciousness significantly.'[51] There was little in his vision about the limitations around air power. Insurgents and terrorists seldom present themselves as lucrative targets for aerial attack. Air power is used to positive effect only indirectly in these types of campaigns, to gather intelligence, shift troops or maintain communication.[52]

To support Halutz's effort, the Israeli Army reactivated its Psychological Warfare Unit. It dropped more than 17 million leaflets over Lebanon. These depicted Sheik Nasrallah as the culprit for the devastation of the war, whether as a scorpion or snake plunging Lebanon into ruin, a coward using civilians as a human shield, or walking off a cliff dragging the symbolic cedar with him.[53] Additionally, Israel sent phone messages to Lebanese civilians, attempting to influence them to blame Nasrallah and dissociate themselves from him:

> Oh Lebanese people, we tell you not to follow Hezbollah. We will continue to strike and no one will bring your prisoners back from Israel except the Lebanese government.
>
> Hassan, have you realised yet that the Israeli army is not as delicate as a spider's web? It's a web of steel that will strangle you!
>
> This is the state of Israel. This resistance...is forcing you to stay at home like rats.
>
> Who is it that's putting your life in danger? Who is using you as human shields?
>
> We don't want to harm you. We're bombing the infrastructure so Hezbollah will have no means of firing its rockets.
>
> We know you wanted to hit Israel, but you have confronted a house made of steel. This is the Israel Defence Force.[54]

This message was part of an overall 'punishment' strategy against both the government of Lebanon and the people of southern Beirut, to raise the costs of supporting Hizballa and alienate Lebanese opinion from the movement that had brought on the war. The punishment was supposed to weaken Hizballa's support base by indicating that Lebanon's suffering was Hizballa's doing. Here was a view of the benefits of escalation. Changing the 'consciousness' of the Lebanese government or society was linked to a military doctrine of retaliating 'in a multiple of the force of the original enemy attack' in response to asymmetrical attacks.[55]

This theory presumed a passive target on the receiving end. It made little allowance for an enemy who could mediate the psychological effects of strategic bombing with its own narrative of the event. It also presumed, against much evidence to the contrary, that the victims of bombing would blame their own internal radicals, rather than the people doing the bombing. Israel neglected an important pattern of air-power history. Although powers conducting bombing raids may wish to coerce a population psychologically and politically into rejecting its own government, this is often not the main effect of the punishment. Despite these intentions, civilians historically have perceived the bomber as the prime aggressor. Punishment creates more public anger towards the assailant than against the 'target government.' And any feelings of hostility or resentment towards the domestic government generated by strategic bombing are overshadowed by the survival instinct for personal safety. Bombing campaigns are more likely to induce political apathy than political subversion.[56]

The gap was wide indeed between the intended and actual results of coercive effects air strikes and punishment strategy. Air raids intended to turn 'domestic anger on Hizballa and force it to back down. Instead, the anger was focused on Israel, which responded by ratcheting up its campaign step by step.'[57] The more the Lebanese responded negatively to bombardment, the more Israel escalated the violence. While it surprised Israel's armoured columns, Hizballah also enjoyed greater dominance in the propaganda war. The world audience saw

> homes and villages destroyed during bombing runs, old people wandering aimlessly through the debris, some tailed by children hugging tattered dolls, Israeli airplanes attacking Beirut airport, Hezbollah rockets striking northern Israel and Haifa—all conveyed live as though the world had a front row seat on the blood and gore of modern warfare.[58]

Through the battle of perception, Hizballah dominated the strategic dimension of the war.

As well as mistaking the enemy for a yielding, passive target, Israel's psychological war also presupposed the existence of a neutral world audience. In contrast, Hizballa was able to mobilise and receive the political support of the international media, and by manipulating images, attract a partisan body of opinion. Some of the photographs and television footage of Israeli atrocities was fraudulent, such as a live civilian who posed as dead, and a child's body that was paraded around bomb sites for photo opportunities. Reuters news agency later admitted that its photographer had used Photoshop to add additional smoke to a shot of downtown Beirut following an air strike on the city, thereby intensifying the image of destruction.[59] Not only was Hizballa prepared to outmanoeuvre Israel in the 'information battlespace', it also benefited from well-placed shapers of opinion, predisposed to reinforce their message.

Nevertheless, the war did inflict real, tangible damage on Lebanese society. Israel claimed that it was conducting the bombing campaign with restraint, while Hizballa claimed that Israel's onslaught was indiscriminate butchery. The truth was somewhere in the middle. Israel avoided the targeting of water-related targets. Despite claims to the contrary, it did not deliberately attack hospitals, mosques or schools. And Hizballa could confidently fortify themselves in urban areas precisely because they knew of the Israeli army's reluctance to kill or wound high numbers of civilians. But Israeli air attacks did gratuitously strike other civilian buildings and homes. It justified this by blaming Hizballa's method of using Lebanese civilians as a shield, and that it had little choice in going after Hizballa structures, rocket launcher sites, and other military objects. On the other hand, Israel also repeatedly attacked ambulances and used land mines and cluster bombs that continued to take civilian lives after hostilities ended.

For the Lebanese victims, the Israeli effort to blame Hizballa was futile. By the time Hizballa had finished with its propaganda effort, Israel's campaign was received as excessive, imprecise and illegitimate. To develop its propaganda campaign, Hizballa has turned to mass marketing techniques, hiring Beirut advertising agency, Idea Creation.[60] Hizballa then capitalised on Israel's 'collateral' destruction with its welfare-reconstruction arm, *Jihad al-Binaa* or 'The Holy Struggle Construction Foundation', undertaking rebuilding efforts quickly after the war and sending its engineers and architects across the country to survey the damage and provide grants to civilian victims, vowing to complete repairs on damaged homes in three months and to replace destroyed homes within a year, an enterprise bankrolled largely by Iran.[61] Such efforts paralleled Hizballa's 'Martyr's Institute', which provides living stipends and education funding for families of dead combatants. They also mirror past efforts, as in 1988–1991, when Hizballa restored over 1,000 homes damaged by Israeli attacks. These welfare provisions enable Hizballa to portray itself as the humanitarian and nationalist protector and provider of the Lebanese people, and indeed as an alternative state within a state.

In sum, Israel's bombing reinforced rather than discredited two of Hizballa's claims: that Israel was attacking Lebanon as a whole, and that Hizballa was the core of Lebanese resistance. This highlights an issue that arises persistently in studies of Orientalism. Weaker parties, like the Sikhs under British rule or the Egyptians under Napoleon, may still be capable of effecting and shaping their image and identity even while subordinate.[62] In this way, the image of the Orient can also be a self-portrait. This becomes particularly significant in a war that is supposed to be directed at cognitive and psychological effects and political consciousness, rather than outright physical collapse.

Making Culture Local

The cultural turn often conflates two things: the need to appreciate the role of culture, and the assertion that there are transnational 'ways of war', such as 'Arab' or 'Western.' But this case study suggests that the two ideas can be contradictory, and need to be decoupled. The differences were dramatic between combating Palestinian irregulars and Lebanon's Hizballa. Hizballa, in fact, developed its warfare from forces that were both more localised and more globalized than the so-called 'Arab' context. Its hybrid form of war evolved not out of peculiarly Lebanese traditions, but from improvisation, internal debate and external patronage. Understanding culture effectively may mean abandoning the notion of an 'Arab' strategic culture altogether.

To appreciate Hizballa's strategic culture, we should abandon generalised concepts of an 'Arab' way of war and be more attentive to change as well as continuity, and externalities as well as indigenous trends. For a start, an Arab 'way of war' presumes common conditions and contexts. One area where this is not the case is in the physical environment. Unlike the desert warfare once chosen by the states of Egypt or Iraq, the topography of Lebanon is different, as mountainous and uneven terrain that can be more effectively occupied by a defender. More broadly, if Hizballa has a culture, it is one of constant self-reinvention. Hizballa's 'way of war', far from being rooted in semi-permanent Lebanese or Shiite traditions, has repeatedly changed since Israel occupied Lebanon in the 1980's. For a start, their capabilities and resources have improved dramatically, and have also expanded. As one Israeli Master Sgt. who fought in Lebanon for sixteen years said, comparing Hizballah then and now 'is like talking about the difference between men who have guns and an army.'[63] Despite popular assumptions that the Sunni-Shia divide in the Islamic world is inexorable, inflexible and hardened, Hizballa draws on both forces. The IDFs expectations that a war with Hizballa would be an Arab-Israeli war were misleading, as Hizballa is partly a Persian phenomenon. Its skills, weaponry and operations are influenced by Iranian patronage, and since Syria's withdrawal from Lebanon in April 2005, both Syria and Hizballa have come under increasing Iranian influence.[64] Its army is trained by the *Pasdarans*, the guards of the Iranian Revolution. Its capabilities and expertise come partly from Iranian veterans of the Iran-Iraq war. Its fighting power is Persian as well as Arab, and Sunni Syrian as well as Iranian Shiite. In turn, the Iranian Army of the war against Iraq was trained by the US. In preparation for this conflict, Hizballa drew on several external influences, carefully studying military history, including the Vietnam War.[65] It then tailored these influences to the precise circumstances in which it would have to combat Israel in its own territory. To appeal to worldwide opinion, and strengthen its case for legitimacy, Hizballa invokes Western martial experiences, comparing itself to America's Revolutionary War against British colonialism or the French resistance against Nazi occupation.[66]

As it has shifted from being an insurgent military force into a multidimensional political and social organisation, so its 'way of war' has proved to be fluid. It has widened its operations, so that where once violent resistance was at the core of its strategy, now it has expanded to charity, patronage and civilian projects—indeed, this shift has been accompanied by re-interpretations of the precise meanings of *jihad*.[67] It moved from a centralised command structure to a decentralised cellular one, where Hizballa delegates authority to small unit leaders, resembling the US Marine Corps more than the rigid behemoths of state armies. When it comes to kidnapping, the tactic that helped to trigger the July War, Hizballa has changed its stance several times, from a willingness to seize hostages, to a tourism-promoting policy of restraint, to a resumption of the method. Thus Hizballa is more than an internal Lebanese phenomenon; it is the by-product of geostrategic realignments in the region.

Conclusion

When Clausewitz looked back on the wars of his fatherland, he asked rhetorically

Would Prussia in 1792 have dared to invade France with 70,000 men if she had had an inkling that the repercussions in case of failure would be strong enough to overthrow the old European balance of power? Would she, in 1806, have risked war with France with 100,000 men, if she had suspected that the first shot would set off a mine that was to blow her to the skies?[68]

In less dramatic vein, would Israel's leaders have attacked Lebanon in July 2006 if they had known that Hizballa would not be smashed like Palestinian militias, but would emerge bloodied but politically stronger, with militant Shiite movements emboldened, Israel's military mystique lowered and its government holding on for life? A powerful state, led by a Prime Minister anxious to display its strength and advised by a Chief of Staff with utopian expectations of air power, entered war unprepared for shocks. Lebanon's Hizballa reacted not as a cultural captive, but as an evolving, adaptive force. The July War has been interpreted as a signpost conflict for the future, pointing towards a post-modern, hybrid and ever more complex environment. But it also points to a simpler and more fundamental danger. Namely, Israel fell prey to the triumphal illusion of control. Halutz and Olmert viewed war as a surgical tool, assuming a patient who was still, pliable, and visible. In fact, the patient turned out to be alert, resistant and unpredictable. And just as the operation began, the lights went out. Israel's very existence had been nourished by a growing confidence not only in its military capabilities, but in the awesome strength it drew from its democratic and dynamic society. But these traits did not give Israel godlike powers. In the face of all evidence and experience to the contrary, Israel's short war and its coercive bombing campaign could not easily uproot a force embedded in Lebanese society, nor could it turn the Lebanese against Hizballa. Decades before, Israel refused to obey the fatalism that the Jewish state could not survive surrounded by mortal enemies. In 2006, Hizballa ignored the script of Arab vulnerability and backwardness, and made its own history.

CONCLUSION

Beyond the Wild East

On the surface, war tears people apart. But if we look closer, it drives them together. There may not be one universal soldier, uniform across time and space. But war has a culture of its own. Even as enemies stress their differences rhetorically, conflict with its reciprocity and strategic interaction creates new syntheses. The story of peoples 'is not national but cosmopolitan; not one, as nationalist myth would have us believe, of separate blocs gradually and belligerently getting to know each other, but of a constant process of cultural and commercial interaction, redefinition of boundaries and mutual enrichment.'[1] 'World history' now moves beyond nations to study patterns of movement, the exchange of goods and ideas, travel literature and maps.[2] Its unit of analysis is not the walled-off tribe or nation, but the nexus of contact between peoples, such as trade routes, oceans, the trail of beliefs and faiths. Ironically, the business of mutual slaughter is an engine of this historical process. Recently in Iraq, the insurgent Islamic Army of Iraq formed a special sniper brigade after downloading a training manual written by a retired US Marine. In their propaganda video, the narrator fuses his world with the sniper's craft. The marksman needs a steady hand, good focus—and faith in Allah.[3] We might call Iraq 'Indian Country' and talk of a separate, savage frontier, but war jumbles people together. Native Americans served under Custer and Petraeus too, and yesterday's rebels of the Sunni triangle are today's American allies.

This matters, because it is tempting to see separation as the grand message of the War on Terror, the wrenching apart of humans who are mutually alien. In its first years the 'War on Terror' evolved as a faith of universalism. Against the predators who struck on 9/11, Atlanticists believed that American power could remake the world in its own image. Its wars of liberation would inspire the spread of democratic freedom and alter the condition of the Arab-Islamic world. Reformers would rise up and banish the furies of extremism that had spawned *jihad*. Instead, the US and its allies became tied down in wars of attrition in foreign lands. The balance of opinion turned against the utopian vision. In the cultural counter-revolution, it is now a sense of the exotic separateness of others that reigns. This 'cultural turn' is not new, but the latest version of an old reflex. For all the differences between America and the European conquerors that came before it, this is one similarity. In reaction to rebellion and resistance, America seeks to weaponise cultural knowledge, to find power in the ability to study, classify, and taxonomize peoples of the East. Western militaries embrace Sun Tzu's advice, 'Know the enemy, know thyself.' The effort to rearm culturally is America's modern attempt to institutionalize this wisdom, pursuing intimate knowledge about foreign societies and turning that knowledge into strategic payoffs. As a hegemon with a global military presence hires anthropologists into its forces, as the Pentagon frames Third World cultures as nests of pathological terror, and as the exotic enemy resurfaces in popular entertainment, the War on Terror marks the 'highest stage of Orientalism.'[4]

As this book has shown, this fascination has an older pedigree, dating from antiquity. 9/11 marked the third post-war 'wave' of interest in non-Western strategic cultures. Scholars once debated the nature and mindset of the Soviet elite and its attitudes towards nuclear war and deterrence. After the Cold War, policymakers and pundits widely depicted the eruption of ethnic and communal conflicts in the Balkans, Africa and the Caucuses as 'medieval struggles over blood and culture.'[5] Now, in the wars unleashed since 9/11, images of the brutal fanatic, the inscrutable Eastern genius, or the noble savage have returned to impress military minds, civilian academics and popular culture. In different forms and intensities, an idea has again taken hold: of the Primordial East driven by visceral or pre-modern urges, against the West, rational and modern.

What can we conclude from this discussion of culture, and what are its practical implications? Several observations should be made. Culture is difficult and prone to oversimplification; we need greater awareness of what inspires our fascination in the first place; and this matters because it is still debated in the public domain and has concrete implications for the wars we are fighting.

First, we can see how difficult culture is to understand or analyse in a way relevant to military affairs, and how easily the discussion can slip into ahistorical myth. That military adventurers still hold up T.E. Lawrence not only as an authority on 'small wars' but as a guidebook to Iraq in the twenty-first century suggests that the image of the timeless Oriental endures.[6] The movement back to culture is potentially valuable. Culture helps define conflict, shaping and constraining choices. The 'cultural turn' should be applauded for encouraging military actors to distance themselves from their own norms to imagine that of others. It is an important corrective to naïve ethnocentrism, and to neo-classical realism, where actors pursue their structural material interests with culture reduced to background music. Yet like all doctrinal shifts, the cultural turn must move beyond utopian expectation and be properly theorized and placed in historical context. If 'know the enemy' is to be a serious endeavour instead of a snappy catch-phrase, there is much more to it than assuming behaviour is necessarily a linear continuum from pre-existing cultural systems, divorced from a fluid strategic context; or that people do not act but are acted upon by impersonal historic forces, taking orders from the culture; or that modes of warfare within cultures are singular and fixed by ancestral habit. The evidence here reveals actors who pursue strategy by reinventing their cultures. War is a power struggle, a deadly reactive dance, and culture is subject to its volatile nature. This is true on many fronts, from the status of women to suicide bombing, from alliance choices to propaganda. Cultural realism enables us to recognize both the power and malleability of symbols and narratives, potent weapons in the hands of skilled users.

As the new *Field Manual* warns, we must guard against the mistake of viewing others only on our own terms. But in the rush to the different, the exotic and the bizarre, Westerners may embrace the opposite error. Instead of assuming sameness, they can regard foreigners as eternally separate and primordial, an alien species with their 'ancient hatreds' or primal urges.[7] The 'Iraq Culture Smart Card', distributed to American troops, laid down the dividing lines between ethnic and sectarian groups, conceiving culture narrowly as 'a force-field of hostilities with no space for mutuality.'[8] Against the fallacy of a world remade in America's image, this is the opposite fallacy, that Arabs or Afghans are archaic curiosities or medieval throwbacks fixed in another time.

Ahistorical myths are insidious because they can be embedded in language. The very term 'Human Terrain' is potentially misleading. 'Terrain' geographically visualizes humans as a space to be mapped and mastered. In effect, the battlespace is imagined as populated by peoples of separate worlds who can be known as part of a 'comprehensive cultural information research system.' This approach may lose sight of the agency of the human subjects being surveyed and the reciprocity of the war relationship. It runs the risk of reducing complex humanity to 'economic, ethnic and tribal landscapes.'[9] Such imaginative geography can overlook the real people who refashion themselves in the overlapping space that we share. Montgomery McFate, an architect of the Human Terrain System, defines the theatre of anthropologized war as a 'tribal zone'[10], a monoculture of 'blood feuds.'[11] Such language falsely partitions the world. A good pedagogy of culture should be attentive to the crossovers and interconnectedness of war, so that culture is not reducible to a discourse of difference and separation.

Enemies at war can look strikingly different, like the Spanish and Aztecs who found each other bizarre at first glance. But the Spanish could only prevail by hiring natives in their thousands. The Aztecs, a ritualized society that tore a heart out of a live victim every day to keep the sun in the sky, and geared its war-making to capturing prisoners for sacrifice, also adapted. They broke with their ethos of close quarter combat and learnt to fire Spanish crossbows, broke their taboos by mobilising women, and broke their traditions to operate at night. A supposedly conservative people, they compromised their ancestral ways and social structure in order to survive. War did not express their pre-existing culture, but forced them to alter it.[12]

What of today? Confronted with the extreme contrast of machetes against machines, or the cult of death against the culture of Pepsi Cola, it is tempting to see a collision of the premodern and post-modern.[13] Yet modernity cuts through all participants, remaking and hybridizing them in the brutal laboratory of conflict. The aims and capabilities of Mohamed Aidid and Osama Bin Laden are made possible by cheap travel, the flow of capital and expertise, access to Western strategic and political thought, and their ability to fuse these with appeals to *jihad* or resistance. It is not helpful to presume that Taliban fighters are necessarily tribal or dogmatically inflexible, that Al Qaeda is a throwback to the seventh century, that gender apartheid, religious protocols or fanaticism dictate Arab warfare, or that Serbians re-enact feuds because they still believe it is 1389. We in turn are shaped by the enemy, emulating their propagandist skills, their small-unit agility, their rhetoric of cosmic conflict. War calls forth imitation and interpenetration, and globalization accelerates this through a worldwide market where states or guerrillas pick among repertoires of ideas, technology and styles. This is not to imply a facile moral equivalence between the US and al Qaeda. It is to observe the irony that even the bitterest enemies teach each other new ways.

Good cultural insight requires greater self-awareness about how and why we analyse the enemy. It is not enough to show that myths about the enemy are empirically flawed. The exotic eastern warrior will not stop being a silhouette in the Western imagination. We therefore need to ask why, to understand what motivates our fascination in the first place, and recognise that these myths are powerful codes through which Westerners debate about themselves. The goal of Western observers should not be to deny their own preconceptions, but to have a more careful dialogue with them. Westerners invoke the figure of the Oriental warrior to praise or criticise the West, or to articulate visions of destiny or decline, regeneration and change. One-dimensional caricatures of Oriental warfare reflect the anxieties, fears, ambitions, confidence or self-doubt of Western observers, from the idealised tribal warrior or steppe horseman, the Eastern mystical genius, to the suicidal fanatic, from the doomed inferior to the supernaturally gifted, ten foot tall adversary.

When Aeschylus wrote of the defeat of Asia in his play *The Persians*, he sought not only to celebrate triumph but to warn Athenians about the dangers of imperial hubris through the example of the humiliated Persian king. When the Navy SEAL Marcus Luttrell penned his memoir about the barbaric Taliban in 2005, he wrote not only to abhor the enemy but to condemn the weakness of America's liberal establishment. He scorned the perceived moral failures of American society by using the brutish Taliban as a lesson in political will and strength. Even the Anglo-American debate about 'small wars' is about much more than a technocratic argument over military practice. With Anglophiles arguing that Britain can play Greece to America's Rome with cultural expertise, it restages the argument between Britons and Americans about their relationship.

As this study has shown, Western visions can be flawed. But misrepresentation is not inevitable. Ideology can also lead to new insights.

Edwardian officers romanticized aspects of Japanese society, but because of their interest in the social roots of military performance, paid careful attention to the Japanese school curriculum and Japanese standards of physical hygiene, as well as transcending the dismissive racism that is a charge so often levelled at Edwardian elites. Because of his interest in improving Western military standards, the Franciscan monk Giovanni di Carpini showed great interest in Mongol military structure. and the rational organization of their military force.

As well as self-awareness, the practitioners of good cultural observation should grasp that those they study are not passive objects of our fascination. In visions of the East, the people who are observed may get a vote in how they are seen. Western images are made also by the enemy. Our frightening views of the Mongols or Balkan warlords are partly a result of their own propaganda efforts. Hizballa succeeded in the July War partly because it adroitly won over world opinion. Gazed upon by the West, non-Westerners have deliberately cultivated their own reputation as ferocious hordes or invincible foes, reinforcing the impression that they are exotic 'others.'

Third, this debate matters because it is still alive in the public domain. As this book neared completion, primordialist versions of culture persisted. After Blackwater mercenaries killed Iraqi civilians, and their bereaved families refused blood money and demanded a trial, the *Los Angeles Times* claimed it was because they were 'traditional' Arabs hung up on honour.[14] As one American pundit replied, 'If an unaccountable band of politically-connected soldiers-of-fortune shot my mother as she was trying to flee from a traffic circle, and the State Department offered me $5,000 in order to make the incident go away, I would not only be angry, I would be exploring my options for revenge.'[15] While fighting reignited in urban, pluralist Lebanon, a respected anthropologist traced it back to a primeval warrior impulse within tribal societies.[16]

But we are also seeing an increasing amount of important and timely criticism, from both professional anthropologists and strategic analysts, of how some policymakers, commentators and practitioners misconceive culture. The sophistication of decades of new thinking in history and anthropology is being brought to bear in the world of strategy. In November 2007, the American Anthropological Association cautioned against structural-functionalist models of culture being employed within the military. Culture, it argued, is best seen as an 'historically contingent, power-laden, dynamic and emerging property of human relations, and the theoretical and methodological entanglements that such a view implies', rather than 'a set of discrete and static elements that can be neatly catalogued, captured, stored, and pulled out to support decision making.'[17] Similar sophistication also emerges in military-strategic thought. A new study from the Strategic Studies Institute conceptualizes culture as a changing negotiation between past and present.[18] And anthropologists working with the new 'Human Terrain Teams' have an opportunity to promote more rigorous concepts of culture.

All of this matters in practical terms. Falling prey to flawed ideas of culture may have strategic costs, while a rethinking of culture can have concrete benefits for militaries. Because this study has stressed the volatility and unpredictability of the war/culture relationship, it is difficult to discern precise policy implications, given that policymakers look to forecast behaviour. Culture is too contested and fluid to operationalise easily. War will always be full of surprises. This point in itself has value. It can check one tendency within militaries, the quest for the 'magic bullet.' If the technology-driven revolution of the 1990s failed to deliver on all of its promises, we should also be cautious about the culture-driven revolution. A more careful reading of history demonstrates that East is not always East.

But in a more indirect sense, cultural realism may offer a certain utility. It can help those who interpret foreign cultures. Consciousness of our own assumptions, attention to change and contradiction within culture can sharpen our ability to observe the enemy acting strategically. This may assist the ubiquitous 'OODA Loop', where militaries must observe, orient, decide and act. By being wary of primordialist visions, and being open to the twists and turns culture can take, we can accelerate the 'observation' and 'orientation' phases. In other words, cultural realism can help us 'watch.' We can more readily recognize, for example, the difference between the Taliban of today and of several years ago, or the continual mutations within 'traditional' societies, or our own role in shaping the environment that the enemy inhabits. This may help at a grand strategic level. In 1945, an awareness of the malleability of culture enabled policymakers to recognize that Japan was not destined to remain a militarist autocracy forever. It could also help in a tactical moment, where the soldier at the checkpoint is not fatally blinded by a misguided expectation of what the suicide bomber might look like.

It is true that we should avoid ethnocentrism, the idea that folks are all like us. But that doesn't mean we should indulge in condescending exoticism, the notion that *we* are strategic, modern and political, whereas *they*, our benighted enemies, are visceral and primitive. That is a denial of common humanity, not to mention the reciprocal nature of war. This is the greatest danger of the 'cultural turn.' In its more crass forms, it recycles old bigotry in the language of political correctness. We should not discard culture, but recognise the dangers it entails, and the promise of richer understandings. After his skeptical study of the notion 'tribe', Morton Fried knew his readers would still use the term, but 'with a twinge of alarm and a new shock of recognition.'[19] Likewise, the word 'culture' will survive. But ideally, for readers of this book, the word will not conjure images of Easterners as archaic relics of the past, suspended in webs of unchanging significance. As they reinvent their culture to survive the carnage, they are warriors without borders.

NOTES

INTRODUCTION

1. Inga Clendinnen, 'Fierce and Unnatural Cruelty: Cortes and the Conquest of Mexico' *Representations* 33 (Winter, 1991), pp. 65–100, pp. 65–6; *Aztecs: An Interpretation* (Cambridge, 1991), p. 269; *Ambivalent Conquests: Maya and Spaniard in Yutacan* (Cambridge, 1989; see also the claims of Spanish chaplain Juan Ginés de Sepúlveda, *On the Reasons for the Just War among the Indians* (1547), http://chss.montclair.edu/~landwebj/105/1sepulve.htm.
2. David Blair, 'The Americans love Pepsi Cola, but we love death', *Daily Telegraph* 24 Sept. 2001.
3. General (Ret) Anthony Zinni, 'How do we Overhaul the Nation's Defence to Win the Next War?' Speech, U.S. Naval Institute, 4 Sept. 2003; 'Non-Traditional Military Missions: Their Nature, and the Need for Cultural Awareness and Flexible Thinking' in Joe Strange (ed.), *Capital 'W' War: A Case for Strategic Principles* (Quantico, VA, 1998), pp. 247–283, p. 267.
4. US Marine Corps, *The Long War: Send in the Marines, A Marine Corps Operational Employment Concept to Meet An Uncertain Security Environment* (Quantico, VA, Jan. 2008), p. 3.
5. Deepak Lal, *In Praise of Empires: Globalization and Order* (New York, 2004), p. xvii.
6. Frank Rich, 'The Two Wars of the Worlds' *New York Times* 3 July 2005.
7. Lee Harris, 'Al Qaeda's Fantasy Ideology: War without Clausewitz', *Policy Review*, 114 (Aug./Sept. 2002), pp. 19–36; likewise, Michael Ignatieff argued that 'The hijackers were more interested in the spectacle of destruction, in violence for its own sake', 'The Challenges of American Imperial Power,' *Naval War College Review*, 56:2 (Spring 2003), p. 56; Ralph Peters, *Beyond Terror in a Changing World* (Mechanicsburg, 2002), pp. 22–65.
8. The self-defined rational, enlightened Westerner is shocked at the photo of four men at Luton Station on 7 July, 2005, calmly preparing to killthemselves and others: John Mackinlay, *Defeating Complex Insurgency: Beyond Iraq and Afghanistan* (RUSI, Whitehall Paper 62, London, 2005), p. 27.

9. Phillip S. Meilinger, 'Clausewitz's Bad Advice' *Armed Forces Journal* (Aug. 2008), pp. 18–21, 39; Richard H. Shultz Jr. and Andrea J. Dew, *Insurgents, Terrorists and Militias: The Warriors of Contemporary Combat* (New York, 2006); Mona Harb and Reinoud Leenders, 'Know Thy Enemy: Hizbullah, 'Terrorism' and the Politics of Perception', *Third World Quarterly*, 26:1, (Feb. 2005), pp. 189–190. Faisal Devji makes the strongest case that the violence of militant jihad is more about self-expression and gestures of martyrdom than about the instrumental pursuit of tangible political goals: *Landscapes of the Jihad: Militancy, Morality, Modernity* (London 2005). As he states, 'Suicide bombing, for instance, is the most individualistic of practices. It is also an ethical gesture that participates only indirectly, if at all, in a solution to the problem it advertises.' Faisal Devji, 'A war fought for impersonal passions' *Financial Times* 25 July 2005. By contrast, it will be argued here that most suicide bombing is an organisational phenomenon and a tool of coercion, relying on the martyrdom impulse but ultimately driven by strategic purpose.
10. As Al Qaeda's chief theorist Ayman al-Zawahiri pronounced, 'If the successful operations against Islam's enemies and the severe damage inflicted on them do not serve the ultimate goal of establishing the Muslim nation in the heart of the Islamic world, they will be nothing more than disturbing acts, regardless of their magnitude, that could be absorbed and endured…' cited in Thomas G. Mahnken and Joseph A. Maiolo (eds), *Strategic Studies, A Reader* (London, 2008), p. 2; see also Colin Gray, *Another Bloody Century: Future Warfare* (London, 2005), pp. 227–8; Youssef H. Aboul-Enein, 'Ayman Al-Zawahiri's Knights under the Prophet's Banner: The al-Qaeda Manifesto', *Military Review* (Jan.-Feb. 2005), pp. 83–5; Christopher Henzel, 'The Origins of Al Qaeda's Ideology: Implications for US Strategy' *Parameters* 35:1 (2005), pp. 69–80, 75–6.
11. For work in this direction, see Keith Stanski, 'So these folks are aggressive': An Orientalist Reading of Western Conceptions of "Afghan Warlords", 2001–present', paper presented at Queen Mary, University of London, 23 May 2008; Tarak Barkawi, 'Orientalism at War', presented at the Sixth Pan-European Conference on International Relations 12–15 Sept. 2007, Turin, Italy; Hans-Henning Kortum, (ed.), *Transcultural Wars: from the Middle Ages to the 21st Century* (Berlin, 2006). I am grateful to Dr Barkawi and Keith Stanksi for permission to cite from their papers.
12. Herodotus, *The Histories* 1.1, 3.38, 7.83, 7.223 (trans. Aubrey de Sélincourt, Harmondsworth, 1954, 2003 edn).
13. National Army Museum (henceforth abbreviated NAM) 9007–76 'Narrative of the disastrous retreat from Kabul by Sgt Major Lissant 37th N.I', p. 2.
14. Cited in Raymond Lamont-Brown, *Kamikaze: Japan's Suicide Samurai* (London, 1997), p. 115.
15. Ellen Knickmeyer, 'Near the Iraqi Desert, Kuwait', *Associated Press*, 19 March 2003.

16. Thus the West's 'Others' have been internal as well as external: see Keith Windschuttle, 'Edward Said's Orientalism revisited', *New Criterion*, 17:5 (Jan. 1999), pp. 30–35.
17. For example, whether Australian Aborigines resisted invasion, or whether their raids were mostly apolitical robberies, forms one front in the 'history wars' over land rights and race relations: Stuart Macintyre, Anna Clark, *The History Wars* (Melbourne, 2003), p. 166; Keith Windschuttle, *The Fabrication of Aboriginal History, Volume One: Van Diemen's Land 1803–1847* (Sydney, 2002), pp. 64–5, 95–116, 122–4; at the anniversary of Spain's conquest of the New World, polemicists debated who was the more barbaric: Arthur Schlesinger Jr. 'Was America A Mistake?' *Newsweek* (Sept., 1992), pp 16–27; how America's white settlers and natives fought, and who introduced scalping to whom, is linked to modern disputes about the legitimacy of European settlement: James Axtell, William C. Sturtevant, 'The Unkindest Cut, or Who Invented Scalping', *The William and Mary Quarterly*, 31:3 (July 1980), pp. 451–472.
18. *The Declaration of Independence of the Thirteen Colonies and the Constitution of the United States of America* (Senate Document No. 79, Washington DC, 1934), p. 3.
19. Harold R. Isaacs, *Scratches on Our Minds: American Views of China and India* (New York, 1958); Andrew J. Rotter, 'Saidism without Said: *Orientalism* and U.S. Diplomatic History', *The American Historical Review*, 105:4 (2000), pp. 1205–1218, 1230.
20. On the etymology of the idea of the West and its role in American education, see David Gress, *From Plato to Nato: The Idea of the West and Its Opponents* (London, 1998), pp. 16, 31–2; see also Alistair Bonnett, *The Idea of the West: Culture, Politics and History* (New York, 2004), pp. 1–13.
21. As Tarak Barkawi argues, 'Orientalism at war in Korea' presented at the Sixth Pan-European Conference on International Relations 12–15 Sept. 2007, Turin, Italy, p. 2.
22. These include Niccoló Capponi, *Victory of the West: The Story of the Battle of Lepanto* (London, 2006); Roger Crowley, *1453: The Holy War for Constantinople and the Clash of Islam and the West* (New York, 2005); Tom Holland, *Persian Fire: The First World Empire and the Battle for the West* (London, 2005); Ernle Bradford, *Thermopylae: The Battle for the West* (Cambridge, 1980, reprinted 2004); more recently, there is Anthony Pagden, *Worlds at War: The 2,500–Year Struggle between East and West* (Oxford, 2008); Ryan Dilley, 'Lessons from Lawrence of Arabia', *BBC News*, 9 April 2004.
23. Nathaniel Fick, 'Books and Battles: A former marine captain in Afghanistan and Iraq tells of the books that helped him most', *Washington Post*, 17 July 2005, BW08.
24. With all caveats noted, this book defines 'West' at present as the United States, Europe, Israel, Australia, New Zealand and South Africa. Good arguments could be made to include Lebanon, India, Japan, the West

Indies or the Philippines, if not wholly as Western, at least strongly Westernized. But part of this book's argument is that these categories are malleable and that through war, we dispute and reformulate their meaning.

25. For example, some enthusiasts of the Occident once portrayed the Germanic peoples of the west Roman Empire as barbaric wreckers from beyond. But scholarship in the era of the EU's integrationist drive now sees them as creative agents who revitalised the defence and culture of Rome. Bryan Ward-Perkins, *The Fall of Rome and the End of Civilisation* (Oxford, 2005), p. 174.
26. Randy Roberts, James S. Olsen, *A Line in the Sand: The Alamo in Blood and Memory* (New York, 2001), pp. 172–3; Susan Prendergast Schoelwer (ed.), *Alamo Images: Changing Perceptions of a Texas Experience* (Texas, 1986), p. 5.
27. Samuel Huntington, *The Clash of Civilizations and the Remaking of World Order* (New York, 1996).
28. Andrew Roberts, *A History of the English-Speaking Peoples since 1900* (London, 2006). The chapter titles hint at the book's view of civilisation as a permanent call to arms: 'First Assault', 'United and Conquering', 'Attritional Victory', 'Fourth Assault.'
29. This was the phrase of philosopher Georg Hegel in his description of the battle of Salamis, 480BC; Georg Hegel, *Philosophy of History*, (trans. J. Sibree, New York: Dover, 1956), p. 257.
30. On the realism of the Iran/Armenia relationship, see Brenda Schaffer (ed.), *The Limits of Culture: Islam and Foreign Policy* (London, 2006), pp. 15, 230–231.
31. Yuval Noah Harari analyses the historical appeal of decisive battles: 'The Concept of Decisive Battles in World History', *Journal of World History*, 18:3 (Sept. 2007), pp. 251–267.
32. From Fouad Ajami, 'The Summoning', *Foreign Affairs*, 72:4 (Sept./Oct. 1993), pp. 2–9, p. 2. Similarly to the argument here, Ajami proposes that 'Nations 'cheat': they juggle identities and interests. Their ways meander. One would think that the traffic of arms from North Korea and China to Libya and Iran and Syria shows this—that states will consort with any civilisation, however alien, as long as the price is right and the goods are ready.'
33. Edward Creasy, *The Fifteen Decisive Battles from Marathon to Waterloo* (New York, 1851, 1881 edn). Creasy's work is replete with the binary image of civilisation-spreading westerners and an archaic, corrupted Orient, linking the 'western energy and superior civilisation' of Alexander with 'Anglo-Saxon commerce and conquest.' Orientals are 'despotic dynasties', 'barbarous hordes', or 'pagan savages from the wilds of Central Asia', pp. 27, 63, 127.
34. Dennis E. Showalter, 'Of Decisive Battles and Intellectual Fashions: Sir Edward Creasy Revisited, *Military Affairs*, 52:4 (Oct. 1988), pp. 206–208.
35. Victor Davis Hanson, *Carnage and Culture: Landmark Battles in the Rise of Western Power* (New York, 2001), which he anticipated in *The Western*

Way of War: Infantry Battle in Classical Greece (Berkeley, 1989), esp. pp. 9–19 and pp. 227–228.
36. Sun Tzu, *The Art of War*, III.18.
37. Joe Klein, 'Good General, Bad Mission', *Time*, 12 Jan. 2007.
38. US Marine Corps, *Small Wars Manual* (Washington, 1940), pp. 13, 18, 28.
39. Ronald Schaffer, 'The 1940 Small Wars Manual and the 'Lessons of History', *Military Affairs*, 36:2 (April 1972), pp. 46–51, p. 48, 50.
40. PRO 30/57/28, Kitchener Papers, Lord Roberts to Kitchener, 28 Dec. 1904, discussed also in David Omissi, *The Sepoy and the Raj: The Indian Army, 1860–1940* (London, 1994), p. 30.
41. PRO WO 28/7/22, General Staff, India, 'Military Report on Afghanistan' 1925, 'Table XXIV, Tribes along group of Routes from Quetta to Kandahar.'
42. Colonel Charles C.E. Callwell, *Small Wars: Their Principles and Practice* (London 1896, 1906 edn), p. 33.
43. For an example of this continuity, strategist Frank Hoffman commends the *Small Wars Manual* of 1940 for being ahead of its time, although he overlooks its stress on race and racial characteristics, substituting the word 'culture': Frank G. Hoffman, 'Small Wars Revisited: The United States and Nontraditional Wars', *Journal of Strategic Studies*, 28:6 (Dec. 2005), pp. 913–940, p. 929.
44. Bernard Brodie, *War and Politics* (New York, 1973), p. 332.
45. Jack Snyder, *The Soviet Strategic Culture: Implications for Nuclear Options* (Santa Monica, 1977); Colin Gray, 'National Style in Strategy: The American Example' *International Security* 6:2 (Fall, 1981), pp. 35–37; Ken Booth, *Strategy and Ethnocentrism* (New York, 1981).
46. Robert Gates, Landon Lecture, Kansas State University, Manhattan, Kansas, 26 Nov. 2007.
47. US Army/Marine Corps, FM 3–24 *Counterinsurgency Field Manual* (Chicago, 2006), foreword, David H. Petraeus and James F. Amos.
48. Jennifer Taw and Bruce Hoffman, *The urbanization of insurgency: the potential challenge to US Army operations* (Santa Monica CA: RAND Corporation, 1994).
49. As Colin Gray argues, 'Out of the Wilderness: Prime Time for Strategic Culture', *Comparative Strategy*, 26:1 (Jan. 2007), pp. 1–20.
50. See Hew Strachan, 'The Lost Meaning of Strategy', *Survival*, 47:3 (2005), pp. 33–54; Philip H. Gordon, *Winning the Right War: The Path to Security for America and the World* (New York, 2007), pp. 1–37.
51. Tim Benbow, *The Magic Bullet? Understanding the Revolution in Military Affairs* (London, 2004), p. 80.
52. House Armed Services Committee, 'Army Transformation, Implications for the Future.' Statement of Major General Robert Scales, July 15 2004, http://www.au.af.mil/au/awc/awcgate/congress/04–07–15scales.pdf; Robert H. Scales, 'Culture-centric Warfare' *Proceedings of the United States Naval Institute* 130:10 (Oct. 2004), pp. 32–36.

53. Leo Docherty, *Desert of Death: A Soldier's Journey from Iraq to Afghanistan* (London, 2007), pp. 191–2.
54. Major General Peter W. Chiarelli, Maj. Patrick R. Michaelis, 'Winning the Peace: The Requirement for Full-Spectrum Operations', *Military Review* (July-Aug. 2005), pp. 4–17, p. 5, 9.
55. Bryan Bender, 'Pentagon studying its war errors', *Boston Globe*, 16 Aug. 2006.
56. Kambiz Fattahi, 'US Army enlists anthropologists', *BBC News*, 16 Oct. 2007.
57. Department of Defense, *Quadrennial Defence Review* (Washington DC, 2006), p. 78; Secretary of Defense Memo, 'Defence Capabilities to Transition to and from Hostilities' 8 Oct. 2004, cited in Steven C. Boraz, 'Behind the Curve in Culture-centric skills' *Proceedings of the United States Naval Institute*, 131:6 (June 2005), pp. 41–45.
58. George Packer, 'Knowing the Enemy: Can Social Scientists redefine the 'war on terror'? *New Yorker* (Dec. 2006), pp. 40–69.
59. Thomas R. Mockaitis, *The Iraq War: Learning from the Past, Adapting to the Present, and Planning for the Future*, Strategic Studies Institute (Feb., 2007), pp. 37–38, 57. Likewise, Lieutenant General Sir John Kiszely, outgoing director of the British Defence Academy, argues that anthropology must inform officer education: 'Learning About Counterinsurgency', *Military Review* (March-April 2007), pp. 5–11, p. 11.
60. Beatrice Heuser, for instance, claims that the Achilles Heel of French failures in Indo-China and Algeria was a 'lack of emphasis on and sympathy for cultural differences' and that culture 'is the key variable in group relations.' 'The Cultural Revolution in Counterinsurgency', *Journal of Strategic Studies*, 30:1 (Feb. 2007), pp. 153–171, pp. 155, 169.
61. Tony Corn, 'Clausewitz in Wonderland', *Policy Review* (Sept. 2006); see also Montgomery McFate, 'Anthropology and Counterinsurgency: The Strange Story of their Curious Relationship', *Military Review*, 85 (March-April 2005), pp. 24–38.
62. John McCain, 'An Enduring Peace Built on Freedom', *Foreign Affairs*, 86:6 (Nov/Dec 2007), pp. 19–34, p. 24.
63. See the debate between Alastair Johnston and Colin Gray: Gray, 'Strategic Culture as Context: The First Generation of Theory Strikes Back', *Review of International Studies*, 25 (1999),pp. 49–69; Johnston, 'Strategic cultures revisited: reply to Colin Gray', *Review of International Studies*, 25 (1999), pp. 519–523.
64. It is espoused by a range of academics and retired officers. It has made its way into respected journals of public policy such as the *Atlantic Monthly* and the *Economist*. It has been taken up by the US military's chief cultural anthropologist. More ambitiously, profound differences between East and West are asserted in academic and popular texts, from Christopher Coker's *Waging War without Warriors* to Robert Kaplan's *Imperial Grunts*.
65. See John Glenn, Darryl Howlett and Stuart Poore (eds), *Neorealism versus Strategic Culture* (Aldershot, 2004) and Michael C. Desch, 'Culture Clash:

Assessing the Importance of Ideas in Security Studies', *International Security*, 23:1, (1998), pp. 141–170.

66. Elizabeth Kier, *Imagining War: French and British Military Doctrine Between the Wars* (Princeton, 1997); Isabel Hull, *Absolute Destruction: Military Culture and the Practices of War in Imperial Germany* (Cornell, 2005); W.P.S. Sidhu, 'Of Oral Traditions and Ethnocentric Judgements' in G.K. Tanham, K.P. Bajpai and A. Mattoo (eds.) *Securing India: Strategic Thought and Practice* (New Delhi, 1996).
67. Basil Liddell Hart, *The British Way in Warfare* (London, 1932); Russell Weigley, *The American Way of War* (Bloomington, 1973).
68. John Baylis, James Wirtz, Colin S. Gray and Eliot Cohen, *Strategy in the Contemporary World* (Oxford, 2007), p. 88.
69. See Risa Brooks and Elizabeth Stanley-Mitchell, *Creating Military Power: The Impact of Culture, Society, Institutions, and International Forces on Military Effectiveness* (Palo Alto, 2007); Theo Farrell, 'World Culture and Military Power', *Security Studies*, 14:3 (July-Sept. 2005), pp. 448–488, esp. 448–456; Stephen Biddle, *Military Power: Explaining Victory and Defeat in Modern Battle* (Princeton, 2004); Allan R. Millett, Williamson Murray and Kenneth H. Watman, 'The Effectiveness of Military Organisations' *International Security*, 11:2 (1986), pp. 37–71.
70. For 'neo-realist' works that reject outright the value of culture and ideology see Kenneth Walz, *Theory of International Politics* (New York, 1979), pp. 124–128; John Mearsheimer, *The Tragedy of Great Power Politics* (New York, 2001).
71. Theo Farrell, *The Norms of War: Cultural Beliefs and Modern Conflict* (London, 2005), pp. 12–15; Jack Snyder, *The Soviet Strategic Culture*, p. 40; Jeffrey W. Legro, 'Whence American Internationalism' *International Organization* 54:2 (2000), pp. 253–289, p. 263.
72. Jeffrey Lantis, 'Strategic Culture: From Clausewitz to Constructivism', *Strategic Insights*, 4:10 (Oct., 2005), pp. 1–16, p. 8; as Ken Booth argues, culture 'Outlast(s) all but major changes in military technology, domestic arrangements or the international environment' in 'The Concept of Strategy Culture Affirmed' in C.G. Jacobsen (ed.) *Strategic Power: USA/USSR* (New York, 1990), pp. 121–128, p. 121; as Theo Farrell argues, culture 'as both professional norms and national traditions, shapes preference formation by military organisations by telling organisational members who they are and what is possible, and thereby suggesting what they should do.' 'Culture and military power', *Review of International Studies*, 24 (1998), p. 407–416, p. 416; Farrell also commented that 'strategic culture must always be viewed and analyzed as an open system. He argues also that culture itself is more or less consistent and admitted that both internal and external shocks occur—and the impact of such shocks is hugely important—but that culture more often than not settles and continues on as a constant norm. Farrell emphasized that if we are ever to attempt to use strategic culture as an analytical independent variable, we

must view it as a fixed, continuous concept.' Elizabeth L. Stone, Christopher p. Twomey, Peter R. Lavoy, *Comparative Strategic Culture*, p. 11.

73. This issue is highlighted in a recent conference report on strategic culture that describes culture as a 'central determinant' of strategic behaviour, but concludes by stressing the 'malleability' of culture with its multiple narratives that could be politically chosen. Elizabeth L. Stone, Christopher p. Twomey, Peter R. Lavoy, 'Comparative Strategic Culture: Monterey California, 21–22 Sept. 2005, Conference Organized by the Center for Contemporary Conflict, U.S. Naval Postgraduate School for the Advanced Systems and Concepts Office of the U.S. Defence Threat Reduction Agency (Center for Contemporary Conflict, 2005), pp. 1, 12.
74. Geoffrey Parker (ed.), *The Cambridge History of Warfare* (Cambridge, 2005), esp. pp. 1–15.
75. John Keegan, *A History of Warfare* (London, 1993), p. 387.
76. As argued by Christopher Coker, *Waging War Without Warriors? The Changing Culture of Military Conflict* (London, 2002), pp. 147–8.
77. Paul Bracken, *Fire in the East: The Rise of Asian Military Power and the Second Nuclear Age* (New York, 1999), p. 130.
78. Geoffrey Parker (ed.), *The Cambridge Illustrated History of Warfare: The Triumph of the West* (Cambridge, 1995).
79. Andrew Bacevich, 'The Islamic Way of War' *The American Conservative*, 11 Sept. 2006.
80. John Poole, *Tactics of the Crescent Moon* (Emerald Isle, NC, 2001), xxviii, p. 5.
81. William Lind, foreword to J. Poole, *Phantom Soldier: The Enemy's Answer to U.S. Firepower* (Posterity Press, 2001).
82. Robert M. Cassidy, *Counterinsurgency and the Global War on Terror: Military Culture and Irregular War* (London, 2006), p. 3.
83. For the argument that the 'logic and rational direction of war are universal', see Michael Handel, *Masters of War: Classical Strategic Thought* (London, 1996), p. 3.
84. Robert D. Kaplan, 'A Historian for Our Time', *Atlantic Monthly*, 299:5 (Jan./Feb. 2007), pp. 78–84.
85. John A. Nagl, *Counterinsurgency Lessons from Malaya and Vietnam: Learning to Eat Soup with a Knife* (New York, 2002); Brigadier Nigel Aylwin-Foster, 'Changing the Army for Counterinsurgency Operations', *Military Review*, 85:6 (Nov.-Dec. 2005), pp. 2–15, p. 9.
86. In 1991, Prime Minister Thatcher reminded President Bush that Britain could help with its political and military knowledge of the Gulf. See Christopher Hitchens, *Blood, Class and Empire: The Enduring Anglo-American Relationship* (New York, 1990, 2004edn), p. xvii.
87. Stephen Castle, 'From Prince Andrew, critical words for U.S. on Iraq', *International Herald Tribune*, 4 Feb. 2008.
88. Edward Said, *Orientalism* (New York, 1978), pp. 6–18.
89. Robert Brightman, 'Forget Culture: Replacement, Transcendence, Relexification', *Cultural Anthropology*, 10 (1995), pp. 509–46, p. 510.

90. Clifford Geertz, *The Interpretation of Cultures* (New York, 1973), p. 5.
91. H. H. Gerth, C. Wright Mills (eds), *From Max Weber: Essays in Sociology* (Oxford, 1958), p. 280.
92. For this 'baseline' definition, see also John H. Bodley, *Cultural Anthropology: Tribes, States and the Global System* (London, 1994); anthropologist Bronislaw Malinkowski in 1931 defined culture as 'inherited artefacts, goods, technical processes, ideas, habits and values.' *Encyclopaedia of the Social Sciences*, 1931, cited in Peter Burke, *What is Cultural History?* (Cambridge, 2006 edn), p. 29.
93. As described by William H. Sewell, Jr. 'The Concept(s) of Culture' in Victoria E. Bonnell and Lynn Hunt (eds) *Beyond the Cultural Turn: New Directions in the Study of Society and Culture* (Berkeley, 1999), pp. 35–61, p. 44; for an example of the insights of this literature, Consuelo Cruz makes a similar argument in the context of modern identity politics: 'Identity and Persuasion: How Nations Remember Their Pasts and Make Their Futures', *World Politics*, 52:3 (April 2000), pp. 275–312.
94. See Renato Rosaldo, *Ilongot Headhunting, 1883–1974: A Study in Society and History* (Stanford, 1980).
95. This definition is derived from A. Macmillan, K. Booth and R. Trood, 'Strategic Culture' in K. Booth and R. Trood (eds) *Strategic Cultures in the Asia-Pacific Region* (Basingstoke, 1999), pp. 3–26, p. 8 and Alastair Johnston, *Cultural Realism: Strategic Culture and Grand Strategy in Chinese History* (Princeton, 1997), p. ix-x, p. 36. Jack Snyder defines strategic culture as 'the sum total of ideas, conditioned emotional responses, patterns of habitual behaviour that members of a national strategic community have acquired through instruction or imitation.' Snyder, *The Soviet Strategic Culture*, p. 8.
96. Recently, Kerry Longhurst defined it as 'a distinctive body of beliefs, attitudes and practices regarding the use of force, which are held by a collective (usually a nation) and arise gradually over time, through a unique protracted historical process.' *Germany and the Use of Force*, pp. 17–18.
97. On this gap between strategic culture literature and sociological and anthropological scholarship, see Iver B. Neumann and Henrikki Heikka, 'Grand Strategy, Strategic Culture, Practice: The Social Roots of Nordic Defence', *Cooperation and Conflict*, 40 (2005), pp. 5–23, p. 17.
98. For example, as Jeffrey Legro acknowledges: 'Reality can be socially constructed, but only with available materials and within existing structures… however, when the contradiction between external conditions and cultural tendencies becomes too great, culture will likely adapt.' *Cooperation under Fire: Anglo-German Restraint during World War II* (Ithaca, 1995), p. 231.
99. Alastair Iain Johnston, 'Thinking about Strategic Culture', *International Security*, 19 (1995), pp. 32–44, p. 38; Brian McAllister Linn, *The Echo of Battle: The Army's Way of War* (London, 2007).

100. Ken Booth, *Strategy and Ethnocentrism*, p. 181.
101. *On the Edge: The Clinton Presidency* (New York, 1994), p. 157; Michael T. Kaufman, 'The Dangers of Letting a President Read', *New York Times*, 22 May 1999.
102. Rone Tempest, 'Right Way to Farm the Classics', *Los Angeles Times*,25 Feb. 2004; Laura Secor, 'The Farmer Classicist and Raisin-Grower Victor Davis Hanson Argues that the USA Needs a Dose of Ancient Greece's Warrior Culture. White House Hawks are Listening.', *Boston Globe*, 25 May 2003, D1; Barton Gellman, *Angler: The Cheney Vice Presidency* (New York, 2008), pp. 249–50; on the linkages between democratic triumphalism and national security policy, see Michael C. Desch, *Power and Military Effectiveness: The Fallacy of Democratic Triumphalism* (Baltimore, 2008), p. 4.
103. My use of the concept of 'cultural realism', which proposes a way strategy is made through ambiguous sets of ideas, should not be confused with that of Alastair Johnston, for whom it specifically refers to how realism is culturally learnt rather than the natural response to an anarchic environment: *Cultural Realism: Strategic Culture and Grand Strategy in Chinese History* (Princeton, 1995).
104. See Statement of Col. Martin Schweitzer, Commander, 4/82 Airborne Brigade Combat Team, US Army, House Armed Services Committee, 24 April 2008, http://humanterrainsystem.army.mil/col_schweitzer_statement.pdf; David Kilcullen, 'Anatomy of a Tribal Revolt', *Small Wars Journal*, 29 Aug., 2007. http://smallwarsjournal.com/blog/2007/08/anatomy-of-a-tribal-revolt; but for its potential fragility, see Austin Long, 'The Anbar Awakening', *Survival* 50:2 (April-May 2008), pp. 67–94.
105. This will be explored in greater depth in later chapters, where this view is evident in the analysis of some psyop specialists, generals, anthropologists and academics.

1. THE EMBATTLED WEST

1. WO 208/1447 'The Japanese Soldier'. An earlier military training pamphlet recalled that 'the Jap won the reputation of a superman' which was 'not deserved,' but Japan remained 'a dangerous and determined enemy whom it would be the greatest mistake to underrate', while still 'inferior to well-trained Allied or German troops.' BDA JSCSC 2745 War Office 'Military Training Pamphlet No. 52, Warfare in the Far East (Provisional), Dec. 1944, para. 15, p. 98.
2. As John Lynn argues, *Battle: A History of Combat and Culture* (Boulder, 2003), p. 23.
3. See A.L. Macfie, *Orientalism: A Reader* (Edinburgh, 2000), p. 6.
4. Edward W. Said, *Orientalism* (New York, 1978).
5. As summarised by Sadik Jalal al-'Azm, cited in Robert Irwin, *For Lust of Knowing: The Orientalists and their Enemies* (London, 2007), p. 285.

6. Tarak Barkawi, *Globalisation and War* (Oxford, 2006), p. 107.
7. Ibn Warraq, *Defending the West: A Critique of Edward Said's Orientalism* (New York 2007); Irwin, *For Lust of Knowing*, esp. pp. 277–310.
8. John MacKenzie, 'Edward Said and the Historians', *Nineteenth-Century Contexts*, 18:1 (1994), pp. 9–25, pp. 12, 15–16; Rosalind O'Hanon and David Washbrook, 'Histories in Transition: Approaches to the Study of Colonialism and Culture in India', *History Workshop Journal*, 32 (1991), pp. 110–28.
9. Daniel Martin Varisco, 'Reading against Culture in Edward Said's *Culture and Imperialism*' *Culture, Theory and Critique*, 45:2 (2004), pp. 93–112, pp. 95–6.
10. Edward Said, *Culture and Imperialism* (New York, 1993), p. xxiv-v.
11. As Said argued, anthropology 'often went hand in glove with a consciously undertaken imperial enterprise' *Culture and Imperialism*, p. 48; see also Talal Asad, *Anthropology and the Colonial Encounter* (London, 1973).
12. Peter Green, *Alexander of Macedon 356–323 BC: A Historical Biography* (Berkeley, 1991), pp. 161–3.
13. Juan Cole, *Napoleon's Egypt: Invading the Middle East* (New York, 2007), pp. 17, 30, 140–5, p. 247. This episode was seminal for the argument of Said's *Orientalism*, p. 86.
14. Michael Oren, *Power, Faith and Fantasy: America in the Middle East, 1776 to the Present* (New York, 2007), pp. 307–8.
15. On this debate, see Kurt Jakobsen, 'Are we there just to help the Army aim better?', *The Guardian*, 13 May 2008; David Vine, 'Enabling the kill-chain', *Chronicle of Higher Education*, 30 Nov. 2007; Roberto J. Gonzalez, 'Towards mercenary anthropology?', *Anthropology Today* 23:3 (June 2007), pp. 14–19; Bryan Bender, 'Efforts to aid US roil anthropology: Some object to project on Iraq, Afghanistan', *Boston Globe*, 8 Oct. 2007; Ralph Peters, 'Politically Incorrect War: US military Leaders Deny Reality', *New York Post*, 18 Oct. 2006.
16. P. J. Rhodes, 'The Impact of the Persian Wars on Classical Greece' in Emma Bridges, Edith Hall and P. J. Rhodes (eds), *Cultural Responses to the Persian Wars: Antiquity to the Third Millennium* (Oxford 2007), pp. 31–47, p. 34.
17. Said, *Orientalism* (New York, 1978), pp. 56–7. This interpretation is broadly followed by Thomas Harrison, *The Emptiness of Asia: Aeschylus' Persians and the History of the Fifth Century* (London, 2000), pp. 103–117; Edith Hall, *Inventing the Barbarian: Greek Self-Definition Through Tragedy* (Oxford, 1989).
18. Aeschylus, *The Persians* (trans. Janet Lembke and C.J. Herington, Oxford, 1981), references in order at lines 52, 71, 399, 658.
19. Simon Goldhill, 'Battle Narrative and Politics in Aeschylus' *Persae*', *Journal of Hellenic Studies*, 108 (1988), pp. 189–93, p. 190.
20. *Persians*, 567.
21. The interpretation here of the *Persians* as a 'supra-national' play is also made by H.D. Broadhead, *The Persae of Aeschylus. With Introduction,*

Critical Notes and Commentary (Cambridge, 1960), p. xviii; Christopher Pelling, 'Aeschylus' *Persae* and History' in Christopher Pelling (ed.), *Greek Tragedy and the Historian* (Oxford, 1997), pp. 1–19.

22. *Persians*, pp. 1340–1349.
23. Herodotus asserts a similar theme: 'the Athenians will not be so very different from the Persians, as imperialism turns out to have its own universally aggressive and brutal characteristics.' Christopher Pelling, 'East is East and West is West—Or Are They? National Stereotypes in Herodotus', *Histos*, 1 (1997). http://www.dur.ac.uk/Classics/histos/1997/pelling.html.
24. As Pelling indicates, there are several clear hints of this weakening of Persian empire, as it mentions islands that would be liberated after 480; Pelling 'Aeschylus *Persae*', p. 12.
25. Rudyard Kipling, *Rudyard Kipling's Verse: Inclusive Edition 1885–1932* (London, 1933), p. 45; Ralph Peters, 'The Counterrevolution in Military Affairs: Fashionable thinking about Defence ignores the great threats of our time', *The Weekly Standard*, 11:2 (6 Feb. 2006). Both of these articles are also compared by Robert Kaplan, 'America's Will to Win' *The American Interest* 11:6 (July/Aug. 2007).
26. Ken Adelman, 'Cakewalk in Iraq' *Washington Post* 13 Feb. 2002, p. A27; Toby Harnden, 'Bush Takes a Top Gun Stance on Western Carrier', *Daily Telegraph*, 3 May 2003; 'Bush: Bring on Attackers of US Troops', *USA Today*, 2 July 2003.
27. As Bob Woodward relates, among Bush's advisors there was great apprehensiveness about Afghanistan, its history of 'rebuffing outside forces' and the prospect of mountain fighting, quagmire and even overspill into Pakistan: *Bush at War* (London, 2002, 2003 edn.), pp. 82–83; but success created momentum and optimism: *Plan of Attack* (New York, 2004), p. 5; on 21 Nov. 2001, the day Bush instructed Rumsfeld to prepare plans for Iraq, he declared that the Taliban were 'on the run', 'President Shares Thanksgiving Meal with Troops' http://www.whitehouse.gov/news/releases/2001/11/20011121–3.html.
28. For the predictions during the crisis of 1990–1991, see Jacob Weisberg, 'Gulfballs: How the Experts Really Blew It' *New Republic* (March 25, 1991), pp. 17–19; Mike Royko, 'Most Experts Really Blew it this Time' *Chicago Tribune*, 28 Feb. 1991, p. 3; Daniel T. Plesch, 'A Military Tragedy' *New York Times* Feb. 8 1991, p. A31; Lawrence Freedman and Afraim Karsh 'How Kuwait was Won: Strategy in the Gulf War' *International Security* 16:2 (Fall 1991), pp. 5–41.
29. Notable exceptions were John J. Mearsheimer, 'A War the United States Can Win—Decisively', *Chicago Tribune*, 15 Jan. 1991, p. 13; 'Liberation in Less than a Week', *New York Times*, 8 Feb. 1991; Barry R. Posen, 'Political Objectives and Military Options in the Persian Gulf', *Defence and Arms Control Studies Working Paper* (Cambridge, Mass. Nov. 1990).
30. As Michael Barnett describes, '...the sight of one Arab state swallowing another whole...caused Arab leaders to proclaim the end of Arab nation-

alism, the need for a"new realism", and the view that state interests were not interchangeable with, and took primacy over some conception of, the Arab national interest.' Michael N. Barnett, 'Identity and Alliances in the Middle East' in Peter J. Katzenstein (ed.), *The Culture of National Security: Norms and Identity in World Politics* (New York, 1996), pp. 400–447, p. 428.

31. For example, Joseph Grew, former US ambassador in Tokyo before the Pacific war, argued that the Japanese were essentially irrational and could never adapt to democracy; while Ed Bodalato, former Marine officer and Defence and Naval attaché to Beirut, Damascus and Nicosia, argues that they have a propensity for conflict because of their childrearing practices, where competitiveness, pressure and a hostile spirit are instilled at an early age. Ian Buruma, foreword, in Ruth Benedict, *The Chrysanthemum and the Sword* (New York, 1946, 2005 edition), viii; Edward V. Badolato 'Learning to Think like an Arab Muslim: a Short Guide to Understanding the Arab Mentality', http://www.blackwaterusa.com/btw2004/articles/0503arabs.html.
32. Cited in Richard J. Reid, 'Revisiting Primitive War: Perceptions of Violence and Race in History', *War and Society*, 26:2 (Oct. 2007), pp. 1–25, pp. 2–6.
33. Steven A. LeBlanc and Katherine E. Register, *Constant Battles: The Myth of the Peaceful, Noble Savage* (New York, 2003), pp. 8–9, 95, 150–151.
34. On the Balkans, Henry Kissinger claimed that 'none of the populations has any experience with—and essentially no belief in—Western concepts of toleration.' 'No US Ground Forces for Kosovo', *Washington Post*, 22 Feb. 1999, p. A15; on the systemic and irrational violence of the Arab character, see David Pryce-Jones, *The Closed Circle: An Interpretation of the Arabs* (London, 1989), pp. 9–10; on Africans, I.M. Lewis depicts Somalis as 'pervasively bellicose', 'doing what they have always done—only with greater access to more lethal weapons', cited in Catherine Besteman, *Cultural Anthropology*, 13:1 (Feb. 1998), pp. 109–120, p. 110.
35. Janice E. Thompson, *Mercenaries, Pirates and Sovereigns* (Princeton, 1994).
36. Beatrice Heuser, *Reading Clausewitz* (London, 2002), pp. 138–42; David B. Ralston, *Importing the European Army: The Introduction of European Military Techniques and Institutions into the extra-European World 1600–1914* (Chicago, 1990); Mark Philip Bradley, *Imagining Vietnam and America: The Making of Postcolonial Vietnam, 1919–1950* (Chapel Hill, 2000), pp. 10–25, 190.
37. See Armstrong Starkey, *European and Native American Warfare, 1675–1815* (Norman, 1998), pp. 92–103; Ian K. Steele, *Warpaths: Invasions of North America* (New York, 1994), p. 3.
38. Matthew C. Ward, *Breaking the Backcountry: The Seven Years' War in India and Pennsylvania 1754–1765* (Pittsburgh 2003), pp. 54, 220–2.
39. J. C. B. *Travels in New France*, cited in George A. Bray III, 'Scalping during the French and Indian War', *Early America Review* 2:3 (Spring/Summer 1998). http://www.earlyamerica.com/review/1998/scalping.html

40. James Axtell, William C. Sturtevant, 'The Unkindest Cut, or Who Invented Scalping', *The William and Mary Quarterly* 31:3 (July 1980), pp. 451–472, 461–2.
41. R. Brian Ferguson, 'Blood of the Leviathan: Western Contact and Warfare in Amazonia' *American Ethnologist* 17:2 (May 1990), pp.237–257.
42. John Childs, *Armies and Warfare in Europe 1648–1789* (Manchester, 1982); Jeremy Black 'Eighteenth-Century Warfare Reconsidered', *War in History*, 1 (1994), pp. 215–232.
43. Hew Strachan, 'A General Typology of Transcultural Wars—the Modern Age' in Hans-Henning Kortüm (ed.), *Transcultural Wars from the Middle Ages to the Twenty First Century* (Berlin, 2006), pp. 85–103.
44. On this, see Alexander Wendt and Michael Barnett, 'Dependent State Formation and Third World Militarisation', *Review of International Studies*, 19 (1993), pp. 321–347; Joao Resende-Santos, 'Anarchy and the Emulation of Military Systems: Military Organisation and Technology in South America, 1870–1914', *Security Studies*, 5:3 (1996), pp. 193–260; Theo Farrell 'World Culture and Military Power', *Security Studies*, 14:3 (2005), pp. 448–488.
45. Barbara Ehrenreich, *Blood Rites: Origins and History of the Passion of War* (London, 1997), p. 141.
46. *The Song of Roland*, trans. Dorothy L. Sayers (Harmondsworth, 1957), p. 87; discussed also in Irwin, *For Lust of Knowing*, p. 41.
47. There is a wealth of literature on this: Bernard Hamilton, 'Knowing the Enemy: Western Understanding of Islam at the time of the Crusades', *Journal of the Royal Asiatic Society*, 3rd series, 7 (1997) pp. 373–387; Margaret A. Jubb, 'Enemies in the Holy War, but Brothers in Chivalry: the Crusaders' view of their Saracen opponents' in Hans van Dijk and Willem Noomen (eds), *Aspects de l'epopee romane* (Groningen, 1995), pp. 251–259; Margaret A. Jubb, *The Legend of Saladin in Western Literature and Historiography* (New York, 2000); John V. Tolan, *Saracens: Islam in the Medieval European Imagination* (New York, 2002), pp. 280–1.
48. Asli Cirakman *From the 'Terror of the World' to the 'Sick Man of Europe': European Images of Ottoman Empire and Society from the Sixteenth Century to the Nineteenth* (New York, 2002), p. 79.
49. M. Hodgson, *The Venture of Islam* (Chicago, 1974), v.3 p. 113; H.A.R. Gibb and Harold Bowen, *Islamic Society and the West: A Study of the Impact of Western Civilisation on Moslem Culture in the Near East* (London, 1950), 1:62. One observer described Ottoman efficiency thus: 'It costs the Grand Signor no more to maintain his army in time of War, then in time of Peace; for he keeps none but his own Soldiers, and the Bashas and others maintain those whom they have brought with them; But it is not the Number alone that makes them gain so many Battels…it is also the valour and strength of the Soldiers.' Cited in Cirakma, *From the 'Terror of the World'*, p. 70.

50. Traveller Antoine Geuffrey in 1542 explained Turkish strength as 'permitted of God, whyche for oure synnes sufferethe thys estate so farre swaruynge from all good pollycie.'Cited in Cirakman, p. 71, for Luther's idea that God punished Christians through the Turks, see p. 84.
51. This theme is developed in detail in the context of 'going native' in American literature and popular culture: Shari M. Huhndorf, *Going Native: Indians in the American Cultural Imagination* (Cornell, 2001), p.4: 'two characters, cleansed of the corruption of European-American life by adopting Indian ways, hold the promise of a new and better white world. It is, in fact, the regeneration of white society that proves the ultimate goal of Dunbar's journey into the primitive.'
52. Jeff Dawson, 'Don't be fooled by the Japanese Swordplay: Ed Zwick's The Last Samurai is a Western at heart' *Sunday Times* 28 December 2003; see also Stefan Lovgren, 'The Last Samurai: Movie Myth or History?' *National Geographic News* 2 December 2003.
53. This genre is explored by David Edelstein, 'Santa Slays: Billy Bob Thornton vs. kids in *Bad Santa*. Tom Cruise vs. capitalism in *The Last Samurai*' *Slate* 4 Dec. 2003.
54. To Jesuit Francis Parkman, the Iroquois people had not escaped 'the confines of a wild hunter and warrior life. They were inveterably attached to it, impracticable conservatists of barbarism, and in ferocity and cruelty they matched the worst of their race.' Images of a primordial warrior folk appealed to those who saw them as 'nature's nobleman' who was purer than European conquerors. Others looked down on the Indian as 'subhuman, waiting fiercely to be wiped out.' Roy Harvey Pearce, *Savagism and Civilisation: A Study of the Indian and the American Mind* (Berkeley, 1988, first edn 1953); for Francis Parkman's quote see pp. 167–8, 'nature's nobleman' and 'subhuman' at p. 179.
55. Thomas Conlan, *State of War: The Violent Order of Fourteenth-Century Japan* (Ann Arbor, 2003), pp. 7, 64, 159, 161, 231; 'Samurai a good film maybe, but good history unlikely', *Oakland Tribune*, 27 Nov. 2003.
56. Beforehand, they had fought foot battles of massed infantry in line formation with leather body armour, large shields and shock weapons such as lances and clubs, as well as the bow. See Frank Raymond Secoy, *Changing Military Patterns of the Great Plains Indians* (Nebraska, 1954, 1992 edn), pp. 6–38; Bernard Mishkin, *Rank and Warfare Among the Plains Indians* (Nebraska, 1992), pp. v-xii, 5–24, 60; Colin Calloway, *One Vast Winter Count: The Native American West before Lewis and Clark* (Nebraska, 2003), p. 267.
57. Barkawi *Globalization and War*, pp. 107–9.
58. J.A. Hobson, *Imperialism: A Study* (London, 1902).
59. As Sally Ledger and Roger Luckhurst argue, *The Fin de Siècle: A Reader in Cultural History c.1880–1900* (Oxford, 2000), p. xvi.
60. These cases, and the problem of peripheral wars causing distress in the metropole, are discussed further in Douglas Porch, *Wars of Empire* (London, 2000, 2006 edn), pp. 41–51.

61. On the rhetoric of small wars in relation to European-Atlantic utopian ideas of the civilizing mission, see Tarak Barkawi, 'On the pedagogy of "small wars"', *International Affairs*, 80:1 (2004), pp. 19–37.
62. Hew Strachan, 'A General Typology of Transcultural Wars—the Modern Age' in Hans-Henning Kortüm (ed.), *Transcultural Wars from the Middle Ages to the Twenty First Century* (Berlin, 2006), pp. 85–103. Likewise, Indian Sikhs' use of heavy artillery surprised and educated the British: Hew Strachan, *From Waterloo to Balaclava: Tactics, Technology and the British Army 1815–1854* (Cambridge, 1985), pp. 123–5.
63. James Belich, *The New Zealand Wars and the Victorian Interpretation of Racial Conflict* (Auckland 1986), p. 295
64. A distinction explored by Christopher Coker, *Waging War without Warriors? The Changing Culture of Military Conflict* (London, 2002), pp. 4–6.
65. National Army Museum (henceforth NAM), Ref. 8305–55, Captain Neville Cameron, Letter 4 Sept. 1898; 'Science Over Barbarians' from Winston Churchill, *The River War: an Account of the Reconquest of the Sudan* (London, 1951 edn.), p. 300; Rudyard Kipling in his poem 'Fuzzy-Wuzzy' also praised the Sudanese combatants in these paradoxical terms, 'You're a pore benighted 'eathen but a first-class fightin' man.'
66. Charles E. Callwell, *Small Wars: Their Principles and Practice* (London, 1896); Alfred Ditte, *Observations sur les guerres dans les colonies* (Paris, 1905).
67. Callwell, *Small Wars*, p. 78.
68. Ibid., p. 148.
69. See also Richard J. Reid, 'Revisiting Primitive War: Perceptions of Violence and Race in History', *War and Society*, 26:2 (Oct. 2007), pp. 1–25, pp. 15–16.
70. Douglas MacArthur, 'Statement to the 51st. Annual Encampment of the Veterans of Foreign Wars' 20 Aug., 1950, cited and discussed further in Tarak Barkawi, 'Orientalism at War', pp. 27–8.
71. Cited in Michael E. Gordon and Bernard E. Trainor, *Cobra II: The Inside Story of the Invasion and Occupation of Iraq* (New York, 2006), p. 447.
72. PRO AIR 5/264, 'Suggested Systems of Attack against Uncivilised Tribes.'
73. Douglas M. Peers, 'Those Noble Exemplars of the True Military Tradition': Constructions of the Indian Army in the mid-Victorian Press', *Modern Asian Studies*, 31: 1 (1997), pp. 109–142, p. 110; see also David Omissi, *The Sepoy and the Raj: The Indian Army, 1860–1940* (London, 1994); Heather Streets, *Martial Races: The Military, Race and Masculinity in British Imperial Culture 1857–1914* (Manchester, 2004).
74. NAM 6702–91–21 Major-General C.J. Mellis, Letters and Notes relating to Expedition to East Africa, March-July 1896, pp. 3–11.
75. Streets, *Martial Races*, p. 2.
76. Akbar S. Ahmed, *Resistance and Control in Pakistan* (London, 1983, 1991 edn), p. 29.

77. Eden Commission and MacMunn quotes from Tony Ballantyne, *Orientalism and Race: Aryanism in the British Empire* (New York, 2002), p. 113.
78. Omissi, *The Sepoy and the Raj*, pp. 27–28.
79. PRO WO287/22, General Staff, India, 'Military Report on Afghanistan', pp. 'C', 524.
80. PRO WO 106/3311 'Notes on Japanese Army 6/1/42–5/8/42', docs.3, and 4, and 8: 'Cypher 122/7 d.23/12, 'Jap: tactics', pp. 2–3; 'low cunning': 'Jap. Army Periodic Notes No. 1 d.27 Dec. 1941, p. 1; 'Ruses': 'Notes on War experience against Japs in Malaya' pp. 1–2.
81. Callwell, *Small Wars*, pp. 30–31.
82. As a liaison officer wrote, 'I do not want to stir up fanaticism, always an awkward factor.' PRO WO 28/372 'Staff diary of the liaison officer to the Abyssinian forces in the Ogaden', Brevet-Major Hon. A.H.C. Hanbury-Tracy, 17 March to 4 Oct. 1901, p. 7.
83. PRO WO 106/21/7 'African No. 916 Confidential' 26 Aug. 1908.
84. NAM 6112–464 'Notes for Guidance, Camel Corps', 1930, p. 2.
85. PRO CAB 127/1 'Lectures given at Staff College Quetta; 'Somaliland 1884–1919' 'Life of Mohamed bin Abdulla Hasan (the 'Mad Mullah') 1868–1918', dated 1922, p. 95.
86. An observer could present Somalis as rational, while also warning against their childishness and propensity to fanaticism, warning that 'nothing but a clean sweep will cure them.' These were the words of Captain R.WC. Blair, whose description of Somaliland in 1903 otherwise portrayed the Somali population as people influenced by material and geostrategic circumstances, caught between British power on the littoral and the Mullah's power in the interior where they relied on pastureland, so that Somalis could ill-afford to lend outright support to the British, and had powerful incentives to co-operate with the Mullah (security, a wife and camels, and loot). PRO WO 106/21/40/13, 'Military Situation: A Few Notes by Capt. R.W.C. Blair', 10.8.03.
87. *Pall Mall Gazette*, 1 Jan. 1885, p. 1, cited in Cynthia Behrman, 'The Afterlife of General Gordon', *Albion: A Quarterly Journal Concerned with British Studies* (Summer, 1971), 3:2, pp. 47–61, p. 49.
88. Richard Slotkin, *The Fatal Environment: The Myth of the Frontier in Twentieth-Century America* (New York, 1985), pp. 8–10, 435–476.
89. Michael A. Elliott, *Custerology: The Enduring Legacy of the Indian Wars and George Armstrong Custer* (Chicago, 2007), p. 4.
90. These historic meanings are explored by Stephen W. Silliman, '"The 'Old West" in the Middle East: US Military Metaphors in Real and Imagined Indian Country,' *American Anthropologist*, 110:2 (2008), pp. 237–247.
91. BDA, JSCSC 1006, 'Notes on Japanese Warfare on the Malayan Front', 9 Jan. 1942, Washington, Military Intelligence Division, War Department, Information Bulletin No. 6 MID 461.
92. Peter Baker, 'Wrong Turn in Nasiriyah Led to Soldiers' Capture Maintenance Company Drove Into Waiting Ambush,' *Washington Post*, April 13, 2003.

93. Robert Kaplan, 'Indian Country: America's military faces the most thankless task in the history of warfare', *Wall Street Journal*, 25 Sept. 2004, A22; discussed further in Elliot, *Custerology*, pp. 278–9.
94. Hans Delbrück, *Warfare in Antiquity: History of the Art of War* (trans. Walter J. Renfroe, Lincoln, 1990), vol. 1, p. 35, 33–39; Gordon A. Craig, 'Delbrück: The Military Historian' in Peter Paret, Gordon A. Craig and Felix Gilbert (eds), *Makers of Modern Strategy: from Machiavelli to the Nuclear Age* (Princeton, 1986), pp. 326–354, 333.
95. William H. Prescott, *The History of the Conquest of Mexico* (London, 1843).
96. Timothy Braatz, 'Clash of Cultures as Euphemism: Avoiding History at the Little Bighorn' *American Indian Culture and Research Journal*, 28:4 (2004), pp. 107–30, p. 114.
97. For the political campaign to divert attention to the battle, see Michael Glover, *Rorke's Drift* (London, 1975, 1997 edn), pp. 125–133.
98. This is the phrase of Peter Cochrane, *Simpson and the Donkey: The Making of a Legend* (Melbourne, 1992), p. 4.
99. Marcus Luttrell, *Lone Survivor: the Eyewitness Account of Operation Redwing and the Lost Heroes of SEAL Team 10* (Little Brown, 2007); 'Hollywood takes on Taliban tome "Lone Survivor"', Reuters, 21 Aug. 2007.
100. Luttrell, *Lone Survivor*, p. 168.
101. Luttrell, *Lone Survivor*, p. 170.
102. In the case of *Black Hawk Down* and other recent films, see Frank J. Wetta and Martin A. Novelli, 'Now a Major Motion Picture: War Films and Hollywood's New Patriotism', *The Journal of Military History*, 67:3 (July 2003), pp. 861–882, 878, 881.
103. Dennis Showalter, 'Imagery and Realism: The Two Faces of Black Hawk Down', *Diplomatic History*, 26 (4) (2002), pp. 649–51, p. 651.
104. Frederico Neiburg and Marcio Goldman, 'Anthropology and Politics in Studies of National Character', *Cultural Anthropology*, 13:1 (1998), pp. 56–81, 57–8; Christopher Shannon, 'A World Made Safe for Differences: Ruth Benedict's *The Chrysanthemum and the Sword*,' *American Quarterly* 47:4 (Dec. 1995), pp. 659–680, 663–4.
105. For an introduction to the literature in both military history and political science, see Lawrence Sondhaus, *Strategic Culture and Ways of War* (London, 2006). For the history of estimates of Japanese military power, see Philip Towle, *From Ally to Enemy: Anglo-Japanese Military Relations, 1900–1945* (Canterbury, 2006); 'British Estimates of Japanese Military Power, 1900–1914' in p. Towle (ed.), *Estimating Foreign Military Power* (London, 1982), pp. 111–139; John Ferris, 'Double-Edged Estimates: Japan in the Eyes of the British Army and the Royal Air Force, 1900–1939' in Ian Gow, Yoichi Hirama and John Chapman (eds), *The History of Anglo-Japanese Relations 1600–2000 Volume III: The Military Dimension* (New York, 2003), pp. 91–108; John W.M. Chapman, 'Britain, Japan and the 'Higher Realms of Intelligence' 1900–1918' in

Ian Gow, Yoichi Hirama and John Chapman (eds), *History of Anglo-Japanese Relations* (New York, 2003), pp. 71–89.

106. As Williamson Murray claims, just as in 1904 most Europeans believed that the Russians would 'easily defeat' the Japanese, 'racial prejudice would lead the West to underestimate Japan's military capabilities right down to Pearl Harbour in 1941.' Williamson Murray, 'Towards World War 1871–1914', in Geoffrey Parker (ed.), *The Cambridge History of Warfare* (Cambridge, 2005), p. 260; Peter Lowe, 'Great Britain's Assessment of Japan Before the Outbreak of the Pacific War' in Ernest May (ed.), *Knowing One's Enemies: Intelligence Assessment Before the Two World* Wars, (Princeton, 1984), pp. 456–475; see also Antony Best, who argues that on the eve of World War Two, intelligence materials reveal that the British War Cabinet rationalised its economic sanctions on the perception that Japan was too weak militarily and too 'overawed by the Anglo-Saxon powers' to confront Anglo-American power: 'Constructing an Image: British Intelligence and Whitehall's Perception of Japan, 1931–1939', *Intelligence and National Security*, 11:3 (July 1996), pp. 403–421, 421.

107. For this revisionist literature, see John R. Ferris, 'Image and Accident: Intelligence and the origins of the Second World War, 1933–1941' in *Intelligence and Strategy: Selected Essays* (London, 2005), pp. 99–137, esp. 121–123; 'Worthy of Some Better Enemy? The British Estimate of the Imperial Japanese Army and the Fall of Singapore, 1919–1941', *Canadian Journal of History*, 28 (1993), pp. 223–56; Thomas G. Mahnken, *Uncovering Ways of War: US Intelligence and Foreign Military Innovation, 1918–1941* (Ithaca, 2002), pp. 42–86; Richard J. Aldrich, 'Britain's Secret Intelligence in Asia During the Second World War', *Modern Asian Studies*, 32:1 (1998), pp. 179–217, esp. 181, 184.

108. Such as French military attaché Colonel Mast, cited in Ferris, *Intelligence and Strategy*, p. 122; British cavalry officer from PRO WO 106/5491, Captain E. Ainger, 'Report on Attachment to Cavalry School, Imperial Japanese Army' 1 Dec. 1930–28 March 1931, pp. 6, 7, 11, 16, 17.

109. See eg. PRO WO 106/5541, 'The Japanese Danger' (paper prepared for M.I.2), 7 July 1936, p. 13.

110. As Ferris argues, 'Worthy of Some Better Enemy? The British Estimate of the Imperial Japanese Army, 1919–1941, and the Fall of Singapore', *Canadian Journal of History*, 28:2 (Aug. 1993), pp. 224–256.

111. Mahnken, *Uncovering Ways of War*, p. 49; though this was not universal: see BDA JSCSC 3310 G.S. Report for D.C.I.G.S. No. 7, 'Considerations from the Wars in Spain and China with regard to certain aspects of Army Policy', para. 62, p. 22: 'the Japanese usually chose bad and therefore unlikely places, for the sake of surprise.'

112. John W. Dower, *War Without Mercy: Race and Power in the Pacific War* (New York, 1986); Craig M. Cameron, *American Samurai: Myth, Imagination and the Conduct of Battle in the First Marine Division, 1941–1951* (Cambridge, 1994), pp. 89–130; Ronald Takaki, *Double*

Victory: A Multicultural History of America in World War II (Boston, 2000).

113. See Emiko Ohnuki-Tierney, *Kamikaze Diaries: Reflections of Japanese Student Soldiers* (Chicago, 2006, 2007 edn), pp. 8–11; Hatsuho Naito, *Thunder Gods: The Kamikaze Pilots tell their Story* (New York, 1989).
114. Vice Admiral Charles R. Brown, cited in Raymond Lamont-Brown, *Kamikaze: Japan's Suicide Samurai* (London, 1997), p. 78.
115. Allison Gilmore shows that Australian and American psychological operations were effective even against an enemy widely assumed to be radically different, partly because PSYOP personnel overcame crude stereotypes. They recognised that only a small minority of Japanese combatants had the psychological profile of samurai fanatics: Allison B. Gilmore, *You Can't Fight Tanks with Bayonets: Psychological Warfare against the Japanese Army in the Southwest Pacific* (Lincoln, 1998), pp. 146–181.
116. See Antony Best, 'Constructing an Image: British Intelligence and Whitehall's Perception of Japan, 1931–1939', *Intelligence and National Security*, 11:3 (July 1996), pp. 403–421; Douglas Ford, 'British Intelligence on Japanese Army Morale during the Pacific War: Logical Analysis or Racial Stereotyping', *Journal of Military History* (April 2005), pp. 439–474; Douglas Ford, 'Strategic Culture, Intelligence Assessment, and the Conduct of the Pacific War: The British-Indian and Imperial Japanese Armies in Comparison, 1941–45', *War in History*, 14:1 (Jan. 2007), pp. 63–96.
117. As Robert B. Edgerton argues, the changing norms of Japanese combatants between the Russo-Japanese war and the Second World War shows that chivalry and brutality are learned behaviours. *Warriors of the Rising Sun: A History of the Japanese Military* (Westview, 1997), esp. pp. 305–325.
118. Hoover Institution of War and Peace, Stanford University: Bonner F. Fellers papers, Writings 1934–58, Box. 1:3, 'The Psychology of the Japanese Soldier' 1935; Box. 1:1 'Answer to Japan', 1944.
119. As discussed by Allison B. Gilmore, *You Can't Fight Tanks with Bayonets: Psychological Warfare against the Japanese Army in the South West Pacific* (Nebraska, 1998), p. 39.
120. For a further discussion of this issue, see Richard H. Minear 'Cross-Cultural Perception and World War II: American Japanists of the 1940's and Their Images of Japan' *International Studies Quarterly* 24:4 (Dec. 1980), pp. 555–580, p. 564.
121. See also John Dower, who argues that in World War Two, Japan was politically divided and physically no fitter than their enemies in the industrial West: John Dower, 'Sensational Rumours, Seditious Graffiti, and the Nightmares of the Thought Police' *Japan in War and Peace: Essays on History, Culture and Race* (London, 1993), pp. 101–154. As Dower argues, police records indicate growing contempt in public opinion for existing authority and even the Emperor.

122. Samantha Power, *A Problem from Hell: America and the Age of Genocide* (New York, 2002, 2003 edn), xx, 282, 302; Stuart J. Kaufman, *Modern Hatreds: The Symbolic Politics of Ethnic War* (Ithaca, 2001); Noel Malcolm, 'Seeing Ghosts', *The National Interest* (Summer 1993), pp. 83–88.
123. Cited in Power, *A Problem from Hell*, p. 282.
124. Colin Powell, 'Why Generals get Nervous', *New York Times*, 18 Oct. 1992, p. A35.
125. Charles King, 'The Myth of Ethnic Warfare', *Foreign Affairs*, 80:6 (Nov./Dec. 2001), pp. 165–170; John Mueller, 'The Banality of Ethnic War', *International Security*, 25:1 (Summer 2000), pp. 42–70.

2. RETHINKING WAR AND CULTURE

1. Robert S. McNamara, *In Retrospect* (New York, 1995), p. 32.
2. For this argument, see further Colin Gray, *Another Bloody Century* (London, 2005), pp. 90–91.
3. As argued by John Robert Ferris, *Intelligence and Strategy: Selected Essays* (New York, 2005), p. 107.
4. Michael Handel, 'The Evolution of Israeli Strategy: The Psychology of Insecurity and the Quest for Absolute Security' in Williamson Murray, MacGregor Knox and Alvin Bernstein (eds) *The Making of Strategy: Rulers, States and War* (Cambridge, 1994), pp. 534–578.
5. Saddam's pre-war decision-making has been reconstructed from new intelligence by Kevin Woods, James Lacey and Williamson Murray, 'Saddam's delusions: The View From the Inside' *Foreign Affairs* 85:3 (May/June 2006), pp. 2–28; Michael R. Gordon and Bernard E. Trainor, *Cobra II: the Inside Story of the Invasion and Occupation of Iraq* (New York, 2006), esp. pp. 55–75; see also Kevin M. Woods, Michael R. Pease, Mark E. Stout, Williamson Murray, and James G. Lacey, *The Iraqi Perspectives Report: Saddam's Senior Leadership on Operation Iraqi Freedom from the Official US Joint Forces Command Report* (Annapolis, 2006), pp. 14–33.
6. See Gerhard L. Weinberg, 'Hitler's Image of the United States', *American Historical Review*, 69:4 (July 1964), pp. 1001–21. On how aggressors can draw false confidence from their sense of cultural supremacy, see Michael P. Fischerkeller, 'David versus Goliath: Cultural Judgments in Asymmetric Wars,' *Security Studies*, 7:4 (Summer 1998), pp. 1–43, which argues that measurably 'weaker' powers initiate conflict against stronger rivals at least partly because of a dangerous confidence that their supposedly greater cultural sophistication could offset military or economic disadvantage. Before Pakistan's attack on India in 1971, against which it was roughly at a 1:3 military disparity, a generation of Pakistani officers were deluded by their faith that this could be overcome by the supposed martial superiority of Muslim over Hindu officers.
7. Carl von Clausewitz, *On War*, 1:1, ed. and trans. Michael Howard and Peter Paret, rev. edn (Princeton, 1984), p. 88.

8. Cited in Dexter Filkins, 'A Region Inflamed: Strategy; Tough new Tactics by US Tighten Grip on Iraqi Towns', *New York Times*, 7 Dec. 2003. See also Andrew Bacevich, 'What's an Iraqi Life Worth?', *Washington Post*, 9 July 2006, B1.
9. 'Can a lull be turned into a real peace?', *Economist*, 15 Dec. 2007, p. 30.
10. As General Anthony C. Zinni stated, 'Cultural Intelligence is the greatest need of the commander on the ground and the one [if lacking] that leads him into more problems', cited in Michael Trabun, *When the West Meets Islam: Cultural Issues and Considerations for Regional Combatant Commanders* (Newport, 2004), p. 14.
11. Zinni's remarks indicate that he viewed pride and masculinity as distinctive Arab sensitivities: 'The biggest mistake the United States made in the war was speaking of "shock and awe." That was a way to say: "Your fate is inevitable. We're going to crush you. The might of America will defeat you. Just surrender and throw down your arms." You don't speak to Arab pride and Arab manhood in this way. That whole psychological business gave them another cause to fight for, more than they would have fought just for Saddam.' See 'The Wrong War at the Wrong Time', *Buffalo News*, 4 April 2003.
12. Donald Kagan, 'Honor, Interest, and the Nation-State' in Elliot Abrams, Donald Kagan (eds), *Honour Among Nations: Intangible Interests and Foreign Policy* (Washington DC, 1998), pp. 1–17.
13. As Michael Desch also argues, 'Culture Versus Structure in Post-9/11 Security Studies', *Strategic Insights*, 4:10 (Oct., 2005), p. 6.
14. 'Army Transformation, Implications for the Future.' Statement of Major General Robert Scales, House Armed Services Committee, 15 July, 2004.
15. Patrick Devenny, Robert McLean, 'The Battle for Basra', *The American Spectator*, 1 Nov. 2005; see also James Ashcroft: 'Hundreds of years of colonial policing had left the experience of interacting with dangerous peoples in the bones of the British Army' *Making a Killing: The Explosive Story of a Hired Gun in Iraq* (London, 2007), p. 42; Danna Harman, 'As Occupiers, Brits bring Experience: Years of Colonial Policing have made soldiers all-rounders' *Christian Science Monitor* 20 May, 2003.
16. T.E. Lawrence, *Seven Pillars of Wisdom: A Triumph* (New York, 1935), p. 38.
17. Mona Mahmoud, Maggie O'Kane and Ian Black, 'UK has left behind murder and chaos, says Basra police chief', *The Guardian*, 17 Dec. 2007.
18. 'Losing Their Way? The British Army suffers from Lack of Soldiers, Lack of Money and Lack of Conviction.' *Economist* 29 January 2009.
19. Rear Admiral Chris Parry, *Countering Irregular Activity within a Comprehensive Approach, Joint Doctrine Note 2/07*, United Kingdom, March 2007, pp. 1.2–1.3.
20. As Alex Marshall argues, 'Imperial Nostalgia, the Liberal Lie, and the Perils of Post-Modern Counterinsurgency' (forthcoming).
21. See David Anderson, *Histories of the Hanged: The Dirty War in Kenya and the End of Empire* (New York, 2005).

22. Ashley Jackson, 'British Counter-insurgency in History: A Useful Precedent?', *The British Army Review*, No. 139 (2006), pp. 14–16; Huw Bennett, 'The Other Side of the COIN: Minimum and Exemplary Force in British Army Counterinsurgency in Kenya', *Small Wars and Insurgencies*, 18:4 (Dec. 2007), pp. 638–664; Hew Strachan, 'British Counter-Insurgency from Malaya to Iraq', *The RUSI Journal*, 152:6 (Dec. 2007), pp. 8–11, p. 10.
23. Andrew J. Birtle, 'The US Army's Pacification of Marinduque, Philippine Islands, April 1900—April 1901,' *The Journal of Military History*, 61 (April 1997), pp. 255–282.
24. William R. Polk, *Violent Politics: A History of Insurgency, Terrorism and Guerrilla War, from the American Revolution to Iraq* (New York, 2007), p. 210.
25. Raphael Patai, *The Arab Mind* (New York, 1971, 2002 edn); Colonel Norvelle Atkine, director of Middle East Studies at the JFK Special Warfare Centre and School at Fort Bragg, who used to brief American military personnel, approvingly introduces the 2001 reprint of *The Arab Mind*. It 'formed the basis of my cultural instruction' as he briefed 'hundreds of military teams being deployed to the Middle East.'
26. McFate defended the text as evidence that torturing Iraqis would provoke the wrath of their kin for cultural reasons: Matthew B. Stannard, 'Montgomery McFate's Mission: Can one Anthropologist possibly steer the course in Iraq?', *San Francisco Chronicle*, 29 April, 2007; see also Emran Qureshi, 'Misreading 'The Arab Mind': The dubious guidebook to Middle East culture that's on the Pentagon's reading list', *Boston Globe*, 30 May 2004.
27. Montgomery McFate, 'The military utility of understanding adversary culture', *Joint Force Quarterly*, 38 (July 2005), pp. 42–48, p. 43 (my italics for 'determined').
28. T.E. Lawrence, 'The 27 Articles', *Arab Bulletin*, 60:20 (20 Aug. 1917), Article 23.
29. This is a criticism that has also been made of 'localist' concepts of culture: see Lila Abu-Lughod, 'Writing against Culture' in R. Fox (ed.), *Recapturing Anthropology: Working in the Present* (Santa Fe, 1991), pp. 137–12, p. 146.
30. US Army/Marine Corps, *Counterinsurgency* (Washington, DC, 2006), Chapter 3, pp. 6–7, Appendix p. 7. For more discussion of classic ethnography, see William H. Sewell Jr., 'The Concept(s) of Culture' in Victoria E. Bonnell and Lynn Hunt (eds) *Beyond the Cultural Turn: New Directions in the Study of Society and Culture* (Berkeley, 1999), pp. 35–61, 53.
31. Carter Malkasian, 'A Thin Blue Line in the Sand', *Democracy*, 5 (Summer 2007), p. 55.
32. Lieut. Colonel Michael Eisenstadt, 'Tribal Engagement: Lessons Learned', *Military Review* (Sept./Oct. 2007), pp. 16–31, 18, 27.

33. 'Taliban Fighters Heard Speaking in British Accents', *Sheffield Telegraph*, 11 Feb. 2008.
34. Michael Scheuer, 'Al Qaeda's Insurgency Doctrine: Aiming for a 'Long War', *Terrorism Focus* 3:8 (28 Feb., 2006), p. 4; Mark E. Stout, Jessica M. Huckabey, John R. Schindler, Jim Lacey, *The Terrorist Perspectives Project: Strategic and Operational Views of Al Qaida and Associated Movements* (Annapolis, 2008), pp.129–30.
35. Lucasta Miller, 'Bound for Glory', an interview with David Campbell, publisher of the Everyman series, *The Guardian*, Review, 13 May 2006, p. 11, cited also in Hew Strachan and Andreas Herberg-Rothe, *Clausewitz in the Twenty First Century* (Oxford 2007), p. 1.
36. Mark E. Stout, Jessica M. Huckabey, John R. Schindler, Jim Lacey, *The Terrorist Perspectives Project* p.76, 124, 126–7
37. Ibid.
38. Gordon Corera, 'Spy lifts lid on Al Qaeda', *BBC News* 16 Nov. 2006: as a former Al Qaeda operative explained, 'recruits were provided with intense and highly comprehensive military training—much of which was based on training manuals of UK and US special forces.'
39. Qutb cited in Stout, *The Terrorist Perspectives Project*, p.125.
40. Abu Bakr Naji, *The Management of Savagery: Most Critical Stage through which the Umma will Pass* (trans. William McCants, 2006, Harvard), part 7, p.18, part 64, p. 28.
41. Cited in Bryanjar Lia, *Architect of Global Jihad: The Life of Al-Qaida Strategist Abu Mus'ab al-Suri* (London, 2007), pp. 3, 263, 485; Al-Suri's Doctrines for Decentralized Jihadi Training *Terrorism Monitor* 5:2 (2007); as Lia explains, tapes of his lectures were transcribed on the web: 'Explanation of the Book 'War of the Oppressed', Khost, Afghanistan, 1998.
42. As Mark Stout shows, 'In Search of Salafist Jihadist Strategic Thought: Mining the Words of the Terrorists' *International Studies Association* Convention, 29 March 2008, p.7.
43. William S. Lind, Col. Keith Nightingale, Captain John. F. Schmitt, Col. Joseph W. Sutton, Lt.Col. Gary I Wilson, 'The Changing Face of War: Into the Fourth Generation', *Marine Corps Gazette* (Oct., 1989), pp. 22–26; William McCants, 'For the Word of God to Be Supreme: Al-Qaida Strategic Thinking and Its Implications for U.S. Policy' (Combating Terrorism Center at West Point, 15 May 2007), at http://web.mit.edu/ssp/seminars/wed_archives_07spring/McCants.htm
44. 'Bin Laden Lieutenant Admits to Sept. 11 and Explains Al-Qa'ida's Combat Doctrine', *Middle East Media and Research Institute*, Special Dispatch 344 (10 Feb. 2002), cited also in John Robb, *Brave New War: The Next Stage of Terrorism and the End of Globalization* (New Jersey, 2007), p. 20.
45. See Raymond Ibrahim (ed.), *The Al Qaeda Reader* (New York, 2007), pp. xxix, xxx, 204, 224.

46. For this and more general discussion of Al Qaeda's modernity, see John Gray, *Al Qaeda and What it Means to be Modern* (London, 2003, 2004 edn), pp. 2, 26, 76; Rohan Gunaratna, *Inside Al-Qaeda, Global Network of Terror* (London, 2002), p. 11; Malise Ruthven, *A Fury for God: The Islamist Attack on America* (London, 2004), p. 91; James L. Gelvin, *The Modern Middle East: A History* (New York, 2007), p. 7.
47. Dexter Filkins, 'Complexity of Iraq insurgency helps it to survive', *International Herald Tribune*, 2 Dec. 2005; Bruce Hoffman, *Inside Terrorism* (Columbia, 2006), pp. 285–289.
48. David E. Kaplan, 'The New Business of Terror', *US News and World Report*, 5 Dec. 2005.
49. Jane Perlez and Pir Zubair Shah, 'Taliban Imperil Pakistani City, a Major Hub', *New York Times* 28 June 2008: '...to win favor with the Taliban, the criminals grow their hair and their beards, and join forces with the militants, they said. In this way, the criminals get protection from the militants for the money they give to the Taliban from their extortion rackets.'
50. Jessica Stern, 'The Protean Enemy' *Foreign Affairs*, 82:1 (July/Aug. 2003), pp. 27–40.
51. See James Forest (ed.), *Teaching Terror: Strategic and Tactical Learning in the Terrorist World* (Oxford, 2006), xii, and Gabriel Weimann, 'Virtual Training Camps: Terrorist's Use of the Internet' in Forest, *Teaching Terror*, pp. 110–133, esp. 119–123.
52. Bin Laden's statement: '...there will be no harm if the interests of Muslims converge with the interests of the socialists in the fight against the crusaders, despite our belief in the infidelity of socialists.' From BBC News online, 'Bin Laden tape: Text' http://news.bbc.co.uk/1/hi/world/middle_east/2751019.stm.
53. Daniel Trotta, 'Rumsfeld: we need to learn from al-Qaeda', *Sydney Morning Herald*, 19 Feb. 2006; National Security Archive, Department of Defence, 'Information Operations Roadmap' Secret [Excised], 30 Oct. 2003. National Security Archive Electronic Briefing Book No. 177.
54. Bruce Hoffman, 'What we can learn from the terrorists', *Global Agenda* (2004), pp. 32–34.
55. Philip Bobbitt, *Terror and Consent: Wars for the Twenty First Century* (New York, 2008), p. 214.
56. On the Algeria comparison, see Rod Thornton, 'Fourth Generation: A "New" form of "warfare"?' in Terry Terriff, Aaron Karp, Regina Karp (eds), *Global Insurgency and the Future of Armed Conflict: Debating Fourth-generation Warfare* (New York, 2008), pp. 87–95, p. 91. Similarly, strategist John Arquila argues that nation-states are fundamentally ill-equipped to counter terrorist networks, that 'it takes a network to fight a network,' so that like Britain developing counter-gangs to crush insurgency in Kenya, America must infiltrate and imitate to bring the enemy down from within.

57. On this pattern of convergence, see Anthony Vinci, 'Becoming the Enemy: Convergence in the American and Al Qaeda Ways of Warfare', *Journal of Strategic Studies*, 31:1 (Feb. 2008), pp. 69–88, pp. 81–83. The US Department of Defence increasingly stresses the role of Special Operations Forces in the war on terror, increasing Special Forces battalions by one third, creating a Marine Corps Special Operations Command, and increased the number and importance of Humint personnel. The *Quadrennial Defence Review*, as Vinci indicates, also foresees a time when all soldiers resemble Special Forces. On the resurgence of Special Forces in the 'war on terror', see Alastair Finlan, *Special Forces, Strategy and the War on Terror* (Abingdon, 2008), pp. 111–139.
58. The 2007 *Pew Global Survey* showed a sharply reduced percentage of Muslims saying that suicide bombing is are often or sometimes justified, declining from 74 percent to 34 percent in Lebanon, from 43 percent to 23 percent in Jordan, and from 33 percent to 9 percent in Pakistan: 'Pew Global Attitudes Project' http://pewglobal.org/reports/display.php?ReportID=256. In the *World Public Opinion Survey* of 2006 in Iraq, overwhelming majorities of Shias and Kurds, and large majorities of Sunnis, reject Al Qaeda and Osama bin Laden: 94% expressed an "unfavourable" view of Al Qaeda, with 82% expressing a "very unfavourable" view: 'World Public Opinion' www.worldpublicopinion.org/pipa/articles/home_page/250.php?nid=andid=andpnt=250andlb=hmpg1.
59. Al Qaeda's training manuals once implored male members not to use women in the '*jihad* business,' but a year into the war on terror, it was reported that they were recruiting Afghan and Middle Eastern women to distribute money and messages to its operatives and provide logistical support. Jack Kelly, 'Al-Qaeda fragmented, smaller, but still deadly', *USA Today*, 9 Sept. 2002; in April 2003, women were undertaking suicide attacks in the name of Al Qaeda: Katharina von Knop, 'The Female Jihad; Al Qaeda's Women', *Studies in Conflict and Terrorism*, 30 (2007), pp. 397–414, 401, 404.
60. Peter Bergen and Paul Cruickshank, 'Lady Killer: Terrorism is no longer a male-only preserve', *TNR Online*, 11 Sept. 2006.
61. Claudia Brunner, 'Occidentalism Meets the Female Suicide Bomber: A Critical Reflection on Recent Terrorism Debates; A Review Essay', *Signs: Journal of Women in Culture and Society*, 32:4 (2007), pp. 957–971.
62. See Jessica Stern, 'When Bombers are Women', *Washington Post*, 18 Dec. 2003; Debra D. Zedalis, *Female Suicide Bombers* (Strategic Studies Institute, Carlisle, June 2004); Diaa Hadid, 'al Qaida uses women as suicide attackers', *Associated Press*, 4 Jan. 2008. I am grateful to Dr Catherine Brown for alerting me to this material.
63. Arnon Regular, 'Mother of Two Becomes First Female Suicide Bomber for Hamas', *Haaretz*, 16 Jan. 2004.
64. Farhana Ali, 'Muslim Female Fighters: An Emerging Trend', *Terrorism Monitor: An In-Depth Analysis of the War on Terror* 3:21 (3 Nov., 2005), pp. 9–11, p. 10.

65. Sprinzak, 'Rational Fanatics', p. 70; Martin Kramer, 'Sacrifice and Fratricide in Shiite Lebanon' in Mark Juergensmeyer (ed.) *Violence and the Sacred in the Modern World* (London, 1992), pp. 30–47, 43.
66. Richard H. Shultz Jr. and Andrea J. Dew, *Insurgents, Terrorists and Militias: The Warriors of Contemporary Combat* (New York, 2006), pp. 5–6, 4, 26; this repeats similar claims made after America's withdrawal from Somalia about the encounter between Western strategy-based rational 'Clausewitzian' war and the non-Western other: Robert J. Bunker, 'Rethinking OOTW' *Military Review* (Nov.-Dec. 1995), pp. 34–41, esp. p. 37.
67. See the 'Sahlins/Obeyesekere' debate, Ganath Obeyesekere *The Apotheosis of Captain Cook: European Mythmaking in the Pacific* (Princeton, 1992); see also Tzvetan Todorov *The Conquest of America: The Question of the Other* (trans. Richard Howard, New York, 1984); Lawrence, 'A Clash of Cultures—The Issues behind the Battle of the Little Big Horn', in *Custer and His Times*, pp. 231–42.
68. This follows the work of Martin van Creveld, who argued as the Cold War ended that Clausewitz's established ideas, especially the trinity of states, peoples and armies, were becoming obsolete, as wars would increasingly be fought within states—by militias or privatised forces—rather than between them. Martin van Creveld, *The Transformation of War* (New York, 1991).
69. As also argued by Mary Kaldor, *New and Old Wars: Organised Violence in a Global Era* (Cambridge 1999); Edward Luttwak, 'Towards Post-Heroic Warfare', *Foreign Affairs*, 74:3 (1995), pp. 109–122, p. 114; Steven Metz, 'A Wake for Clausewitz: Toward a Philosophy of 21st Century Warfare', *Parameters*, 24 (Winter 1994–5), pp. 126–32.
70. Clausewitz, *On War* 1:3 (ed. and trans. Michael Howard and Peter Paret, rev. ed. Princeton, 1984), p. 76.
71. Cited in Bernd Wegner, 'The Ideology of Self-Destruction: Hitler and the Choreography of Defeat', *Bulletin of the German Historical Institute*, 26:2 (Nov. 2004), pp. 18–34, 29–30.
72. An argument made by Christopher Daase, 'Clausewitz and Small Wars' in Hew Strachan and Andreas Herberg-Rothe (eds), *Clausewitz in the Twenty-First Century* (Oxford, 2007), pp. 182–105; M.L.R. Smith, 'Strategy in an Age of 'Low-Intensity' Warfare' in Isabelle Duyvesteyn and Jan Angstrom (eds), *Rethinking the Nature of War* (London, 2005), pp. 28–64; Stuart Kinross, 'Clausewitz and Low-Intensity Conflict', *Journal of Strategic Studies*, 27 (2004), pp. 35–58.
73. Carl von Clausewitz, *On War*, p. 479.
74. On Aidid and the highly instrumental warfare of Somalia, see Isabelle Duyvesteyn, *Clausewitz and African War: Politics and strategy in Liberia and Somalia* (New York, 2005), pp. 51–53, 75–93; on Aidid's career, see Andrew Purvis, 'Wanted: Warlord No.1', *Time*, 28 June 1993.
75. On the fluidity of Somali clan and ethnic politics, see Anna Simons, *Networks of Dissolution: Somalia Undone* (Boulder, 1995), p. 114: 'Conven-

iently...these same subtle distinctions could obversely and opportunistically be used to revive historical grievances...'

76. John Stone makes a similar case in applying the trinity to the Srebrenica massacre, showing that it was not simply an expression of undying ancient hatred and vengeance, but a Trinitarian war, where there was policy (Serb leaders deliberately planned and directed act of ethnic cleansing designed to cripple the opponent), passion (hatreds mobilized within Serb executioners) and friction (the unexpected release of the footage to international horror) all played a role: 'Clausewitz's Trinity and Contemporary Conflict', *Civil Wars*, 9:3 (Sept. 2007), pp. 282–296
77. Paul Bracken, *Fire in the East: The Rise of Asian Military Power and the Second Nuclear Age* (New York: HarperCollins, 1999), p. 130.
78. Jeremy Black, 'Determinisms and Other Issues', *The Journal of Military History*, 68:4 (Oct 2004), pp. 1217–1232; John Lynn, *Battle: A History of Combat and Culture: From Ancient Greece to Modern America* (Boulder, 2003), pp. 29–73.
79. Edward Luttwak, *Strategy: The Logic of War and Peace* (Cambridge, 2003), pp. 5–7, 120–30.
80. See Felix Gilbert, 'Machiavelli: The Renaissance of the Art of War' in Peter Paret, *Makers of Modern Strategy: From Machiavelli to the Nuclear Age* (Princeton, 1986), pp. 11–31.
81. Niccolo Machiavelli, *Discourses on the First Ten Books of Titus Livius*, 7:XL.
82. As Christopher Lynch suggests, 'Interpretive Essay', in his translation of Niccolo Machiavelli, *Art of War* (Chicago, 2003), pp. 179–226, esp. 195–200.
83. For appeals to Clausewitz and his philosophy, see Michael I. Handel, *Masters of War: Classical Strategic Thought* (London, 1992, 1996 edn.), esp pp. 1–17; Michael Howard 'The Influence of Clausewitz' in Carl von Clausewitz, *On War*, pp. 27–45.
84. Alistair Johnston, *Cultural Realism: Strategic Culture and Grand Strategy in Chinese History* (Princeton, 1995), esp. pp. 175–242.
85. Russell Weigley, *The American Way of War: A History of United States Military Strategy and Policy* (Bloomington, 1973), which has been countered by Brian M. Linn, '*The American Way of War* Revisited', *Journal of Military History*, 66 (April 2002), pp. 501–33.
86. Basil Liddell Hart, *The British Way in Warfare* (London, 1932). Strategist Basil Liddell Hart framed British strategic culture as a legacy of maritime and commercial power avoiding major continental commitments. But this proved a misleadingly selective use of history in the narrow context of European wars, to present the First World War as an aberration. Britain's military past was more colonial and thus its experience of land war more intensive, and its naval power at times insufficient to support an ally's land operations, than Liddell Hart admitted. Michael Howard, 'The British Way in Warfare: A Reappraisal," in *The Causes of Wars and Other Essays* (London, 1983), pp. 189–207; Hew Strachan, 'The British Way in

Warfare' in David G. Chandler (ed.), *The Oxford History of the British Army* (Oxford, 1994), pp. 399–416.

87. See Jeffrey Record and Fritz Stern on this point, 'The Use and Abuse of History: Munich, Vietnam and Iraq', *Survival*, 49:1 (Spring 2007), pp. 163–180; 'Imperial Hubris: A German Tale' *Lapham's Quarterly*, 1:1 (Winter, 2008), pp. 205–210, p. 206.
88. Max Boot, *The Savage Wars of Peace: Small Wars and the Rise of American Power* (New York, 2002).
89. James Kurth, 'Iraq: Losing the American Way' in Gary Rosen (ed.), *The Right War? The Conservative Debate on Iraq* (Cambridge University Press, 2005), pp. 36–48.
90. John Keegan, 'In this war of Civilisations, the West will prevail', *Daily Telegraph*, 8 Oct., 2001.
91. Harold E. Raugh Jr., review, 'Phantom Soldier', *Infantry Magazine* (Winter, 2003).
92. Harry G. Summers, Jr., *On Strategy: A Critical Analysis of the Vietnam War* (Novato, 1982), p. 1.
93. Quote from Philip Sabin, *Lost Battles: Reconstructing the Great Clashes of the Ancient World* (London, 2007), xi, also p. 29.
94. BDA JSCSC 2751, 'Japanese Ruses, issued by the GSIHQ Fourteenth Army March 1944.' Slim encouraged his troops that as they were more imaginative than the Japanese, they would outsmart them at deception: 'Don't be content merely to laugh at his clumsy ruses, think up some hot ones of your own and put them over on him.'
95. Maurice D'Aoust, 'Hoodwinked During America's Civil War: Confederate Military Deception,' *Civil War Times* (June 2006), pp. 42–50.
96. Clausewitz, *On War*, p. 203.
97. Some argue that this agonist mode of hoplite warfare then faded: William K. Pritchett, *The Greek State at War* (Berkeley, 1971), pp. 186–7: 'warfare seems sometimes to be a game in which all that is involved is a fair fight with equal weapons on a plain'; see also Victor Davis Hanson, 'Hoplite Battle as Ancient Greek Warfare: When, Where and Why?' in Hans van Wees (ed.) *War and Violence in Ancient Greece* (London, 2000), pp. 201–232.
98. Peter Krentz, 'Deception in Archaic and Classical Greek Warfare' in *War and Violence in Ancient Greece*, pp. 167–200, the Brasidas example p. 174. In the Peloponnesian war, Krentz identifies 37 instances of attacks based on deception or surprise, outnumbering the two set-piece infantry battles at Delium and Mantinea; Odysseus' and Achilles' ethos are discussed in Everett Wheeler, *Stratagem and the Vocabulary of Military Trickery* (Leiden, 1988), xiv; deception and surprise are discussed further in John Drogo Montagu, *Greek and Roman Warfare: Battles, Tactics and Trickery* (London, 2006), pp. 67–81.
99. Nikolaos Ladis, 'Assessing Greek Strategic Thought and Practice: Insights from the Strategic Culture Approach', doctoral dissertation, University of Southhamption (2003).

100. Robert Kagan, *Paradise and Power: America and Europe in the New World Order* (London, 2003), pp. 27–42.
101. Wheeler, *Stratagem*, translation and commentary on Polybios' text (42.47.4–9) on p. 24, on Caesar at p. 56, on Valerius and Hannibal pp. 15–16.
102. See Barry Strauss, *Salamis: The Greatest Naval Battle of the Ancient World, 480 BC* (London, 2005), pp. 171–253.
103. Jonathan Mirsky, 'John Keegan tells us that Westerners "fight face to face" while Orientals prefer"ambush and deceit." Really?', *The Guardian* 10 Oct. 2001.
104. See for example J.M. Post, 'When Hatred is Bred in the Bone: Psychocultural Foundations of Contemporary Terrorism', *Political Psychology*, 26.4 (2005), pp. 615–636.
105. Larry Schweikart, *America's Victories: Why the US Wins Wars and Will Win the War on Terror* (London, 2006, 2007 edn), pp. 20–22; likewise, Bernard Lewis portrays the suicide bomber as a symptom of an underlying cultural malaise: 'What Went Wrong', *The Atlantic Monthly*, 289:1 (Jan. 2002), pp. 43–45.
106. Ehud Sprinzak, 'Rational Fanatics', *Foreign Policy*, 120 (Sept./Oct. 2000), pp. 66–73, p. 69.
107. See Julian Madsen, 'Suicide Terrorism: Rationalising the Irrational', *Strategic Insights*, 3:8 (Aug., 2004), pp. 1–6; Robert Pape, 'The Strategic Logic of Suicide Terrorism', *American Political Science Review*, 97:3 (Aug. 2003), pp. 343–361.
108. Ehud Sprinzak, 'Rational Fanatics', *Foreign Policy*, 120 (Sept./Oct. 2000), pp. 66–74.
109. Conference, 25 June 1944, cited in Richard B. Frank, *Downfall: The End of the Imperial Japanese Empire* (London, 1999), p. 179.
110. Lee Glendinning, 'RAF pilots asked to consider suicide flight', *Guardian* 3 April 2007.
111. This point is made in another context by Peter Layton, who distinguishes between the conquering waves of Islamic armies and navies in the medieval period and the 'asymmetrical' response of contemporary Islamic terrorists to Western power. Peter Layton, 'A new Arab Way of War', *US Naval Institute Proceedings*, 129:3 (March 2003), pp. 62–65.
112. Anthony Beevor, *Berlin: The Downfall 1945* (London, 2002), p. 238.
113. J.F. Verbruggen, *The Art of Warfare in Western Europe during the Middle Ages* (Oxford, 1977), pp. 327–335; Sean McGlynn, 'The Myths of Medieval Warfare', 44:1 *History Today* (1994), pp. 28–34.
114. As Colin Gray argues, 'Out of the Wilderness: Prime Time for Strategic Culture', *Comparative Strategy*, 26:1 (Jan. 2007), p. ii.
115. Karl Marx, '18th Brumaire of Louis Napoleon', in Karl Marx and Friedrich Engels, *Selected Works in Two Volumes* (Moscow, 1958), vol. 1., p. 247.
116. Ann Swidler, 'Culture in Action: Symbols and Strategies', *American Sociological Review*, 51:2 (April 1986), pp. 273–286,p. 277; 'Cultural

Repertoires and Cultural Logics: Can they be Reconciled?', *Newsletter of the American Sociological Association*, 16:2 (Winter 2002), pp. 6–8.

117. Amartya Sen, *Identity and Violence: The Illusion of Destiny* (New York, 2006), p. 103.
118. I am grateful to Tim Bird for discussion on this point: unpublished paper, 'Implications and Conclusions: A Comprehensive Approach', *International Studies Association Conference*, Chicago 2007.
119. A point also made by Michael Desch, 'Culture versus Structure in Post-9/11 Security Studies', *Strategic Insights*, 4:10 (Oct. 2005), pp. 1–7, p. 6.
120. Martin J. Muckian, 'Structural Vulnerabilities of Networked Insurgencies: Adapting to the New Adversary', *Parameters*, 36:4 (Winter 2006/7), pp. 14–25; Stephen Biddle, 'Seeing Baghdad, Thinking Saigon', *Foreign Affairs*, 85:2 (March/April 2006), pp. 2–14; Jeffrey Record and W. Andrew Terrill, *Iraq and Vietnam: Differences, Similarities and Insights* (Carlisle, 2004), p. 2.
121. Michael Howard, 'A surge of their own: Iraqis take back the streets', *The Guardian*, 20 Dec. 2007.
122. Reidar Visser, 'Historical Myths of a Divided Iraq', *Survival*, 50:2 (2008), pp. 95–106.

3. WATCHING THE RISING SUN: OBSERVING JAPAN AT WAR

1. For general histories of the war, see Richard Connaughton, *The War of the Rising Sun and the Tumbling Bear* (London, 1991); Ian Nish, *The Origins of the Russo-Japanese War* (Harlow, 1985).
2. Richard H. Minear also argues for the importance of domestic politics on perceptions of Japan in World War II: 'Cross-Cultural Perception and World War II: American Japanists of the 1940's and Their Images of Japan', *International Studies Quarterly*, 24:4 (Dec. 1980), pp. 555–580.
3. For an overview of the relationship between Japanese history and Said's theories, see Richard H. Minear, 'Orientalism and the Study of Japan' *Journal of Asian Studies* 39:3 (1980), pp. 507–517.
4. See Michael Howard, 'Men against Fire: The Doctrine of the Offensive in 1914' in p. Paret (ed.), *Makers of Modern Strategy from Machiavelli to the Nuclear Age* (Oxford, 1986), pp. 510–527, esp. 522; see also Tim Travers, *The Killing Ground: The British Army, the Western Front, and the Emergence of Modern Warfare, 1900–1918* (London: 1987), pp. 43–4; Jack K. Snyder, *The Ideology of the Offensive: Military Decision Making and the Disasters of 1914* (Ithaca, 1984); S.P. MacKenzie, 'Willpower or Firepower? The Unlearned Military Lessons of the Russo-Japanese War' in David Wells and Sandra Wilson (eds), *The Russo-Japanese War in Cultural Perspective, 1904–5* (Wiltshire, 1999), pp. 30–41; Philip Towle, 'British Observers of the Russo-Japanese War' (Discussion Paper, Suntory Centre, London, Symposium on Aspects of the Russian-Japanese War, July 1998);

Gary p. Cox notes, 'Of Aphorisms, Lessons and Paradigms: Comparing the British and German Official Histories of the Russo-Japanese War', *Journal of Military History*, 56:3 (July 1992), pp. 389–401;

5. These were noted, for example, by naval historian and geostrategist Julian S. Corbett, *Maritime Operations in the Russo-Japanese War 1904–1905* (Intelligence Division, Admiralty War Staff 1915, reprinted 1994, US Naval Institute), pp. 397–8.

6. As one senior officer in Hong Kong would argue in 1937, the 'Jap soldier' 'seems a very different man to the Jap of the Russo-Jap War...against a European Power I don't believe you'd see him for dust except on the most unequal terms.' WO 106/2380, Col. N.M.S. Irwin to Col. R.B. Pargiter, 14 Oct. 1937; see also WO 208/1383, 'Memorandum by Military Intelligence Department', 23 Feb. 1939. Both cited and discussed in Ferris, 'Worthy of Some Better Enemy?', pp. 237–238, 241.

7. F.J. Norman, *The Fighting Man of Japan: The Training and Exercises of the Samurai* (New York, 1905), p. 1.
8. B.W. Norregaard, *The Great Siege: The Investment and Fall of Port Arthur* (London,1906), p. 302.
9. Ian Hamilton, *A Staff Officers' Scrap Book* (London, 1906), pp. 7–8
10. Ibid., p. 9.
11. Ibid., pp. 13–14.
12. NAM 9405–10–1–1 Captain D.S. Robertson, 'Some Notes on Japanese Infantry in the Manchurian War', pp. 1, 2, 6, 12; (Observer, 16 Feb.-16 May 1905), written 31.01.1908.
13. LHA 15/1/17, Ian Hamilton Papers, p. 5: 'Look into their hearts, and no great gulf separates the Turkish, German, Russian, British peasantry. It is when you come to the men in tall hats and frock coats, superficially twin brethren, that the contrast in ideals becomes startling.'
14. LHA 15/1/17, Ian Hamilton Papers, 7(c).
15. Liddell Hart Archives, 3/1/2, Ian Hamilton, Diary of the Russo-Japanese War, Part 1, 26 July 1904, pp. 2–3.
16. LHA 16/33/1, Ian Hamilton Papers, Transcript of Speech made by General Sir Ian Hamilton to the London Press Club on Thursday 10 Nov. 1921. He also warned against loosening the alliance in an earlier speech, in LHA 16/32/2, Transcript of Speech by General Sir Ian Hamilton at a Dinner given to him by the Lord Mayor of Manchester at the Town Hall on Friday, 15 July 1921.
17. War Office Papers, Public Record Office 33/432 (Henceforth abbreviated PRO WO) 'Extracts from the Diaries of Officers Attached to the Japanese Army, 2nd series, 1907, Major J.A. Somerville.
18. Jay Luvaas, *The Education of an Army: British Military Thought 1815–1940* (London, 1965), p. 299
19. 'The Soul of a Nation', *The Times*, 4 Oct. 1904, p. 6.
20. Those observing officers subsequently killed in the Great War were listed on a tablet at St Andrew's Church, Tokyo, on 14 April 1922: Major

Charles Allix Lavington Yate, VC (King's Own Yorkshire Light Infantry, killed 20 Sept. 1914); Captain Reginald Wickham Harland (Hampshire Regiment, killed 30 Oct. 1914); Lieutenant-Colonel Everard Ferguson Calthrop (Royal Artillery, killed 19 Dec. 1915); Major James Lawson Mitchell (Royal Artillery, killed 16 March 1916); Captain Philip Wood (89th Punjabis, killed 5 April 1916); Major William Hugh Simpson (93rd Burma Infantry, killed 17 April 1916); Captain Percy Montague Clifton Wilde (Royal Marine Artillery, killed 31 May 1916); Major Guy Bertram Oliver (Royal Artillery, killed 29 Sept. 1916); Lieutenant-Colonel Herbert Francis George Carter (Kings Own Yorkshire Light Infantry, died 28 Feb. 1919).

21. Balck's opinions were recorded by Captain Ashley Barrett, who summarised British interpretations of the implications of the war: 'Lessons to be Learned by Regimental Officers from the Russo-Japanese War', *Journal of the Royal United Service Institute* (July-Dec 1907), pp. 799–823.
22. 'An old Japanese (a Samurai) told me that before the Meiji era, if one man had a quarrel with twenty and drew his sword, the twenty would run away, even though there were Samurai among them.' PRO WO 33/432 Report of Captain p. W. North, in General Staff, War Office, 'Extracts from the Diaries of Officers attached to the Japanese Army' (1907), pp. 35–38.
23. PRO WO 106/6150 Lecture, Col. J.A.L. Haldane 'Japanese and Russian Intelligence Systems', March 1909.
24. Colonel Charles Ross, *An Outline of the Russo-Japanese War 1904, 1905* (London, 1912), pp. 486–8
25. Ibid., pp. 82–3
26. Captain Ashley W. Barrett, citing McCullagh, 'With the Cossacks', in 'Lessons to be Learned', above n23, p. 817.
27. 'During the night attacks the Russians lost many men through such slimness on the part of the Japanese as our men suffered from when fighting the Boers—Captain Soloviev on one occasion losing heavily when his company approached a Japanese trench from which some one had called in excellent Russian: '"Come on, brothers, we are all Russians here".' Barrett, 'Lessons to be Learned', above n19, p. 815, citing Captain Soloviev, 'Personal Observations of a Russian Company Commander' published in the *Revue Militaire des Armees Etrangeres*; on feints and the silence of Japanese prisoners of war, Barrett cited Colonel Haldane, 'Lessons from the Russo-Japanese War' (in Barrett, 'Lessons to be Learned', above n19, at p. 818).
28. Ian Hamilton, 'Battle of the Ya-Lu (Chiu-lien-cheng) and the events leading to it', General Staff, War Office, *Reports from Officers Attached to the Japanese Forces in the Field, 1906* (London, 1906), vol. 1, pp. 67–9.
29. Captain Ashley W. Barrett, citing McCullagh, 'With the Cossacks', in 'Lessons to be Learned', above n23, p. 800.
30. See Richard Stites, 'Russian Representations of the Japanese Enemy' in J.W. Steinberg, B.W. Menning, D. Van der Oye, D. Wolff, S. Yokote

(eds), *The Russo-Japanese War in Global Perspective: World War Zero* (Leiden, 2005), pp. 395–411; see also Evgenii Yurievich Sergeev, 'Russian Military Intelligence in the War with Japan, 1904–05' in Steinberg, *The Russo-Japanese War*, pp. 281–304.

31. 'A Plea for History', *The Times* Sept. 10 1904.
32. Philip Towle, *From Ally to Enemy: Anglo-Japanese Military Relations, 1900–1945* (Kent, 2006), p. 51; 'British Estimates of Japanese Military Power, 1900–1914' in p. Towle (ed.) *Estimating Foreign Military Power* (London, 1982), pp. 111–139.
33. 'Efficiency of the Japanese Navy' dated 18 Feb. 1935, cited in A.J. Marder, *Old Friends, New Enemies: The Royal Navy and the Imperial Japanese Navy—Strategic Illusions, 1936–1941* (Oxford, 1981), p. 346.
34. Captain R. Toke, Assistant Military Attache, Tokyo, 25 Oct. 1904, in General Staff, War Office, Reports from Officers Attached to the Japanese Forces in the Field, (1906) vol. 2, pp. 539–546, pp. 544–6.
35. John Woulfe Flanagan claimed in the *The Times* that Japan's 'old chivalrous spirit has led her to disdain the prosecution of war for merely monetary considerations.' *The Times* 30 Aug. 1905. One of the leading British admirers of Japan, Alfred Stead, claimed that war for territory or money was 'abhorrent' to the 'Japanese mind' *Bushido* and the 'instincts of the samurai.' 'Japan in the Far East', *Fortnightly Review*, 78 (1905), p. 597.
36. British Japanist F.S.G. Piggott would continue to write as an apologist for Japanese foreign policy and the noble national character of Japan, and for the 'war party' of militarists who became politically dominant, denying atrocities or blaming them on anyone other than the perpetrators:; F.S.G. Piggott, *Broken Thread: An Autobiography* (Aldershot: 1950), pp. 364–5, 373. For another positive account of Japanese behaviour written decades after the war, see Captain M.D. Kennedy, *The Military Side of Japanese Life* (London, 1924), p. 240.
37. See Edward S. Miller, 'Japan's other Victory: Overseas Financing of the Russo-Japanese War' in *The Russo-Japanese War in Global Perspective*, pp. 465–485.
38. Stewart Lone, 'Between Bushido and Black Humour', *History Today* (Sept. 2005), pp. 20–27.
39. As argued by Yoshihisa Tak Matsusaka, 'Human Bullets, General Nogi, and the Myth of Port Arthur' in *The Russo-Japanese War in Global Perspective*, pp. 179–201.
40. PRO WO 33/447 'Extracts from the Diaries of Officers', Captain R.T. Toke, p. 40.
41. These statistics were analysed by Barrett, 'Lessons to be Learned', above n19, pp. 820–1: The Japanese lost 57,000 men from wounds and 15,000 from sickness (deaths from sickness being less than one fourth the total loss), a ratio of 1 (wounded): 0.26 (disease) compared to the South African war, where 18,000 were admitted to hospital for wounds, with 400,000 admissions for treatment of disease, a ratio of 1 (wounded): 22

(disease). With regards to intestinal/enteric cases, Britain had approximately 41,000 recorded cases in South Africa, compared to 193 for the Japanese.

42. See John F. Howes (ed.), *Nitobe Inazo: Japan's Bridge Across the Pacific* (Oxford, 1995), pp. 13–14.
43. For recent accounts of the pictorial and cultural history of the war, see Frederic Sharf, Anne Nishimura Morse and Sebastian Dobson, *A Much-Recorded War: the Russo-Japanese War in History and Imagery* (Boston, 2005); David Wells and Sandra Wilson (eds), *The Russo-Japanese War in Cultural Perspective, 1904–5* (Wiltshire, 1999).
44. Emperor Meiji was presented like Austria's Franz Joseph I, standing in command over his armed forces. The cavalry charge against the prestigious Russian Cossacks suggested that Japan's horsemen were the equals of the West's equestrian elites. They also took earlier depictions of western colonial wars and superimposed their own iconography over it. One picture juxtaposed Japanese medical treatment with Russian barbarity, the Japanese Red Cross signifying the harmony of Japan with recognised norms. See Sharf, Morse and Dobson, *A Much-Recorded War*, above n45, n46.
45. Social Darwinism had a range of possible inflections: see Paul Crook, *Darwinism, War and History: The Debate over the Biology of War from the 'Origin of Species' to the First World War* (Cambridge, 1994). An anonymous writer wrote in the *Royal Engineers Journal* that 'We may assume that the Darwinian theory as to the survival of the fittest is as true of nations as it is of individuals, and that the fittest nation is the one that is best able to hold its own on the battlefield.' 'The Nation and the Military Spirit' by 'Bushido', *Royal Engineers Journal* 4 (1906), pp. 89–91.
46. See the *Report of the Inter-Department Committee on Physical Deterioration* (1904); Anne Summers, 'Militarism in Britain Before the Great War', *History Workshop Journal* 2(1976), pp. 104–123; Geoffrey R. Searle, *The Quest for National Efficiency: A Study in British Politics and Political Thought, 1899–1914* (London, 1990).
47. Hew Strachan, *The Politics of the British Army* (Oxford, 1997), p. 41.
48. B.W. Norregaard *The Great Siege: The Investment and Fall of Port Arthur* (London, 1906), pp. 135–6, 307–8.
49. Hamilton, *Staff Officer's Scrap Book*, p. 5.
50. H.H. Wilson's history of the war doubted whether an army recruited 'largely from towns can show the same fibre as one drawn from country districts.' It envied the tenacity of colonial troops drawn from rural populations, and feared the loss of the fighting qualities of Wellington's forces. H.H. Wilson, *With the Flag to Pretoria: A History of the Boer War of 1899–1900* 2 vols (London 1900–1902), v. 2, p. 704.
51. 'Education in Japan', *The Times*, 2 Nov. 1905.
52. NAM 1996–10–123 Lt A.P. Wavell, 'The Strategic and Tactical Lessons of 1815, 1862, 1866 and 1870 compared with those of South Africa and Manchuria', Staff College Paper, July 1910.

53. As much as 50% of the curriculum in fifth grade was devoted to these topics. See Toshio Iritani, *Group Psychology of the Japanese in Wartime* (New York, 1991), pp. 160–84; Edward J. Drea, 'In the Army Barracks of Imperial Japan', *Armed Forces and Society*, 15:3 (Spring 1989), pp. 329–348.
54. PRO WO 106 /5515 'General Report on the Japanese System of Military Education and Training.' This document remained confidential until 1972.
55. PRO WO 106/5515 'General Report' pp. 9–10.
56. PRO WO 106/5515, 'General Report,' 'Concluding Remarks', p. 23.
57. PRO WO 106/5515, 'General Report' p. 56.
58. Murray made these comments after an address by Sir George Arthur about military education, in which he was critical of Sir George's view that fundamental racial differences placed limits on the extent to which Japanese education could be imitated. 'Education in Relation to the Army', *Journal of the Royal United Services Institute*, 51:1 (1907), pp. 1190–1224, esp. 1211, 1221.
59. As Matsusaka suggests, 'Human Bullets', above n37, p. 200.
60. As Best notes, *British Intelligence and the Japanese Challenge in Asia, 1914–1941* (New York, 2002), p. 19; see also Towle, 'British Estimates of Japanese Military Power' in *Estimating Foreign Military Power* (London, 1982), pp. 125–8.
61. WO106/6273 General Staff 'Report on the Japanese Staff College March 1908' paras 60(1), 99, 102.
62. Brevet Major Sir Alexander Bannerman, 'The Creation of the Japanese National Spirit' *Journal of the Royal United Services Institute*, 54 (Jan.-June 1910), pp. 697–719.
63. With very rough figures, he argued that 1 in 70 Japanese were liable for military service in 1721, the earliest figure in the official census, whereas before the standing army and militia system was introduced, up to 1 in 4 of the population were classed as liable for service.
64. Bannerman, 'Creation of the Japanese Spirit', pp. 707–8.
65. Bannerman, 'Creation of the Japanese Spirit', p. 706.
66. Captain C.A.L. Yate, Kings Own Yorkshire Light Infantry, 10 Jan. 1906, 'The Peace Training of the Japanese Army' in General Staff, War Office, *Reports from Officers Attached to the Japanese Forces in the Field*, (London, 1906), vol. 5, pp. 265–74, 268–9.
67. Captain C. Slack, comment, 'Creation of the Japanese National Spirit', above n61, p. 716. Slack had spent two years in Japan after the Russo-Japanese war.
68. Lieutenant Carlyon Bellairs, comment, 'Creation of the Japanese National Spirit', above n61, pp. 711–713.
69. Strachan, *The Politics of the British Army*, p. 40.
70. Bannerman 'Creation of the Japanese National Spirit', above n62, p. 707.
71. Yoshihisa Tak Matsusaka, 'Human Bullets', above n42, p. 200.

72. Colonel J.H. Rosseter, comment, 'The Creation of the Japanese National Spirit', above n62, p. 713.
73. This is discussed further by R.J.Q. Adams, 'The National Service League And Mandatory Service in Edwardian Britain', *Armed Forces and Society*, 12:1 (Fall 1985), pp. 75–94, 62.
74. See A. Smith, 'The 'Sacred' Dimension of Nationalism', *Millennium*, 29:3 (2000), pp. 791–814; George Mosse, *Fallen Soldiers: Reshaping the Memory of the World Wars* (Oxford, 1990).
75. As discussed in Bernard Brodie, *War and Politics* (London, 1974), p. 332.
76. See Gerhard L. Weinberg, 'Hitler's Image of the United States', *American Historical Review*, 69:4 (July 1964), pp. 1001–21, also discussed in Fischerkeller 'David Versus Goliath', p. 5.
77. Captain Ashley W. Barrett, citing McCullagh, 'With the Cossacks', in 'Lessons to be Learned', above n19, p. 823.
78. For a survey of the Liberal press in Britain and its war ideology, see I.C. Wills, *England's Holy War: A Study of English Liberal Idealism During the Great War* (New York, 1928); for the origins and popularity of the language of sacrifice, see also Max Jones, *The Last Great Quest: Captain Scott's Antarctic Sacrifice* (Oxford, 2003), esp. pp. 233–245.

4. THE GHOST OF GENGHIS: MONGOLS AND THE WESTERN IMAGINATION

1. Vietnam Veterans Against the War, Statement by John Kerry to the Senate Committee of Foreign Relations, 23 April 1971: http://www2.iath.virginia.edu/sixties/HTML_docs/Resources/Primary/Manifestos/VVAW_Kerry_Senate.html
2. Jörg Friedrich, *The Fire: The Bombing of Germany 1940–1943* (trans. Allison Brown, New York, 2006), p. 118.
3. 'Genghis' is a later European corruption, but given that this chapter is mainly about Western perception, it appears in the title.
4. See D.A. DeWeese, 'The influence of the Mongols on the Religious Consciousness of Thirteenth-Century Europe', *Mongolian Studies*, 5 (1978–9), pp. 41–78.
5. Ata Malik Juvaini, *Genghis Khan: The History of the World Conqueror* (trans. J.A. Boyle, Seattle, 1997), p. 105.
6. Edward Gibbon, *The History of the Decline and Fall of the Roman Empire* (1776–1788, ed. J.B. Bury, London 1900, 1920 edn), vol. 7, chapter 64, p. 4.
7. Kevin Stuart, *Mongols in Western/American Consciousness* (Lampeter, 1998), p. 3; see also Antti Ruotsala, *Europeans and Mongols in the Middle of the Thirteenth Century: Encountering the Other* (Helsinki, 2001).
8. For a recent study of Mongol warfare and a summary of the twentieth-century Western reception of it, see Timothy May, *The Mongol Art of War: Chinggis Khan and the Mongol Military System* (Yardley, 2007), pp. 138–147.

9. See in particular Azar Gat, *A History of Military Thought: From the Enlightenment to the Cold War* (Oxford, 2001), esp. pp. 646–695, and 'Liddell Hart's Theory of Armoured Warfare: Revising the Revisionists', *Journal of Strategic Studies* 19:1 (March 1996), pp. 1–30; Alex Danchev, *Alchemist of War: The Life of Basil Liddell Hart* (London, 1998); John Mearsheimer, *Liddell Hart and the Weight of History* (Cornell, 1988); Brian Bond, *Liddell Hart: A Study of his Military Thought* (Aldershot, 1977, 1991 edn).
10. Rudi Paul Lindner, 'Nomadism, Horses and Huns', *Past and Present*, 92 (Aug. 1991), pp. 3–19.
11. In a letter to Major-General Hobart 19 June, 1948, Liddell Hart claimed that after his original article in *Blackwoods* in May 1924 about Chinggis Khan and Subotai prompted the Germans 'to bring out a number of studies of the Mongol campaigns—which no one had gone to before for military lessons', Liddell Hart Archives [Henceforth abbreviated LHA] 13/37.
12. LHA 1/466–471, letters dated 12 Nov. 1935, 4 April 1951, 2 July 1959, in which Liddell Hart praised Douglas MacArthur for his prescient faith in armoured forces and recognition of the significance of the Mongol precedent, and tried to coax MacArthur into acknowledging that Liddell Hart's writing had provoked these thoughts.
13. As Liddell Hart said in his letter to Macarthur in Nov. 1935, 'I do not know of any modern books in which Genghis Khan's military significance has been treated.' This would have been news to graduates of Russia's military academies.
14. See Chris Bellamy, 'Heirs of Genghis Khan: The Influence of the Tartar-Mongols on the Imperial Russian and Soviet Armies', *RUSI Journal*, 128 (March 1983), pp. 52–60. Bellamy's analysis of the Mongols focussed on the same military-operational qualities of Mongol warfare as Douglas MacArthur, Liddell Hart and other modern admirers: speed, self-sufficiency, and indirection, while he also stressed their strategic planning, intelligence gathering, and psychological warfare, approvingly citing Douglas MacArthur's statements: *The Evolution of Land Warfare: Theory and Practice* (London, 1990), pp. 193–199.
15. Captain Dana J.H. Pittard, 'Genghis Khan and 13th-Century Air Land Battle', *Military Review*, 66 (July 1986), pp. 18–27.
16. James Chambers, 'Horsemen of the Apocalypse', *The Times*, 23 April 2005.
17. Sean J.A. Edwards, *Swarming on the Battlefield* (Washington, 2000), pp. 28–32; John Arquilla and David Ronfeldt, *Swarming and The Future of Conflict* (Santa Monica, 2000), pp. 25–45.
18. See Peter Jackson, *The Mongols and the West*, p. 150.
19. Cited in John Block Friedman, *The Monstrous Races in Medieval Art and Thought* (Harvard, 1981), p. 95. On Latin Christians' view of lands beyond the Islamic Near East, see J.R.S. Phillips, 'The Outer World of the European Middle Ages' in Stuart B. Schwarz (ed.), *Implicit Understand-*

ings. Observing, Reporting and Reflecting on the Encounters between Europeans and Other Peoples in the Early Modern Era (Cambridge, 1994), pp. 23–63.

20. See Erik Hildinger, 'The Mongol Invasion of Europe', *Military History*, 14:2 (June 1997), pp. 38–44.
21. Charles Oman, *A History of the Art of War in the Middle Ages* (London, 1924), vol. 2, pp. 316–335.
22. The words of William of Rubruck, cited in Peter Jackson, *The Mongols and the West 1221–1410* (Harlow, 2005), p. 139.
23. This typology is sketched out by Stephen Morillo, 'A General Typology of Transcultural Wars—the Early Middle Ages and Beyond' in Hans-Henning Kortüm (ed.), *Transcultural Wars from the Middle Ages to the Twenty-First Century* (Berlin, 2006), pp. 29–42, esp. p. 34.
24. As Jackson suggests, *The Mongols and the West*, pp. 5, 31.
25. Richard A. Gabriel, *Genghis Khan's Greatest General: Subotai the Valiant* (Oklahoma, 2004), pp. 28–9.
26. Giovanni di Plano Carpini, *The Story of the Mongols Whom We Call the Tartars* translated by Manuel Komroff (ed.) *Contemporaries of Marco Polo: Consisting of the travel records to the Eastern Parts of the World of William of Rubruck [1253–1255]; The Journey of John of Pian de Carpini [1245–1247] and The Journal of Friar Odoric [1318–1330]* (London, 1928, 1929 edn), Chapter 16 'Of Their Spies, and How they may be Resisted', p. 50.
27. Giovanni di Plano Carpini, *The Story of the Mongols*, p. 49.
28. Richard A. Gabriel, *Genghis Khan's Greatest General*, xi.
29. Peter Hopkirk, *The Great Game: On Secret Service in High Asia* (London, 1990, 2006 edn), pp. 11–12. Hopkirk's account of Russian fears of Mongol conquest and rule invokes classic themes of hostile military Orientalism—the Mongols were like 'molten lava' destroying everything in sight, practised 'black propaganda', and were rumoured to enjoy cannibalism and slicing off the breasts of captured virgins for senior Mongol commanders.
30. Cited in David Wells, Sandra Wilson (eds), *The Russo-Japanese War in Cultural Perspective* (Houndmills, 1999), p. 112.
31. Richard Brietman, 'Hitler and Genghis Khan', *Journal of Contemporary History*, 25 (1990), pp. 337–351. As Breitman suggests, Hitler was influenced by Michael Prawdin's 1934 bestseller, *Tschingis Chan, der Sturm aus Asien* that portrayed Chinggis as a civilising empire-builder.
32. Douglas MacArthur, Annual Report of the Chief of Staff for fiscal 1935, cited in Frank C. Waldrop (ed.), *MacArthur on War: His Military Writings* (London, 1943), pp. 305–6, quotations p. 306.
33. As discussed also in Michael Schaller, *Douglas MacArthur: The Far Eastern General* (Oxford, 1989), p. 247. On MacArthur ignoring the fact that the Chinese were also effectively fighting a limited war in the peninsula, see John Edward Wiltz, 'The MacArthur Hearings of 1951: The Secret Testimony', *Military Affairs*, (Dec. 1975), pp. 167–173.

34. Douglas MacArthur, 'Statement to the 51st. Annual Encampment of the Veterans of Foreign Wars' 20 Aug., 1950, cited and discussed further in Tarak Barkawi, 'Orientalism at War', pp. 27–8. I am grateful to for permission to cite from Barkawi's paper.
35. Robert D. Kaplan, *Imperial Grunts: The American Military on the Ground* (New York, 2005), p. 94.
36. Liddell Hart Archives, (henceforth abbreviated LHA) LH 15/1/2/2, Letter, BLH to 'Lattimore', 12 March 1965.
37. See Basil Liddell Hart, *The Memoirs of Captain Liddell Hart* (London, 1965), vol. 1, pp. 74–5.
38. LHA 11/1948/31'Lightning War and Decisively Deep Penetration (1948?)'
39. LH 11/1948/31'Lightning War and Decisively Deep Penetration'; Basil Liddell Hart, *Sherman: Soldier, Realist, American* (New York, 1929); for his later studies, see *The Decisive Wars of History: A Study in Strategy* (Boston, 1929).
40. For a study of the 'indirect approach', see Alex Danchev, 'Liddell Hart and the Indirect Approach', *Journal of Military History*, 63 (1999), pp. 313–337.
41. B.H. Liddell Hart, *The Decisive Wars of History: A Study in Strategy* (Boston, 1929), pp. 153–154.
42. LHA, II/1947–48, 11/1948/35 'The Influence of Analogies of the Evolution of Armoured Warfare'
43. LH II/1947–48, 11/1948/36 'The Development of Armoured Infantry—'Tank Marines'
44. B.H. Liddell Hart, *Great Captains Unveiled* (London, 1927), p. 1.
45. See Timothy May, *Mongol Art of War*, p. 16.
46. Liddell Hart, *Great Captains*, p. 17.
47. B. H. Liddell Hart, *Great Captains Unveiled*, p. 31–33.
48. *Great Captains* p. 32.
49. Steven Stinemetz, 'Clausewitz or Khan? The Mongol Method of Military Success', *Parameters*, 14:1 (Spring 1984), pp. 71–80.
50. LHA 1/499, Sir Ivor Maxse, letter to Liddell Hart, 3 Oct. 1927, p. 46.
51. As Thomas Barfield argues, *The Perilous Frontier: Nomadic Empires and China, 221BC to AD 1757, Studies in Social Discontinuity* (Oxford, 1989), p. 203.
52. Gabriel, *Genghis Khan's Greatest General*, p. 46.
53. Clausewitz, *On War*, pp. 230–231.
54. The issue of the primacy of surrender over body count is further discussed in Niall Ferguson, 'Prisoner Taking and Prisoner Killing: The Dynamics of Defeat, Surrender and Barbarity in the Age of Total War', in George Kassmeris (ed.), *The Barbarisation of Warfare* (London, 2006), pp. 126–158.
55. See Alan D. Beyerchen, 'Clausewitz, Nonlinearity and the Unpredictability of War', *International Security*, 17:3 (Winter 1992), pp. 59–90.
56. Liddell Hart, *The Ghost of Napoleon* (London, 1933), p. 120.

57. Liddell Hart's chapter in *Great Captains* was based on an earlier essay, 'Two Great Captains: Jenghiz Khan and Subutaï' *Blackwoods Magazine* (May 1924), pp. 644–59.
58. LHA 15/12/2 88–90 Lectures by Col. G.M. Lindsay for Royal Tank Corps, Lecture, undated, but probably from 1925, 'Précis of Lecture on Tanks and their Co-operation with Other Arms'
59. LHA15/12/2 Lecture, Lindsay, 'Tanks and their Co-operation with Other Arms', 'Part VII The Future', p. 119.
60. LHA 15/12/13 Lindsay/Hobart correspondence, Letter Hobart to Linsday, 10 July 1925.
61. Ibid., Letter Lindsay to Hobart, 21 Aug. 1925.
62. Quoted in Liddell Hart, *Memoirs*, vol. 1, p. 129.
63. Similarly, an article of the same period by an officer (in the Royal Tank Corps, which was probably influential on his perspective) cited Liddell Hart as one source, also hardly mentioned sieges, focussing instead on 'sudden swift blows' and the 'instantaneous exploitation of success.' Capt. E.W. Sheppard, 'The Military Methods of the Mongols', *Army Quarterly*, 18 (1929), pp. pp. 305–315.
64. LHA 15/1/2/5 'The Mongol Practice of Warfare.'
65. See Michael Howard, *The Listener*, 28 Dec. 1972, p. 894; cited along with Spencer Wilkinson's private correspondence in Azar Gat, *A History of Military Thought: From the Enlightenment to the Cold War* (Oxford, 2001), p. 684. For a more sustained critique of Liddell Hart's interpretation of Sherman, see Albert Castel, 'Liddell Hart's *Sherman*: Propaganda as History', *The Journal of Military History*, 67 (April 2003), pp. 405–26.
66. Spencer Wilkinson, 'Killing No Murder: An Examination of Some New Theories of War', *Army Quarterly* (Oct., 1927), pp. 14–27, p. 22: 'The modes of fighting are always conditioned by the weapons and by the structure of armies. From the earliest times until the end of the eighteenth century armies were solid masses covering only a tiny space in the vast theatre of war. An army took a long time to form in order of battle, so long that during the process an enemy who preferred not to fight could march away. Malborough's correspondence is full of complaints of the difficulty of inducing the enemy to accept battle.'
67. Brian Bond, *Liddell Hart: A Study of His Military Thought* (Aldershot, 1979, 1991 edn), p. 57.
68. This incident is mentioned in a discussion about the relationship between Mongol warfare and terrain in Edwards, *Swarming on the Battlefield*, p. 30; Oman, *Art of Warfare* p. 327.
69. On Mongol logistics, see May, *Mongol Art of War*, pp. 58–69.
70. On this shortcoming of *Blitzkrieg*, see Mary R. Habeck, *Storm of Steel: The Development of Armour Doctrine in Germany and the Soviet Union, 1919–1939* (Cornell, 2003), xvii.
71. Robert Citino, *The German Way of War: From the Thirty Years' War to the Third Reich* (Kansas, 2005), p. 305.

72. Robert Foley, *German Strategy and the Path to Verdun: Erich von Falkenhayn and the Development of Attrition, 1870–1916* (Cambridge 2005), pp. 14–38, esp. p. 36; Stig Förster, 'Facing 'People's War': Moltke the Elder and Germany's Military Options after 1871', *Journal of Strategic Studies*, 11 (1988), pp. 209–30.
73. LHA 15/12/13 Lindsay/Hobart correspondence, Hobart to Lindsay, 10 July 1925.
74. LH 11/1948/35 'The Influence of Analogies of the Evolution of Armoured Warfare.'
75. *Great Captains*, p. 33.
76. As Gat notes, 'Liddell Hart: Revising the Revisionists', pp. 19, 21.
77. On this debate, see J.P. Harris, *Men, Ideas, and Tanks: British Military Thought and Armoured Forces, 1903–1939* (Manchester, 1995) and J.S. Corum, *The Roots of Blitzkrieg: Hans von Seeckt and German Military Reform* (Lawrence, 1992).
78. For fuller discussion of the differences between theory and practice in the evolution of armoured warfare from the interwar period through to the Second World War, see Max Boot, *War Made New: Technology, Warfare and the Course of History 1500 to Today* (New York, 2006), pp. 213–240.
79. LHA 13/37, Letter, Hobart to Liddell Hart, 20 June 1948.
80. On the interwar context in which German armoured warfare innovation developed, see Williamson Murray, 'Armoured Warfare: The British, French and German experiences' in Williamson Murray and Allan Millet (eds), *Military Innovation in the Interwar Period* (Cambridge University Press, 1996), pp. 6–49, page 7 for a summary of the revisionist view of the explanation for innovation.
81. Basil Liddell Hart, *Deterrent or Defence: A Fresh Look at the West's Military Position* (New York, 1960), p. 198.
82. Liddell Hart, *Paris, or the Future of War* (London, 1925), pp. 46–8.

5. EXOTIC ENEMY? AMERICA, THE TALIBAN AND THE FOG OF CULTURE

1. Thucydides, *The Peloponnesian War* (trans. Richard Crawley, New York, 2004), 1.76.2.
2. Declan Walsh, Jamie Wilson, 'US fears backlash after TV documentary shows soldiers burning Taliban corpses', *The Guardian*, 21 Oct. 2005.
3. PSYOPS expert cited in Kelton Rhoades, who also questions the interpretation of this incident, 'The Cultural Variable in the Influence Equation' in *The Public Diplomacy Handbook* (2008), p. 10.
4. Marine Corps reverence for the dead discussed in J.E. Lendon, *Soldiers and Ghosts: A History of Battle in Classical Antiquity* (Yale, 2005), p. 3; K.W. Nolan, *Operation Buffalo* (New York 1991), pp. 298–302.
5. Colin Gray, 'Comparative Strategic Culture', *Parameters*, 14 (1984), pp. 26–33, 26.

6. For general accounts of the war of 2001 and what followed, see William Maley, *Rescuing Afghanistan* (London, 2006); Sean M. Maloney, *Enduring the Freedom: A Rogue Historian in Afghanistan* (Dulles, 2005); Anthony Davis, 'How the Afghan War was Won', *Jane's Intelligence Review*, 14 (1 Feb. 2002), pp. 6–13.
7. Cited in Boot, *War Made New*, p. 383.
8. CNN Transcript, 23 Nov. 2001, 'Afghan Warfare is 'Bizarre', http://transcripts.cnn.com/TRANSCRIPTS/0111/23/ltm.15.html.
9. Davis, above n1, p. 1.
10. 'Mullah Omar pledges to kick out US', *APS Diplomat Recorder*, 13 Sept. 2002; Can Merey, 'Mullah Omar warns Western forces', *Rediff News*, 23 Oct. 2006.
11. Johanna McGeary, 'The Taliban Troubles', *Time* 23 Sept. 2001.
12. Paul Titus, 'Honor the Baloch, Buy the Pashtun: Stereotypes, Social Organisation and History in Western Pakistan', *Modern Asian Studies*, 32:3 (July 1998), pp. 657–687, p. 662.
13. Akbar S. Ahmed, *Resistance and Control in Pakistan* (London, 1983, 1991 edn), pp. 133–4.
14. America's 10th Mountain Division, for example, was taught that Pashtuns are 'a fierce people who are themselves often divided and whose first loyalty is to family and tribe.' John Kifner, 'Tough G.I.'s Go to War with Afghan ABCs', *New York Times*, 16 Feb. 2006. The *Economist* also depicts Pashtuns thus: 'His honour besmirched—and here's the problem for American's—a Pushtun is obliged to have his revenge, or *badal*... If Pashtunwali is about more than killing, its strictures are still remarkably unforgiving. Many Tajiks, like Pashtuns, would die before the suffered a slight.' 'Honour Among Them: The Pashtuns Tribal Code', *Economist*, 22 Dec. 2006. For other assessments that stress the role of tribal codes in Taliban behaviour, see Col. Patrick Donahue, Lt. Col Michael Fenzel, 'Combating a Modern Insurgency: Combined Task Force Devil in Afghanistan', *Military Review*, (March-April 2008), pp. 25–40; Brigadier Feroz Hassan Khan, 'Rough Neighbours: Afghanistan and Pakistan', *Strategic Insight* (Jan., 2003), p. 5.
15. Fouad Ajami, 'The Summoning' *Foreign Affairs* (Sept./Oct. 1993), pp. 2–9.
16. As described by Stephen Tanner, *Afghanistan: A Military History from Alexander the Great to the Fall of the Taliban* (Cambridge, Mass., 2002), p. 304.
17. President George W. Bush, 'Address to a Joint Session of Congress and the American People', 20 Sept. 2001, White House Website, accessed 16 May 2007.
18. Rowan Scarborough, 'War on Terrorism in 'Cleanup' Phase', *The Washington Times*, 2 May 2003.
19. Tim McGirk, 'The Taliban on the Run', *Time*, 28 March 2005.
20. Helene Cooper, 'Taliban will be defeated, Rice assures Afghanistan President', *Deseret News (Salt Lake City)*, 29 June 2006.

21. Victor Davis Hanson, *Carnage and Culture: Landmark Battles in the Rise of Western Power* (New York, 2001), pp. 456–465. Likewise, John Birmingham argued that the power of the Western way of war was manifested in the success of Australian Special Forces in Operation Anaconda as they co-ordinated air-strikes to relieve beleaguered American troops, and exploited their mobility and surveillance net to project 'overwhelming presence' beyond their numbers. Australia's military culture, he argued, inherited the west's practices of 'decisive shock battle, civic militarism, technological innovation, civilian audit and dissent', so that it is heir 'to the Greek hoplites who voted as sovereign individuals to fight against the slave armies of Xerxes.' John Birmingham, 'A Time for War: Australia as a Military Power', *Quarterly Essay*, 20 (2005), pp. 23–24.
22. As estimated by a Johns Hopkins University Study, the infant mortality rate dropped from 165 to 135 deaths per 1000 live births. Alisa Tang, 'Afghan infant deaths fall by 40,000 a year since ousting of Taleban', *Scotsman*, 28 April 2007.
23. President George W. Bush, 'President Bush Discusses Progress in Afghanistan, Global War on Terror', Statement 15 Feb. 2007, White House website, accessed 24 May, 2007.
24. *World Public Opinion*, 11 Jan. 2006, 'New WPO Poll: Afghan Public Overwhelmingly Rejects al-Qaeda, Taliban, Strongly Supports US and International Presence, Believes Pakistan is Allowing Taliban to Operate There'; Gary Langer, 'Poll: Four Years After the Fall of the Taliban, Afghans Optimistic about the Future', *ABC News*, 7 Dec. 2005; more recently, one poll cited by *The Economist* reported that levels of consent in Afghanistan were still high, with roughly 70% of Afghans supporting the presence of American military forces in Afghanistan: 'Afghanistan: Policing a Whirlwind', *The Economist*, Dec. 15 2007, pp. 31–33, p. 31.
25. Milton Bearden, 'Afghanistan, Graveyard of Empires', *Foreign Affairs*, 80:6 (Nov./Dec.) 2001, pp. 17–30.
26. R.W. Apple, Jr., 'A Military Quagmire Remembered: Afghanistan as Vietnam', *New York Times*, 31 Oct. 2001; Stephen Tanner, *Afghanistan: a Military History from Alexander the Great to the Fall of the Taliban* (New York, 2002); Frank Holt, *Into the Land of Bones: Alexander the Great in Afghanistan* (London, 2005).
27. See Antonio Giustozzi, *Koran, Kalashnivok and Laptop: the Neo-Taliban Insurgency in Afghanistan 2001–2007* (London, 2007); Barnett R. Rubin, 'Saving Afghanistan', *Foreign Affairs*, 86:1 (Jan./Feb. 2007), pp. 57–78
28. Michel Comte, 'Afghans 'pessimistic' about NATO, *Middle East Times*, 29 May 2007.
29. Tom Coghlan, 'Taliban mutilate Afghans for helping US', *Daily Telegraph*, 19 March 2007; for the Taliban conducting an armed information operation, see the remarks of David Kilcullen, Australian counter-insurgency expert at the State Department, reported in George Packer, 'Knowing the Enemy: Can Social Scientists Redefine the 'War on Terror'?, *New Yorker* (18 Dec. 2006), pp. 61–69; and David Kilcullen, *The Accidental*

Guerrilla: Fighting Small Wars in the Midst of a Large One (London, 2009).

30. As Sean Maloney notes, 'Conceptualising the War in Afghanistan: Perceptions from the Front, 2001–2006', *Small Wars and Insurgencies*, 18:1 (2007), pp. 27–44, p. 39.
31. See Thomas Elkjer Nissen, *The Taliban's Information Warfare: A Comparative Analysis of NATO Information Operations (Info Ops) and Taliban Information Activities* (Royal Danish Defence College, 2007), pp. 8–9.
32. As Guistozzi warns in *Koran, Kalashnikov and Laptop*, p. 35.
33. Sean D. Naylor, 'The waiting game: A Stronger Taliban lies low, hoping to leave Afghanistan' *Armed Forces Journal*, 143:7 (2006), pp. 30–38.
34. Thomas H. Johnson and M. Chris Mason, 'Understanding the Taliban and Insurgency in Afghanistan', *Orbis*, 51:1 (2007), pp. 71–89.
35. National Security Archives, Defence Intelligence Agency, Cable 'IIR [Excised]/Veteran Afghanistan Traveller's Analysis of Al Qaeda and Taliban Exploitable Weaknesses', 2 Oct. 2001, p. 5 (Recently declassified, accessed online, 7 May 2007.).
36. For more on the background and origins of the Taliban, see Neamatollah Nojumi, *The Rise of the Taliban in Afghanistan: Mass Mobilisation, Civil War, and the Future of the Region* (New York, 2002), esp. pp. 119–124.
37. For a summary of Al Qaeda and its ideology, see Mary Habeck, *Knowing the Enemy: Jihadist Ideology and the War on Terror* (Yale, 2006).
38. The 9/11 attack inflicted damage on developing nations that, in an interdependent world, plunged millions more people into poverty and starvation. The World Bank estimated that damage to developing nations were greater than the US economy as a result of a sharp fall off in tourism, increases in transport, insurance and security costs, and reduced demand for agricultural products, while 40,000 children would die from hunger or illness as a result, and that a million people would fall below the 'extreme poverty' line. 'World Bank says Poor Nations Will Suffer Worst Economic Toll', *New York Times*, 2 Oct. 2001.
39. Thomas H. Johnson and M. Chris Mason, 'Understanding the Taliban and Insurgency in Afghanistan', *Orbis*, 51:1 (2007), pp. 71–89, p. 80.
40. Ibid, p. 88. On the significance of Mullah Omar and the argument that Mullah Omar's 'charismatic leadership was founded on his commanders' and followers' belief in his divine guidance through night dreams', see Iain R. Edgar, 'The "true dream" in contemporary Islamic/Jihadist dreamwork: a case study of the dreams of Taliban leader Mullah Omar', *South Asian Studies*, 15:3 (Sept. 2006), pp. 263–272.
41. Charles Haviland, 'Ex Taliban media leader defects', 10 June 2007 http://www.afgha.com/?q=node/3188; 'High Profile Taliban defector blames Bin Laden' 25 Nov. 2001 http://www.cbc.ca/world/story/2001/11/25/defect_blame011125.html;
42. Ismat Hasan Sulfo, *Karari: The Sudanese Account of the Battle of Omdurman* (trans. Peter Clark, 1980), p. 9.

43. James Dobbins, 'Testimony before Senate Foreign Relations Committee' in *Ending Afghanistan's Civil War*, 8 March 2007 (Santa Barbara, 2007), p. 4.
44. Ahto Lobjakas, 'Afghanistan: NATO Sees 'Tribal' Nature To Taliban Insurgency', *Radio Free Europe*, 20 July 2007.
45. Steven Pressfield, 'Tribalism is the Real Enemy in Iraq', *Seattle Intelligencer*, June 18, 2006; *The Afghan Campaign* (London, 2007).
46. Andre Beteille, 'On the Concept of Tribe', *International Social Science Journal*, 32:4 (1980), pp. 825–28; Morton H. Fried, 'The Myth of Tribe', *Natural History*, 84:4 (April 1979), pp. 13–18.
47. Antonio Giustozzi, 'The resurgence of the neo-Taliban', *Open Democracy*, 17 Dec. 2007.
48. Antonio Guistozzi, *Koran, Kalashnikov and Laptop: The Neo-Taliban Insurgency in Afghanistan*, pp. 47–48; see also Joshua Foust, 'The Myth of Taliban Tribalism', 15 July 2008, http://www.registan.net/index.php/2008/07/15/the-myth-of-taliban-tribalism/.
49. General James L. Jones, Ambassador Thomas R. Pickering, *Afghanistan Study Group Report: Revitalising our Efforts, Rethinking our Strategies* (Washington, 2008), p. 29.
50. Robert H.E. Gooren, 'Soldiering in unfamiliar places: The Dutch Approach', *Military Review*, 86:2, (March/April, 2006), pp. 54–60.
51. Scott Petersen, 'Afghan Fighters put Survival over Loyalty', *Christian Science Monitor*, 19 Oct. 2001;
52. Anthony Lloyd, 'The mysterious Afghan warlord trusted to spread peace in a divided province', *The Times*, 12 Jan., 2008.
53. For an example of Afghan defection politics, see Scott Peterson, 'Afghan Fighters Put Survival over Loyalty', *Christian Science Monitor*, 19 Oct. 2001: 'We joined the mujahideen [Northern Alliance] because the Taliban are going to withdraw, and will disappear in the near future', says Khan Mohamed, a father of two, who effected from the Taliban with Malang. 'From the time the US attacks began, day by day the Taliban are becoming weaker.' Sniffing the wind four years ago, as the Taliban moved north, Mr. Mohamed's unit defected from the mujahideen to the Taliban, because there was "no way to bring food" to their village of Shukhi if they resisted, he says. And because 'we had no choice.' See also David Rennie, 'Defectors plan to strap bombs to their bodies', *Daily Telegraph*, 26 Nov. 2001, who reports the reasons one Taliban deserter gave: 'He offered no grand defence of their defection. The Taliban lost their power, and their morale. They were falling, so it was better for us to join the Northern Alliance.'
54. Sean Maloney argues, 'Conceptualising the War in Afghanistan: Perceptions from the Front, 2001–2006', *Small Wars and Insurgencies*, 18:1 (2007), pp. 27–44, p. 44; Mark Sappenfield, 'Taliban Leaves Tribal Roots for al Qaeda Tactics', *Christian Science Monitor*, 1 Aug. 2007.
55. Shah M. Tarzi, 'President Bush Versus the "Irrational" Taliban: The Dilemma of American Coercive Diplomacy', Presentation, International Studies Association Annual Conference, March 2006, p. 29.

56. NSA 'Islama' 06863, 'U.S. Embassy (Islamabad), Cable, "Afghanistan: Demarche to Taliban on New Bin Laden Threat," Sept. 14, 1998, Secret, pp. 1, 2; At one stage, the Taliban Foreign Minister intimated that they would consider swapping Bin Laden in exchange for formal recognition, saying that most of the Taliban wanted to be rid of him. NSA State 028054 'U.S. Department of State, Cable, "Taliban Deliver Letter from Muttawakil; Say They Will Comply With Office Closing in New York," Feb. 15, 2001, Confidential, p. 3.
57. NSA 'Islama' 07665, U.S. Embassy (Islamabad), Cable, "Usama Bin Laden: High-Level Taliban Official Gives the Standard Line on Bin Laden With a Couple of Nuances, In Oct. 11 Meeting With Ambassador," Oct. 12, 1998, Secret, p. 2.
58. Gordon McCormick, 'Things Fall Apart: The Endgame Dynamics' of Internal Wars', New York, 2007, p. 2.
59. For an overview of the frequent or common preconditions for successful insurgencies, see John Ellis, *From the Barrel of a Gun: A History of Guerrilla, Revolutionary and Counter-Insurgency Warfare, from the Romans to the Present* (London, 1995, pp. 235–244) and David Galula, *Counterinsurgency Warfare: Theory and Practice* (Westport, 1964, 2006 edn), pp. 11–25. Robert Thompson, *Defeating Communist Insurgency: The Lessons of Malaya and Vietnam* (New York, 1966).
60. RAND draft document cited in Seth G. Jones, 'Pakistan's Dangerous Game', *Survival*, 49:1 (Spring 2007), pp. 15–33, p. 16. Insurgencies that have lost or been deprived of external support have succeeded only 17% of the time, while those without state support but supported by non-state actors and diaspora groups won a third of the time.
61. Tim Albone, Claire Billet, 'Ruined poppy farmers join ranks with the Taleban', *The Times*, 27 Feb 2007.
62. See Paul R. Kan, 'Webs of Smoke: Drugs and Small Wars', *Small Wars and Insurgencies*, 17:2 (2006), pp. 148–162.
63. Michael Fumento, 'Afghanistan: the Winnable War', *Washington Times*, 27 June, 2007.
64. On the evolving form of 'complex insurgency' as opposed to the classical insurgency, see John Mackinlay, *Defeating Complex Insurgency: Beyond Iraq and Afghanistan* (London, 2005), pp. 19–31; David Kilcullen, 'Counterinsurgency redux', *Survival*, 48:4 (2006), pp. 111–130. For the metaphor of a 'bazaar of violence', see John Robb, *Brave New War: The Next Stage of Terrorism and the End of Globalisation* (New York, 2007); for more on cyber-mobilisation, see Audrey K. Kronin, 'Cyber-Mobilization: The New *Levée en Masse*', *Parameters*, 36:2, (2006), pp. 77–87.
65. NSA Washington (Afghanistan 'extras' box 4) Declassified telegram, 'Consultations on Afghanistan' 30 June 1985, NEA Special Assistant Dunbar.
66. 'Living under the Taleban', *Afghan Recovery Report, Institute for War and Peace Reporting* (4 April, 2007), 249; see also Guistozzi, *Koran, Kalashnikov, and Laptop*, p. 72.

67. Noor Khan, 'Taliban to open their own schools in the south', Associated Press, 22 Jan. 2007; Tim Albone, 'Taleban in $1m drive to open schools', *The Scotsman*, Mon 22 Jan 2007; Can Merey, 'Taliban plan "education offensive" in Afghan fight', *Deutche Presse Agentur*, 24 Jan 2007.
68. Mullah Yusuf, a senior commander in Andar, told *Rolling Stone* that once the Taliban had expelled the Americans, they would relax their harsher strictures, so that 'girls will be allowed to go to school, and women will be allowed to work.' Nir Rosen, 'How we Lost the War we Won', *Rolling Stone*, 30 Oct. 2008; Taliban spokesmen told British journalist James Fergusson that the Taliban set up girls' schools in Wardak, and that they burn schools that teach girls 'pornography.' James Fergusson, *A Million Bullets* (London, 2008), p.314. Significant here is the desire of the Taliban to present themselves as supporting their version of proper Islamic girls' education, a shift from their prior stance.
69. Taliban spokesman Qari Yousuf Ahmadi, speaking to the BBC, cited in Merey, 'Taliban plan 'education offensive', above.
70. Cited in Can Merey, 'Taliban plan 'education offensive', above.
71. FM3–24 *Counterinsurgency* (Marine Corps Warfighting Publication), 1–32.
72. Barnett Rubin, cited in Noor Khan, 'Taliban to open their own schools in the south', above.
73. Romesh Ratnesar, 'The Afghan Way of War', 11 Nov. 2001. See also Robert Kaplan, *Imperial Grunts: The American Military on the Ground* (New York, 2005), p. 201, who had lived with the Afghan mujahedin in the 1980s, explaining that no male would be taken seriously if he had not grown a beard.
74. Cited in Claudio Franco, 'In Remote Afghan Camp, Taliban Explain How and Why they Fight', *San Francisco Chronicle*, 21 Jan. 2007.
75. For example, see Anthony Davis, 'Foreign Fighters step up Activity in Afghan Civil War', *Jane's Intelligence Review*, Aug. 2001, pp. 14–17, p. 15: 'UF sources, however, believe that, more recently, losses and the uncertain military effectiveness of these volunteers have tempered both the enthusiasm at source and the demand from commanders within Afghanistan.'
76. NSA 01310 'DOD News Briefing', Secretary of Defence Donald H. Rumsfeld, 25 Sept., 2001, p. 4.
77. Scott Baldauf, Ashran Khan, 'New Guns, New Drive for Taliban: Rebel Leader says they can Now Shoot Down US Aircraft', *Christian Science Monitor* (26 Sept. 2005).
78. Graeme Smith, 'More Taliban fighters agree on suicide bombings', *Toronto Globe and Mail*, 5 April 2008.
79. Ibid.
80. The figures and findings are drawn from a five-month study of suicide bombings in Afghanistan from 2001–2007, cited in Brian Glyn Williams and Cathy Young, 'Cheney Attack Reveals Taliban Suicide Bombing Patterns', *Terrorism Monitor*, 5:4 (March 1, 2007).

81. Cited in an interview by Sami Yousafzai and Ron Moreau 'The Taliban's New Weapon: Suicide Bombers', *Newsweek*, 16 April 2007.
82. Ibid.
83. As was noted in a report by Abdul Rasheed, NSA Washington, 'Afghan Nation: Strategy, Tactics and Organisation' submitted to Office of Under Secretary of State for Defence for Policy, 15 Jan. 1989: '...the Mujahidin have...made an attempt to refrain from combat activity that can cause civilian losses.'
84. See Ron Synovitz, 'Taliban and Al Qaeda—Provincial vs. Global', Radio Free Europe, 25 Aug. 2004.
85. Lawrence Wright, *The Looming Tower* (London, 2006), p. 287.
86. Syed Saleem Shahzad, 'Pakistan makes a deal with the Taliban', *Asia Times*, 1 March, 2007.
87. Syed Saleem Shahzad, 'Pakistan, the Taliban and Dadullah', *Pakistan Security Research Unit*, Brief No. 3, 2007.
88. Sami Yousafzai and Ron Moreau, 'By the Book: Taliban Fighters Play by Their Own Rules', *Newsweek*, 3 Dec. 2006; Urs Gehriger, 'Layeha (Regelbuch) fuer die Mudschaheddin', *Die Weltwoche*, 16 Nov. 2006.
89. Traces of lessening support of the freedom fighters by the Afghan populace were visible. At fault were excesses by individual groups of freedom fighters: rape of women and confiscation of money and food 'in the name of help for the holy war.' Additionally, former thieves, highwaymen and robbers continued their old tricks after they became freedom fighters. National Security Archive, Washington, CIA Report, Aug 1983, regraded from confidential to unclassified (info report not finally evaluated Intel), Incoming FOIA, Box. #1.
90. Joe Sharkey, 'Word for Word/www.taliban.com; Allah is Good, Technology is Bad. Visit our Web Site,' *New York Times*, 25 Oct. 1998.
91. BBC News Online, 'Afghan Taleban commander killed', 13 May 2007.
92. See the online report of Tom Perriello, based on 'a dozen or so interviews with security experts from various Embassies, UN offices, NGOs, and the Afghan government' at http://thecenturyfoundation.typepad.com/aw/2007/07/tom-perriello-c.html#more, posted on 12 July 2007.
93. Steve Tatham, 'Hearts and Minds: Time to Think Differently', *Naval Review*, Vol. 96, No. 4 (Nov. 2008), pp. 329–30.
94. Reported in Yosseff Bodansky, 'The New Phase of Afghanistan's War', *Defence and Foreign Affairs Strategic Policy*, 8 (2005), pp. 4–6.
95. Fred Burton, 'Combat Season 2007: the Taliban's Metamorphosis', *Stratfor*, 7 March 2007.
96. Tom Coghlan, 'Karzai questions Nato campaign as Taliban takes to hi-tech propaganda', *The Independent*, 23 June 2006.
97. See Olivier Roy's seminal work on the shift from fundamentalism to Islamism: *Globalised Islam: The Search for a New Umma* (London, 2004).
98. Jonathan Foreman, 'Defeat in the Information Battle Space: The Western Media, Wittingly or Not, are Aiding our Enemies' *National Review Online* 17 May, 2007.

99. For the argument that the 'logic and rational direction of war are universal', see Michael Handel, *Masters of War: Classical Strategic Thought* (London, 1996), p. 3.
100. As phrased by Stephen Peter Rosen, 'Military Effectiveness: Why Society Matters', *International Security*, 19:4 (Spring 1995), pp. 5–31.

6. THE DIVINE VICTORY: HIZBALLA, ISRAEL AND THE 2006 'JULY WAR'

1. For more partisan accounts, see Gilbert Achcar and Michael Warschawski, *The 33–Day War: Israel's War on Hezbollah in Lebanon and its Aftermath* (London 2007); Charles Krauthammer, 'Israel's Lost Moment', 4 Aug. 2006, *Washington Post*, p. A17.
2. Alon Bed-David, 'Iran supplied Zelzal-2 rockets to Hizballa', *Jane's Defence Weekly*, Aug. 16, 2006, p. 5.
3. CNN 'Israel authorizes 'severe' response to abductions' 13 July 2006.
4. Estanislao Oziewicz, 'Did Israel Underestimate Hezbollah?', *Toronto Globe and Mail*, 1 Aug. 2006.
5. Dina Kraft, 'The Displaced: Israeli Refugees Seek Friends and Families', *New York Times*, 31 July 2006.
6. Ian Black, 'Grave Failings All Round', *Guardian*, 30 Jan. 2008.
7. 'Nasrallah Wins the War: Bad News all Round, Especially if More of Israel's Neighbours Come to Believe in Hizballa's Methods', *The Economist*, 17 Aug. 2006.
8. Tom Lasseter, 'US Made Hezbollah Stronger, Analysts say', *The Slate*, 10 Dec. 2006.
9. Figures from 'The blame game: Unity ended when the fighting died' *Economist* 17 Aug. 2006.
10. Israel's aims are discussed in Anthony H. Cordesman, George Sullivan and William D. Sullivan, *Lessons of the 2006 Israeli-Hezbollah War*, Center for Strategic and International Studies, Significant Issues Series, 29:4 (Washington, 2007), pp. 4–32; Jim Quilty, 'Israel's War against Lebanon's Shi'a', *The Middle East Report*, 25 July 2006.
11. 'The War in Lebanon: Strategic Consequences', *Strategic Comments*, 12:6 (July 2006), pp. 1–2; Matt Matthews, 'Interview with BG (Ret.) Shimon Naveh' (Operational Leadership Experiences Interview Collection, Combat Studies Institute, Fort Leavenworth, Kansas, 7 Nov. 2007), p. 7.
12. 'English Summary of the Winograd Commission Report', 30 Jan. 2008, *New York Times*; Anthony H. Cordesman, George Sullivan and William D. Sullivan, *Lessons of the 2006 Israeli-Hezbollah War*, Center for Strategic and International Studies, Significant Issues Series, 29:4, (Washington, 2007), pp. 67–75.
13. Lt. General Michael D. Maples, Director, Defence Intelligence Agency, 'Current and Projected National Security Threats to the United States', Statement for the Record, Senate Select Committee on Intelligence, 11 Jan.

2007; Yaakov Katz, 'IDF: Hezbollah Almost at Full Strength', *Jerusalem Post*, 21 Dec. 2006.

14. See Avi Kober, 'The Israel Defence Forces in the Second Lebanon War: Why the Poor Performance?', *Journal of Strategic Studies*, 31:1 (Feb. 2008), pp. 3–40; Sarah E. Kreps, 'The 2006 Lebanon War: Lessons Learned', *Parameters*, 37:1 (2007), pp. 72–85.
15. Efraim Inbar, 'How Israel Bungled the Second Lebanon War', *Middle East Quarterly* (Summer 2007), pp. 57–65.
16. Hew Strachan, 'Strategy and the Limitation of War', *Survival* 50:1 (2008), pp. 31–54.
17. Benjamin Netanyahu, 'No Ceasefire: Remove Hezbollah's Missiles—or destroy them,' *Wall Street Journal*, 23 July 2006.
18. James Orr, 'Bush Condemns Hizballa and Hamas in Knesset Speech', *Guardian*, 15 May 2008.
19. Sean Yoong, 'Ahmadinejad: Destroy Israel, End Crisis', *Washington Post*, 3 Aug. 2006.
20. Kenneth Pollack, *Arabs at War: Military Effectiveness, 1948–1991* (Lincoln, 2002), pp. 561–574.
21. Norvelle B. De Atkine, 'Why Arabs Lose Wars: Fighting as you Train, and the Impact of Culture on Arab Military Effectiveness', *Middle East Quarterly* (Dec. 1999), 6:4; Lawrence Sondhaus, *Strategic Culture and Ways of War* (New York, 2006), pp. 88–89.
22. This debate is summarised in Michael C. Desch, 'Democracy and Victory: Why Regime Type Hardly Matters', *International Security*, 27:2 (2002), pp. 5–47.
23. Yigal Allon, *The Making of Israel's Army* (London, 1970), p. 63, cited and discussed also in Michael C. Desch, *Power and Military Effectiveness* (Baltimore, 2008), p. 95.
24. Avi Kober, 'From Blitzkrieg to Attrition: Israel's Attrition Strategy and Staying Power', *Small Wars and Insurgencies* (June 2005), pp. 216–240; p. D. Feaver and C. Gelpi, 'How Many Deaths Are Acceptable? A Surprising Answer,' *Washington Post*, 7 Nov. 1999, B-3.
25. Estanislao Oziewicz, 'Did Israel Underestimate Hezbollah?', *Toronto Globe and Mail*, 1 Aug. 2006.
26. As reckoned by Stephen Biddle and Jeffrey A. Friedman, *The 2006 Lebanon Campaign* (2008), p. 76, as calculated from J. David Singer and Melvin Small, *The Correlates of War Project: International and Civil War Data, 1816–1992* (Ann Arbor, 1994).
27. Examples of its colourful rhetoric include Sheik Hassan Nasralla stating 'We have discovered how to hit the Jews where they are the most vulnerable. The Jews love life, so that is what we shall take away from them. We are going to win because they love life and we love death.' (As reported by Jonathan Chait, 'Who Says War has to be Proportional', *Los Angeles Times*, 23 July 2006.) Hizballa's television station, Al Manar, also broadcast a series based on the anti-Semitic forgery, *The Protocols of the Elders*

of Zion (see Sebastian Usher, 'Hezbollah's Passion Play', BBC News, 14 May 2004).

28. Magnus Ranstorp, 'The Strategy and Tactics of Hizballah's Current "Lebanonization Process"', *Mediterranean Politics*, 3:1 (Summer 1998), pp. 103–134.
29. See Frank G. Hoffman, 'Conflict in the 21st. Century: The Rise of Hybrid Wars', *Potomac Institute for Policy Studies* (Arlington, Dec. 2007), pp. 35–43.
30. See Martin Van Creveld, *The Sword and the Olive: A Critical History of the Israeli Defence Force* (New York, 1998), p. 344.
31. Adam Garfinkle, 'Culture and Deterrence', *Foreign Policy Research Institute*, 25 Aug. 2006, http://fpri.org/enotes/20060825.americawar.garfinkle.culturedeterrence.html.
32. Jonathan Finer, 'Israeli Soldiers Find a Tenacious Foe in Hezbollah', *Washington Post*, 8 Aug. 2006, p. 1.
33. From Greg Myre, 'Israel's Wounded Describe Surprisingly Fierce, Well-Organized and Elusive Enemy', *New York Times*, Aug. 12, 2006, p. A5.
34. Cited in Matt. M. Matthews, *We Were Caught Unprepared: The 2006 Hizballa-Israeli War*, The Long War Series, Occasional Paper 26, US Combined Arms Centre, Combat Studies Institute Press, Fort Leavenworth, Texas, p. 43.
35. Ari Shavit, 'A Spirit of Absolute Folly', *Haaretz*, 16 Aug. 2006.
36. Col. David Eshel, IDF Ret., 'Israel Lebanon War One Year Later: Electronic Warfare in the Second Lebanon War', *The Journal of Electronic Defence* (July 2007), pp. 27–34.
37. Stephen Biddle and Jeffrey A. Friedman, *The 2006 Lebanon Campaign and the Future of Warfare: Implications for Army and Defence Policy* (Strategic Studies Institute, 2008), pp. 8–24, 73.
38. Thom Shanker, 'New Enemy Gains on the Pentagon', 30 July 2006, *New York Times*; Nicholas Blanford, Daniel McGrory, Stephen Farrell, 'Tactics that have Kept the Middle East's Most Powerful Army at Bay', *The Times*, 10 Aug. 2006.
39. According to Israeli Army Spokesman Miri Regev, they 'already knew about the network': Matthew Kalman, 'Israel set war plan more than a year ago: Strategy was put in motion as Hizballa began gaining military strength in Lebanon', *Chronicle of Foreign Service*, 21 July 2006.
40. Uzi Mahnaimi, 'Humbling of the Supertroops Shatters Israeli Army Morale', *The Times*, 27 Aug. 2006.
41. 'Hez hacked Israeli Radios' http: //www.defensetech.org/archives/002785.html.
42. Inbar, 'How Israel Bungled the Second Lebanon War', p. 57.
43. Col. David Eshel, IDF Ret. 'Israel Lebanon War One Year Later', p. 32; *Ha'aretz*, 4 Nov. 2006.
44. Cited in Matthews, *We Were Caught Unprepared*, p. 49, 63.
45. Alon Ben-David, 'Debriefing teams brand IDF Doctrine "Completely wrong"', *Jane's Defence Weekly*, 3 Jan. 2007, p. 7: 'The IDF's undisputed

success in suppressing Palestinian terrorism increased commanders' self-confidence and drove them to underestimate their Lebanese opponent.'

46. General cited in Andrew Exum, *Hizballah at War: A Military Assessment* (Policy Focus #63, Dec. 2006, Washington Institute for Near East Policy), p. 10.
47. Alon Ben-David, 'Limited Israeli Achievements Made in Lebanon', 16 Aug. 2006, *Jane's Defence Weekly*, 16 Aug. 2006, p. 4.
48. Cited in Edward Cody and Molly Moore, 'The Best Guerrilla Force in the World: Analysts Attribute Hezbollah's Resilience to Zeal, Secrecy and Iranian Funding', *Washington Post*, 14 Aug. 2006, p. A01.
49. See Ranstorp, 'The Strategy and Tactics of Hizballah's Current 'Lebanonization Process'', pp. 103–134.
50. Thom Shanker, 'To Disarm Shadowy Guerrilla Army, Israeli Air Power May Not be Enough', *The New York Times*, 20 July 2006, p. A10.
51. Ze'ev Schiff, 'The Foresight Saga', *Haaretz*, 18 Aug. 2006.
52. James S. Corum and Wray R. Johnson, *Airpower in Small Wars* (Lawrence, 2003), p. 8.
53. SGM Herbert A. Friedman, 'Psychological Operations During the Israeli-Lebanon War 2006', from *Psywar.org*, 26 Nov. 2007, pp. 3–4.
54. Cited in SGM Herbert A. Friedman, 'Psychological Operations', p. 19.
55. L. Drake 'Continuity and Change in Israeli Foreign Policy' in R.K. Beasley, J. Kaarbo, J.S. Lantis, and M.T. Snarr (eds), *Foreign Policy in Comparative Perspective: Domestic and International Influences on State Behaviour* (Washington DC 2002), pp. 190–216, 199–201.
56. See Robert Pape, *Bombing to Win: Airpower and Coercion in War* (Ithaca, 1996), p. 25; William M. Arkin, 'Divine Victory for Whom? Airpower in the 2006 Israel-Hezbollah War', *Strategic Studies Quarterly* (Winter 2007), pp. 98–141, 103.
57. 'The Blame Game: Unity Certainly Ended When the Fighting Died', *The Economist*, 17 Aug. 2006
58. Marvin Kalb and Carol Saivetz 'The Israeli-Hezbollah War of 2006: The Media as a Weapon in Asymmetrical Conflict' (Research Paper Series, Feb. 2007), p. 4.
59. Sheera Claire Frenkel, 'Reuters Admits Doctoring Beirut Photo', *Jerusalem Post*, 6 Aug. 2006; Daryl Lang, 'Reuters Says Freelancer Manipulated Lebanon Photos', *Photo District News*, 7 Aug. 2006; *The New York Times* was forced to retract a photo in which a supposedly dead man was actually a rescue worker who was alive in other photographs of the same event: 'Corrections: For the Record', *New York Times* 9 Aug. 2006; a Lebanese rescue worker was shown on German television carrying a dead boy from one scene to another: Marvin Kalb and Carol Saivetz, 'The Israeli-Hezbollah War of 2006', p. 26.
60. Kevin Peraino, 'Winning Hearts and Minds: The New War in Lebanon is a Propaganda Battle, and Hizballa is Coming out on Top. Some Tips From a Master', *Newsweek*, 2 Oct. 2006.

61. Jeffrey Stinson, 'Lebanon relief effort raises houses, questions', *USA Today*, 17 Dec. 2006.
62. Richard Fox, *Lions in the Punjab: Culture in the Making* (Berkeley, 1985); Harjot Oberoi, *The Construction of Religious Boundaries: Culture, Identity and Diversity in the Sikh Tradition* (Chicago, 1994); Juan Cole, *Napoleon's Egypt: Invading the Middle East* (New York, 2007), pp. 247–248.
63. Jonathan Finer, 'Israeli Soldiers Find a Tenacious Foe in Hezbollah', *Washington Post*, 8 Aug. 2006, p. 1.
64. 'The War in Lebanon: Strategic Consequences', *Strategic Comments*, 12:6 (July 2006), pp. 1–2.
65. Edward Cody and Molly Moore, 'The Best Guerrilla Force in the World', p. A01.
66. Magnus Ranstorp, 'The Strategy and Tactics of Hizballah's Current 'Lebanonization Process'' *Mediterranean Politics* 3:1 (Summer 1998), pp. 103–134, p. 116.
67. Judith Palmer Harik, *Hizballa: The Changing Face of Terrorism* (New York, 2004, 2005 edn), pp. 58–9.
68. *On War*, 581.

CONCLUSION

1. Fred Halliday, *100 Myths About the Middle East* (London 2005), p.14.
2. As John Darwin suggests, *After Tamerlane: The Rise and Fall of Global Empires 1400–2000* (London 2007, 2008 edn) p.12; Sanjay Subrahmanyam, 'Connected Histories: Notes towards a Reconfiguration of EarlyModern Eurasia' *Modern Asian Studies* 31:3 (1997), pp.735–762, p.740.
3. Robert Watson, 'Iraqi rebels learn from US sniper guru.' *Telegraph* 29 October 2006.
4. Stephen Graham, 'Cities and the War on Terror' M. Sorkin, *Indefensible Space*. (New York, 2008), p.1–28; Mike Davis, *Planet of Slums* (London, 2006), p.205–6.
5. The words of US Deputy Secretary of State Strobe Talbott, Address at Bucharest University, Romania, 19 March 1998, cited in Brenda Schaffer (ed) *The Limits of Culture: Islam and Foreign Policy* (MIT, 2006), p.12.
6. For example, Charles Blackmore, a former British Army counter-terrorism expert, claims that the book is still valid because Iraq remains 'feudal and tribal.' Ryan Dilley, 'Lessons from Lawrence of Arabia', BBC News 9 April 2004.
7. See Gerald Segal, 'Strategy and 'Ethnic Chic', *International Affairs* 60:1 (1984), pp. 15–30.
8. Derek Gregory, 'The Rush to the Intimate: Counterinsurgency and the Cultural Turn in Late Modern War' *Radical Philosophy* 150 (2008), p.9.
9. These are the official phrases of the Human Terrain System project: Jacob Lipp, Lester Grau, Karl Prinslow, Don Smith, 'The Human Terrain System:

a CORDS for the 21st. century' *Military Review* (September-October 2006), pp.8–15.

10. Montgomery McFate, 'The Military Utility of Understanding Adversary Culture' *Joint Force Quarterly* 38 (July 2005), p. 42–48, p.43.
11. Lucy Stallworthy, 'Experts Apply Anthropology to Iraq', *United Press International* 1 February 2006.
12. See Christopher Ebert, 'Adaptability and the Shock of the New: the Response of the Mexica to Cortes' Invasion', *Ex Post Facto*, 6 (1997), accessed online at http://userwww.sfsu.edu/~epf/; Inga Clendinnen, 'Fierce and Unnatural Cruelty: Cortes and the Conquest of Mexico' *Representations*, 33 (1991), p. 65–100; George Raudzens, 'So Why Were the Aztecs Conquered, and What Were the Wider Implications? Testing Military Superiority as a Cause of Europe's Preindustrial Colonial Conquests' in *War in History* (1995) 2:1, p.87–104.
13. As Michael Evans describes, 'From Kadesh to Kandahar: Military Theory and the Future of War' *Naval War College Review* 56:3 (Summer 2003), p.132–150.
14. Borzou Daragahi and Raheem Salman, 'Blackwater Shooting Highlights a US, Iraq Culture Clash' *Los Angeles Times* 4 May 2008.
15. Spencer Ackerman, at http://thinkprogress.org/attackerman/2008/05/05/blackwaterisheretohelp accessed 11 May 2008.
16. Philip Carl Salzman, 'Clashes in Beirut' in *Middle East Strategy at Harvard*, http://www.spme.net/cgi-bin/articles.cgi?ID=4007: 'How can we understand this factional pattern of institutionalized fragmentation and oppositional conflict? My suggestion is that this pattern reflects the "tribal spirit" of Arab culture, manifested in self-help corporations for defense and the advancement of interests, and for which men have a primarily obligation to engage in military action. Each man has a duty to be a warrior, and most take pleasure in the glory of it.'
17. American Anthropological Association, *Commission on the Engagement of Anthropology with the US Security and Intelligence Communities, Final Report*, 4 November 2007, p.22.
18. Sheila Miyoshi Jager, *On the Uses of Cultural Knowledge* (Strategic Studies Institute, Carlisle, 2007), p.9.
19. Morton H. Fried, *The Notion of Tribe* (Columbia, 1975), p.114.

INDEX